THINKWELL

CU00407982

BROADLAKE

Ed Bingham was born in 1978, in Pembury, Kent. He graduated in 2000 from the University of Southampton with a degree in English & Philosophy and is a member of The Good Ship Band, an acoustic rock project formed in 2009. Ed has two sisters and is the middle child of an insurance broker and travel consultant. *Broadlake* - a novel within a novel - is his first work of fiction, which he spent copious amounts of time editing in the bath. When not in the bath, he teaches guitar, songwriting and music production, and is a signed songwriter with NorthStar Music and Post House Music.

'Ed Bingham has constructed an ingenious murder mystery that brings reason to rhyme in a style that is reminiscent of TS Eliot and the experimental fiction of BS Johnson. Employing a 'smoke and mirrors' approach to the murder case, the deceased narrator simultaneously weaves into his epic poem an account of his own downfall. *Broadlake* is an inventive novel that is just that – novel.'

David Stephens, author of *The Disappeared*

'In 2023 *Broadlake* remains an enigma. It is 'a novel in rhyming prose' of uncertain provenance and purpose. If, like me, you enjoy tales told by unreliable narrators, you may well be drawn in.'

Jonathan Vischer, author of
The Wonderful Discovery of Elizabeth Sawyer

'I confess my heart sank when asked to review Ed Bingham's brilliantly original debut novel, *Broadlake*. Not so much for the content matter – drunken Englishmen, personal tragedy, and outback Australia are subjects I know too much about – but because of its form. To write (almost) an entire novel in epic rhyming form is highly ambitious, dangerously naïve or perhaps the work of a madman – and possibly all three. However, I need not have worried. Such is the writer's mastery of his craft that far from detracting from the narrative, the central themes (murder mystery, grief, childhood trauma) are aided by Bingham's woozy, lyrical style. Never has a grim Greek package holiday been so exquisitely evoked; rare indeed the author who can juxtapose moments of pure comedy and heart-wrenching tragedy whilst maintaining the same consistency of voice. This labour of love is the work of a uniquely gifted talent.'

Mark Liam Piggott, author of
Kidology: The pre-cretinous era

'Intricate and intriguing. Easily captures the imagination.'

Kate Rizzo, literary agent, Greene & Heaton

'An extraordinary novel. Reaching back to the tradition of Pope, this is a brave and courageous reimagining of what the contemporary novel can be.'

Alan Kane Fraser, author of *The Muse of Hope Falls*

'*Broadlake* is a masterpiece in originality, creativity and storytelling. Ed Bingham explores humanity with exquisite insight, touching every possible aspect of human life, and presents it like a delicate dessert. The premise of this novel is a dream for a writer to have and a joy for the reader to find. The work has everything to put poetry back centre stage. I hope it receives all the awards it deserves.'

Ann Chettle, author of *Japheth & Josephina*

'A very ambitious piece of work. Good writing and original ideas.'

Susie Maguire, author of *The Short Hello*

'This novel is dirty, wild, too trippy and brazen. Reading it is akin to lying on the back of a motorbike while scrambling around a sodden landscape. Encore!'

Ade Kolade, ex-researcher at The University of Manchester

'An excellent and remarkable book.'

James Essinger, author of *Ada's Algorithm*

'Dip your head beneath the water or spume of what Bingham has created, hold your breath, and come up a changed, disparate man. His work is a literary baptism – especially for those in the pews or those watching on.'

Jeff Weston, author of *Wagenknecht*

Ed Bingham

BROADLAKE

THIRD EDITION

THINKWELL BOOKS

Curated by Jeff Weston.

Cover design by Alejandro Baigorri.

Interior formatting by Rachel Bostwick.

Published by Thinkwell Books, U.K.

First printing edition 2023.

To Freddie & Lily

'The truth is rarely pure and never simple.'

- Oscar Wilde, *The Importance of Being Earnest*

The Liger Critical Series

Broadlake

Third edition

A novel in rhyming prose

**An authoritative text
Background, sources and criticism**

**Edited by
David Balkan**

**Analysis by
Michael Anthrup**

**Foreword by
Jay Burgess**

LIGER BOOKS . *New York* . *London* . *Sydney*

First published in Great Britain in 2004 by
Liger Books Limited
23 Acklam Road London W10 5QZ

Printed in England by
Bluefire Ltd., St Ives plc

Copyright c 2004, 2006, 2023 by Liger Books, Inc.

A CIP record for this book is available from the British
Library

ISBN 978-1-7396-6815-0

Liger Books Inc. 17 Astoria Boulevard New York NY 11102
Liger Books Ltd. 23 Acklam Road London W10 5QZ
Liger Books Ltd. 431 George Street Sydney NSW 2000

Contents

Foreword

Upon being asked to edit *Broadlake* for its third edition, I was taken with the prospect of reinvigorating one of the most contentious texts of the last twenty years; a work that, in the light of unprecedented events, has risen from obscurity to capture both the critics' and public's imagination. However, after some deliberation it became evident that it would be quite inappropriate to modify or abridge the second edition, with its accompanying analysis by Michael Anthrup. I felt that the latest revelations surrounding the author would be best served by unveiling the Bracewell murder case in its original context. Consequently, I have made minimal alterations to the text itself and Michael's analysis, merely italicising any commentary of my own and appending an epilogue to lend a degree of resolution to this most fluctuating of literary and legal sagas.

Jay Burgess, March 2023.

Note on the author and text

It is with some trepidation that I introduce an author by confessing scarce little knowledge of the individual in question. The omission of the writer's name from *Broadlake*'s credits is neither a typographical error nor an editorial blunder, but a stark reminder of the ongoing inquiry into his identity. While it is believed that he was English and approximately thirty-two years old when he died, his name and the finer details of his background have remained elusive. Such a dearth of particulars is by no means due to insubstantial scholarly research or cursory forensic investigation. Indeed, what we do know of the author owes much to the painstaking work of the late David Balkan, the book's champion and editor, and the Northern Territory Police following the author's death in August 2002 and in conjunction with the trial of Ivan Damascus in January 2005. Ultimately, the paucity of biographical information is the result of many supposed facts regarding *Broadlake*'s author being recently called into question. This has served to keep the truth at arm's length; a state of affairs mirrored by the novel's narrator as he searches for reasons behind his own fate in the early exchanges of Part 1.

Following the manuscript's discovery beside the author's decomposed corpse in August 2002, it was retained as evidence by the Northern Territory Police. Having completed their initial investigation that November, Balkan, an English lecturer from The University of Melbourne who had been following the case in the national press, requested to see the manuscript. With the permission of the Australian Legal Commission it was released to him in December 2002 and, seeing potential in the work, he edited it over the subsequent seven months. Were it not for Balkan it is highly unlikely that the text we have come to know as *Broadlake* would have even entered the public domain, let alone have become embroiled in the Bracewell murder trial. From the outset, Balkan encountered immense difficulties in not only producing a coherent narrative from the disordered and, in some places, barely legible document, but also in finding a publisher willing to take on the novel; one that, on the surface at least, was not commercially viable due to its unconventional form.

Nonetheless, Otherworld, a small forward-looking Sydney publishing house, believed there was a market for the book's eclectic style and in December 2003 an extract appeared in *Otherworld - First Sight*, a circular showcasing the publisher's forthcoming releases.

One of the most pressing issues facing Balkan upon *Broadlake*'s publication was the verification of events relating to the manuscript's discovery in the basement of a house on Larapinta Drive, Alice Springs, Australia. Introducing the *First Sight* extract, Balkan stated that "without authenticating the circumstances in which the manuscript was found the very integrity of the text is called into question". He was mindful of what may have appeared a well-worn scenario: "the-bundle-of-papers-found-in-a-dark-room-beside-a-dead-body", as writer and critic Jacob Manson branded the setup in his review in 2003. Balkan was eager for the book to be judged solely on its literary credentials and not be viewed as, in Manson's words, "a crass publicity stunt". He therefore insisted that a copy of the official police report, detailing the discovery of the author and his belongings, was made available by Liger Books upon publication and on request thereafter.

As well as providing fundamental details such as the man's cause and time of death (see Part 1 Introduction), the report also confirmed that the manuscript had, beyond all reasonable doubt, been written by the deceased. Although the corpse had entered the third stage of human decomposition, namely active decay, traces of black Qwerty ink were detected on the man's left index finger and thumb; a direct match of the ink used to write *Broadlake*.

Yet, despite Balkan's efforts to prove the text was genuine, many remained sceptical. Jacob Manson was one of several to question whether the papers released to Balkan by the Northern Territory Police were the "sole source" of what he would fashion into *Broadlake*, inferring that the text is an amalgamation of the author's and Balkan's work. Such a claim can largely be dismissed by comparing the published version with a copy of the manuscript kept in police records; the book's adherence to the original papers is evident throughout. Nevertheless, Manson's assertion is arguably upheld since, according to him, "a number of pages being inconveniently lost following Balkan's death has, conveniently for those advocating the authenticity of the book, ensured that the text's clear and inexcusable manipulation cannot be proven."

Overriding Manson's reservations over the book's authenticity, he was even more disparaging of its literary merits. "The 'whodunit' resulting from the discovery of the body is relatively incidental in comparison to the question of who wrote it. The 'whodunit' terminology is wholly applicable to this matter, since the very act of writing such a monstrosity befits that of a heinous crime." It may seem unnecessary to give a platform to such vitriolic criticism, but such views exemplify the contrasting reactions the book received on its full publication in April 2004. For example, Edith Ratchet acclaimed the book's "ceaseless invention and bypassing of literary convention", whilst Catherine Bates labelled the text "a crude and solipsistic clever-clever novel - a failed attempt in sophisticated post-modernism by a dilettante floating on the edges of literacy". In equally conflicting assessments, Damien Grey believed *Broadlake* to be the "raw masterpiece of an unheralded maverick" whereas the unremitting Manson condemned "the incessant cannibalisation of *The Catcher in the Rye*" before slating the book's breezy, colloquial style: "The sub-Salinger doggerel is so spare it must be the most unpoetic poetry ever to be perceived as such - I have seen better verse on a toilet door." Yet, as critic and investigative journalist, Arthur Hamlin, has countered in his authoritative book, *The Kookaburra Killer*, "the novel is not written in standard poetic form but rhyming prose, which ironically gives the author poetic license to control the form as he sees fit." Such is Hamlin's influence, we shall return to his reflections on both the text and its writer throughout the course of the novel.

Putting critical opinion aside, let us focus briefly on *Broadlake*'s involvement in the trial of Ivan Damascus. It must be emphasised that the outcome of the case was by no means swayed by the book's contents alone. Although the text was invaluable in providing, amongst other things, a motive for the

2002 murder of Rose and Mary Bracewell in Alice Springs, much of the incriminating evidence stemmed from events relating to the author's own death. Furthermore, when the book was cited by Damascus' defence, proceedings were plagued by whether *Broadlake* was admissible in a court of law. For submitting a novel as evidence represented something of a first, although diaries had been used to help determine legal cases before: in September 1995 in Orange County, California, Richard Overton was convicted of murdering his third wife, Janet Overton, largely due to evidence from his own diary. Although the entries (which had been recovered via forensic computer analysis from a seemingly empty computer disk) did not categorically say that he was planning to poison his wife, they did contradict statements that Richard Overton made in court with reference to his marriage. These inconsistencies were instrumental in convincing the jury that Overton was lying and would lead to his conviction.

More recently, in June 2005 in Fresno County, also in California, in a case that concluded just weeks before the end of the Bracewell case, Marcus Wesson was convicted on nine counts of first-degree murder. The victims, who had all been shot once in the eye, were his daughters and nieces, coupled with their children whom he had fathered. The diary entries of his daughter, Kiani Wesson, were referenced by the prosecution to illustrate her father's abusive and incestuous tendencies, and the observations reinforced the forensic evidence presented to the court.

There have also been cases where potentially incriminating diary evidence has been excluded, possibly resulting in a miscarriage of justice. In July 1857 in Glasgow, Scotland, Madeleine Smith was accused of murdering her lover, Pierre Emile L'Angelier. Notes made by L'Angelier in a diary that could have inculpated Smith were excluded as evidence and she was found not guilty.

The Bracewell case judge, Mr Justice Ronald Stewart, thus had to consider several factors. Firstly, it would have to be proven that evidence could legitimately be extrapolated from a text high on chicanery and black humour. Secondly, the defence had to demonstrate that the text was authoritative in itself - i.e. the writer's intended version. Hence, Balkan's role was again brought under tremendous scrutiny regarding the number of substantive edits made (consciously changed meanings or additions), and the accidental variants he effected during his revisions (spelling, punctuation and capitalisation). This in turn was reliant on the fact that what he was correcting was the author's own work and not of his own doing.

Even after Mr Justice Stewart had considered these issues and allowed *Broadlake* to be submitted as evidence, Balkan's credibility was still called into question. What is more, the man who in many respects gave *Broadlake* to the world was one of those most undermined by the challenge to its fictional status in June of this year. Perhaps, in hindsight, Balkan would have chosen to reserve *Broadlake*'s eclecticism for a discerning few, rather than see the book he championed on the grounds of its literary flair become part of something so sinister. That said, perhaps he would have found the novel's impact on the Bracewell case fitting testimony to the text's ability to operate on a number of levels. Either way, neither *Broadlake*'s author nor Balkan could have anticipated the consequences of their work.

Michael Anthrup, December 2005.

Part 1 Introduction

The investigation into the author's death

On 28th August 2002 the body of *Broadlake*'s author was discovered in the basement of 38 Larapinta Drive, Alice Springs; a timber-framed one-level property, typical of many found in the residential areas of the town. Uninhabited at the time, it is believed that the author gained entry to the premises via an unsecured bedroom window on the south side of the building. In addition to a rotten window frame and faulty lock, a detached rusted shutter latch was found by police on the sandstone patio below; inspiration, some have advocated, for the broken apartment shutter described by the author in 2.5.

The reason behind the man's presence in Alice Springs seemed clear. At the heart of The Red Centre of Australia, 350,000 tourists a year base themselves in the town in order to visit the nearby sights, converging on Ularu, or as it is better known, Ayer's Rock. Hence, when the body was found it was believed to be that of a traveller. As suggested by the two half-empty bottles of Bell's and Teacher's whisky, coupled with the vomit found on and around the corpse, an autopsy confirmed that the man had partly drunk himself to death, "aspirating his gastric contents". The forensic pharmacologist assigned to the case, Dr Jeremy Back, estimated that the deceased's Blood Alcohol Concentration had risen to around 0.45%, nine times greater than Australia's legal driving limit of 0.05%. (The latter figure equates to 0.05 grams of alcohol per 100 millilitres of blood.) The autopsy also revealed that the deceased had ingested lethal levels of arsenic, or arsenic trioxide as it is most commonly found. It appeared that *Broadlake*'s author had taken his own life but, in view of the poison involved, the police were left with no choice but to treat the death as suspicious.

The man had been dead for "between 21 and 22 days", according to the pathologist Dr James Radcliffe, prompting a problematic investigation into his identity. Despite traces of Qwerty ink being detected on the man's left hand, his facial features had decayed beyond all recognition, a process exacerbated by the extreme heat in the basement. (Although it was not yet summer, when temperatures often reach 40°C between October and March, it had averaged 33.6°C that August.) In addition, the passport and identity cards found in the man's black Nike rucksack were all deemed to be counterfeit. The body was thus, to appropriate legal parlance, a John Doe.

The police's best hopes of a positive identification lay with the Alice Springs community. Staff at Lambert's off-licence and the general store on Todd Street both recognised the man in the deceased's counterfeit passports. However, given he had been merely a customer, neither of the two parties knew his name. Scores of travellers were also scrutinised but these inquiries proved similarly fruitless. By the time the corpse had been found and questioning had begun, the flux of tourists meant that many of the potential witnesses had most likely moved on. Consequently, no one from either the indigenous population or backpacking community knew the identity of the deceased. This included the owner of the house in which the body was found. The man in question, Rupert Tome, was awaiting the renovation of the kitchen and bathroom whilst living at his principle residence in Perth, and when visiting on the weekend of 28th August he had been drawn to the basement by the putrid smell. Amongst the corpse and his belongings, Tome came across an assortment of discarded food packaging, indicating that the man had been living down there for some time.

The Northern Territory Police were called to the scene and, on examining the body, officers found *Broadlake*'s tattered manuscript bound together by frayed yellow string beside the author's Nike rucksack. It lay on top of two objects: a UK edition of *The Times*, dated May 6th 1999, which was open at reports of cricket's County Championship; and an empty pack of Librium, a benzodiazepine used in the treatment of anxiety and panic disorders. The dedication page lay separately under the man's left hand, yet could only be recognised as such by the words "To" and "family" which were still just visible beneath the otherwise defaced writing. What the author originally wrote here, and the likely reason for its defacement, would only come to light at the end of the

Damascus trial. Lastly, loose within the manuscript between pages 106 and 107, a black and white photograph of a burnt-out car was found alongside two unused strips of the antidepressant paroxetine.

Compounding the issue of identity, the man's nationality seemed clear yet was likewise unproven. Staff at Lambert's off-licence and the general store on Todd Street confirmed that the man had an English accent. At the time of his death, he was also in possession of two counterfeit UK passports and, as stated, a British newspaper, *The Times*. Moreover, upon the police's initial reading of the manuscript, the protagonist's intimate portrayal of English family life seemed to provide further clarification of the author's origins. Yet when the man's details were passed on to the Metropolitan Police Service Missing Persons Bureau (METMPB) in London, and then subsequently the National Missing Persons Helpline (NMPH), not a single lead was found. This indicated that either the man was not English after all or that he had become estranged from his loved ones; a set of circumstances that drew parallels with the "familial troubles" of *Broadlake*'s protagonist, as outlined in 1.0 and expounded in later chapters. After three months of unproductive investigations into his identity, the body was buried at the Alice Springs Garden Cemetery on the South Stuart Highway. Consistent with book's fictional world often imitating reality - coincidentally or otherwise - the author's roadside grave is uncannily similar to that of the book's narrator; a site first described in verses 4 and 5 of the novel's opening page.

Inevitably, the precarious concoction of facts and speculation now affect whether we view the text as solely escapism or grounded in a nefarious reality. I hope, therefore, that supplementing the novel's six parts with further analysis will help forge a clearer understanding of how the perception of *Broadlake* has vacillated over time, and will provide an insight as to how the book became entwined in the Bracewell murder case.

Broadlake

1.0

Life is long, my friend, interminably long.
Whatever the score you're scuppered, I fear:
Whether dead at twenty or ninety going strong
It's nothing on the time that you do down here.

With death comes time to focus on life:
Midst cheap rotting wood and weed-choked earth,
We retrace our stories, regret ever rife,
A tardy attempt to defend our worth.

Recalling the past becomes our future,
Eternal life granted despite heresy.
It's no Elysium and, in our stupor,
We're left to varnish our faint legacy.

Yet where I once lay in a tranquil corner
Now borders a slip road to the A34;
Our occasional listeners - fair-weather mourners -
Struggle to hear above the carriageway roar,

The pounding on high, quaking us, the entombed.
Years past you would catch the blithe purl of the stream
But now I'm afraid that pleasure is doomed.
So here's the Big Question, or so it would seem:

Where did my End, if you like, begin?
Where - where exactly - did it all go wrong?
Even now I'm not sure, that is the thing;
Conclude as I might, the doubts play on.

Some ascribe this to plain naivety,
Ignoring the adage of "best made plans".
Some, of course, will gladly come at me
With lines about life dealing out "harsh hands".

Some see the damage and swiftly scoff
Then draw air between teeth like a handyman
Wondering how much he can rip you off:
"Well," they say, "life is hard." Some are a fan

Of sketchy theories that imply,
"I have no clue how things reached this state
So instead I will let the truth pass by
And talk of coincidence, destiny or fate."

Me, I crave Facts, foolproof explanation,
I like to see the logic, the justification.
And often I can, that I will assert,
Before riddles and enigmas subvert

The truths and, once more the rudderless bard,
I find myself turning to those terms I hate:
Naivety, harsh hands, life being hard,
Coincidence, destiny and, yes, fate.

Now such conjecture has moved many on
But I trust you're still there? Hello? Hair-lo-owe?
Oh, not again, don't tell me you've gone?
Today of all days, I beg of you, no!

Or do I sense that you have stayed for more?
Is that you above the ten o'clock chime?
Talking of which, so we're done by half four
It's vital I keep an eye on the time;

Even the dead are in a hurry today.
Come closer, my friend, we'll get underway.
Since you are giving me another whirl,
Let's address childhood then meet The Girl.

Though averse to dredge my upbringing's ills
And join a club many millions strong
- The Miserable Childhood as old as the hills -
It's crucial I do not string you along.

Familial troubles, we had our share,
No doubt more than some and less than others.
Our family hailed from the old school where
Children are nurtured by protective mothers,

Knocked by fathers shorn of compassion;
Former toiling to thwart the latter's effects.
Yet we were not miserable, as is the fashion,
Through poverty or violence, the usual suspects.

No, we were miserable - how can I say it? -
In the middle-class sense of the word.
In essence we had everything, in a way it
Was crazy we felt aggrieved; quite absurd.

We were, on paper, "a close-knit family",
Blessed with olds who'd do all that they could
To set us on our way and thereby happily
Forsake their comforts for a greater good.

And yet still somehow our daily dialogue
Hit on one state at regular juncture:
"I am depressed/You are depressed..." A monologue
That on many occasion would puncture

The post-row silence. By tea it was rare
To not have progressed beyond the third person;
"We are depressed" the prevailing fare
As supper was served and the mood would worsen,

The gloom leaving visitors as they went
To freely conclude the conjugation.
Seeing so many, on the surface, content,
We drew comparisons - no, shared a fixation -

That the whole world had a "normal" family
And in turn wondered why we did not.
Such quandaries were frequent, maddeningly
So at social events that would alas blot

Otherwise perfectly unsociable weekends
(Misanthropy struck at a tender age).
At functions I would be urged to make friends;
School talk/small talk was all the rage.

Why, some say the turning point was one "do".
Very little happened - it's hardly *Plot City* -
But maybe it explains my dilemma to you
Without labouring over the nitty-gritty.

It was a bash at the Such's, world-class bores,
Prime candidates for the dinner party circuit.
Being the cricket season it was raining once more,
Yet we held firm as if conditions were perfect.

Often sister Lara would be press-ganged, too,
But, only turning twelve the previous weekend,
She was home with Elaine, daughter of Sue,
Another party guest and Mother's great friend.

As dentures chattered in praise of our host,
A bitter gust ruptured the bloom-weaved trellis.
A clinked glass announced the birthday toast
And we huddled like penguins on the terrace.

Beneath the ruins of a wind-whipped parasol,
Dick Such blabbered - frankly unpardonable.
The guests were consoled by third-rate alcohol
And the thought it would end, though that was arguable.

We'd toast an aeon later with dregs of wine
And the hum of fevered prattle resumed.
Rain clouds were carried off on the force nine
As I tramped to the pond, gladly marooned.

I eyed the wisteria-swathed Georgian manor:
Fronting the porch, buffed like sports day prizes,
Four hairdresser cars outshone our banger;
One, I presumed, for each midlife crisis.

The band, Angry Salad, a three-chord quintet,
Now shook the marquee - wide open to the gale -
So I had the misfortune of catching their set.
A guest tore outside, as if fleeing from jail,

All flapping comb-over and turkey neck chin,
Dashing, no less, from the face-melting blare.
A buoyed baldie followed and, armed with a gin,
Began jiving with a plastic garden chair.

"Sonny," he hollered, "how are we doing?"
I groaned as I wrestled my blown-out brolly.
"Made pals, have we now?" A cursory viewing
Of the quagmire confirmed Dad's patent folly:

An exclusion zone of circa fifty yards
Rendered his questions somewhat inane.
With more hope of finding friends on Mars,
Avoiding others was the name of the game.

Beaming, Dad ditched his plastic partner
And wagged his glass towards Angry Salad.
"Marvellous," he slurred with booze-fuelled ardour.
His smile, though, drooped as his face turned haggard.

"Dad, they're like two bands playing at once,"
The crotch-wielding crooner wrecking *Hungry Heart*.
"Poppycock, best thing I've heard in months."
I'd heard better tunes in a two-tone fart.

"Where's drummer boy from?" "What do you mean?
London, I imagine, like the rest of the guys."
"Not English, though, is he? Not one of the team.
*Keen*yan, I reckon." I rolled my eyes.

"Nothing's more common, I've always believed,
Than unsuccessful men with talent."
I longed to scarper but lingered, intrigued.
"Why you saying that? Did you hear me?" He hadn't.

Dad grappled his flies: "Sorry, sonny, what?"
"What you said about unsuccessful men."
"Oh, it's nothing important, it's really not."
"Well, if it's nothing important, then - "

"Come on!" And, propped on a felled tree trunk,
He implored me to dance, follow his steps,
As he waltzed to the band's arrhythmic funk,
Sending my ire to uncharted depths.

"Oh, come on," he urged, "come on, sonny."
"I don't want to. And don't call me sonny."
"Have some fun while you have the chance."
He pincered my arm. "Dance, boy, dance!"

My simmering anger brought to the boil
- I'd been happy having a miserable time -
From his grasp I'd gruffly recoil
And, eyeing my watch, down more wine.

Our untimely set-to was over at last,
But I wasn't as yet out of the woods.
Dad's wish to dance suddenly passed
For he'd spied amongst the great and the good

An old colleague of his from yesteryear.
"Bertie," he boomed, "Bertie, old boy!"
His victim, cowering, contrived not to hear,
But, cornered and looking suitably coy,

Sidled on over, sage tie askew.
Drizzle on his cheek may as well have been tears.
"Bertie, old chap, how the hell are you?
I have not seen you in over ten years."

Stalling and clearly musing, Thank God,
A fresh squall loosened the garage guttering.
"Really?" he said as I thought, Lucky sod,
And Bertie squirmed, recalling the suffering.

"Bert left Kline & Co then moved to Dover.
Finally had enough of the darn rat-race."
Introduced and with niceties over,
Dad slapped my thigh then continued apace.

"With luck he'll join the business one day."
He was urging me to mirror his grin.
"How about it?" he purred. "Whaddya say?"
Modulating tone, I simply gave in.

"Sure," I quailed, curtained locks wind-plumed.
Dad glossed over my equivocal reply.
"Still enjoying married life, I presume?"
"Enjoying?" blinked Bertie, straightening his tie.

As if he sought to avoid the query,
Bertie reverted to Kline & Co.
"How's Will these days, Will McCleary?
Doing well is he?" "Sickeningly so.

Earning silly money, I hear he was made - "
"I meant is he happy and in good health?"
"Golly, old chap, no idea, I'm afraid."
Bertie attempted to excuse himself:

"Look, it's been - " "Anyway, enough of Will.
Goodness me, we should be talking family.
How is everyone? Your dear wife, Jill?"
"Oh, she's alright. Still with us sadly."

"No need to be so down in the dumps.
Life can't be that bad, surely, old fellow?"
Dad dealt my arm two Tysonesque thumps
Before broadcasting, approaching a bellow:

"These whippersnappers are lucky indeed.
Girls, school, sport - the best years!" he burst.
True, they *should* be the best but for my breed,
Virgin + misfit + sub = worst.

"We're doing alright now, aren't we, sonny?"
Less a question, more hopefully stated,
I looked at him like a startled puppy,
And maffled a denying, belated,

"Yes." Dad, however, seemed none too fussed
For, as if being tugged away by a gust,
He'd taken off to speak to Mother's friend, Sue.
" 'Scuse me, Bertie. What a fabulous do!"

I was poised for further stilted conversation
But Bertie now appeared far more at ease.
"So," he resumed, "I see your aspirations
Rather differ from Pa's. It would seem that he's

Got you nailed down as a future head.
When pressed on the subject I saw your alarm."
"Oh, was it obvious?" "Obvious?" he said.
Bertie edged closer and gripped my arm.

"It was like watching someone," he wheezed,
"Gaily agreeing to be shot at dawn."
His chortle was dampened by the Arctic breeze.
"So how do you hope to earn your corn?"

"Through songs, books - " "Ah," he laughed wryly
Then turned to view Dad gabbing with Sue.
Shaking, Bertie stooped, quaffing beside me.
"You know," he said, flicking mud from his shoe,

"Years ago, against advice of my betters,
Before grasping I didn't have what it takes,
I saw myself as a man of letters,
My scribblings akin to Donne's or Blake's.

Failure pained me for years but, you see,
How many of us, when we look back on life,
Became the man we believed we'd be?
Before gravity set in, before the wife,

I thought my pen would change the world."
He frowned, shivering, as again he laughed.
"If I could feel my toes - boy, they'd be curled.
What I *did* learn, though, dabbling with the craft:

If, brainstorming, you're not drawn to think
Your tale's a world-beater, something of a first,
It is barely worth another drop of ink.
It won't be - it could be up with the worst -

But anything less is pure extravagance.
Producing bad books - any art for that matter -
Is tantamount to cerebral flatulence!"
His finale curtailed the trembled natter

Of legal beagle, Ray Jenson, supping Chablis.
"What's worse, though," he rallied, "are those frauds
Who dare to proclaim, 'I've a novel in me.' "
"Where it should stay," I said in accord.

"You read Hitchens! Learned fellow!" he blasted.
"You know the sort: when they're out at night,
They talk up books they've barely started
And, sure as death, they will never write.

It's bad enough hearing plots of a caper
That some amateur has actually written,
Let alone one they'll only commit to paper
'If they have time'." He scowled in derision.

"Then some claim it's a 'massive achievement'
Just to *finish* a book: 'You gave it a shot.'
That's so bloody British." I umm in agreement.
"Any witless, semi-literate twot

Can shit three hundred pages of drivel.
That's no damn achievement, for God's sake,
That's a damn waste of paper." I watched him swivel
As a crater-faced waiter dolled out cake.

Whilst he chomped I saw Dad leaving Sue
To catch up with a fast-fleeing Mother.
She brushed him off, as if to shoo
Away a fly, and went to gas with Ros' brother.

"To top it," spat Bertie, starting to sweat,
"Some who find a fool with whom to publish
Don't have the time, it seems, so they get
Some 'ghosty' instead to pen their rubbish.

Back in my day they'd be told to bog off.
You had to at least *write* to be a writer.
Nowadays, I swear, you so much as cough
And the market's seized by a ghosted blighter

Effing and blinding to six-figure deals,
All kinky sex and drug-taking habits.
Many write solely to shock now, I feel,
First line to last buggers at it like rabbits."

Glugging corked fizz to quell his rage,
I spied Ros Such nibbling strawberries and cream,
Bearing an expression that by this stage
Had morphed from vexed squirrel to the face in *The Scream*.

Worse, a twitchy Mother looked none too well;
Or perhaps she was just upset with Dad.
Ros' brother was clueless but I could tell.
I motioned to speak to her. "Bertie, I had - "

"Something else, m' boy, and this one's for free:
Is every book now a blasted 'bestseller'?
Only last week on our nth shopping spree
Jill bought some books from this Cockney feller,

Then bound up to say what a bargain they were.
'Look at these, dear, I got them in a deal.
Bestsellers!' " he cheeped, lampooning her.
"I asked her their names but she just squealed,

'Oh, I don't know, *The*...I don't know...
But they're bestsellers, dear, aren't they nice?'
I tried to tell her bargains are only so
If you *want* them and they're a good price,

Not *because* they're cheap. But would she listen?
Mark my words - screw political correctness -
Balls to it," he growled, forehead aglisten,
"And pardon my cynicism and directness,

But if you ever experience married life
You'll find one defective institution.
Lord, brace yourself, here comes the strife."
Jill was waylaid, a stay of execution.

"She thinks," he whispered, "I have a compulsion
To give into her, say her ways are reasonable,
That I should not be alarmed at her repulsion
Of what seconds before she found agreeable.

Last week, to ward off her hourly outburst,
I did one thing sure to win her affection
- Some housework without being asked to first -
But of course it failed her forensic inspection.

I often take walks, such is my pique.
I pace the long beach beneath The White Cliffs.
These days I do it at least twice a week,
So frequent they've become, these ghastly tiffs.

I try joking but no - droll mares, I fear,
Are rarer than men who send Christmas cards."
He peeped up at Jill who, aptly austere,
Was hounding our doctor, Amy Bernards,

And her son, Paul, gutting a baguette.
"Tell me," the matter still in contention,
"How many comical girls have you met?"
I assumed it a rhetorical question.

As Bertie rattled on Mother shot by,
Barely acknowledging me to boot.
Seeing her upset, dabbing bloodshot eyes,
I was set to slink off and give pursuit

But Rev Snow grabbed her, clutching some Teacher's.
"Why God made the most incompatible creatures
Live together I will never understand.
He must *like* being begged for help by the damned."

I sniggered as, at last, Bertie's wife
Set free Doc Bernards and a lip-licking Paul.
"He's sweet," Jill cooed as he brandished a knife.
"Fucking children," fizzed Bertie, "they're just small.

Make no mistake, they bring untold joy,
But equally can they be little runts.
Don't let those blue eyes fool you, m' boy,
Even Hitler was a cute baby once."

At that, Paul bent the blade's buttered end,
And, censured promptly, down came the red mist.
He looked like the kid who loves telling friends
That Father Christmas doesn't exist.

Jill advanced by way of a scuttle.
"So who have you been harassing, my dear?"
Unable to muster the feeblest rebuttal,
Bertie drew a blank, itching his ear,

And - with aspect more wake than party -
Circled the rim of his champagne flute.
A senior moment, I stepped in sharply,
Bluffing my way as he stayed on mute.

"Hello, my name's - " "Pleasure, really is.
But it's time we chatted to Ros now, dear."
Frogmarched away, necking his fizz,
Bertie sneaked a wave as I poached a beer.

Viewing the porch as the front door slammed,
I watched Dick Such, Britain's dullest man,
Talking the ear off poor Ray Jenson
Whilst stroking the bonnet of his penis extension.

As the band butchered *Help!* then *Hey Jude*,
Fresh rain sent outsiders to the marquee.
Although hungry as ever for solitude,
My seclusion was worrying even me.

Such troubles I endured like no other.
I was that son who, quite beyond help,
Was slipped Kipling's *If* by his mother
In the vague hope I'd be saved from myself.

As two girls neared I sought introductions.
Approaching, though, they were questioning why
Ready meals came without Aga instructions,
So I thought better of it and slid by.

I snuck into the rammed, fuggy marquee,
Polluted by the band's atonal drone.
Eavesdropping on the nearest standee,
A bejewelled dame was parading the stone

Winking at the heart of her new ring.
"It's the fuck factor," she said of a broad soul,
Built like a piano, air-humping a bin,
Clapping like a seal round the tent's central pole.

"It's all about cash flow, you see, Rowena.
He provides the cash, I provide the flow."
Her stitch 'n bitch buds howled like hyenas
As a voice slammed her need to steal the show.

"Quite agree," I chimed, "mother from hell."
Whilst Salad dismantled *Easy Lover*
Our brewing contempt began to swell.
"Imagine if she really was your mother.

I mean, Christ," I sneered, shaking my head,
And we chortled as one at our despair.
Yet his mirth was strained. "Actually," he said,
"She is my mum. And that's my dad there.

Lord of the Prance," he garbled, cockeyed,
And my laughter dwindled as I nearly died.
I peered down into my froth-lined glass
And, grovelling, stared at the trampled grass.

"Don't worry," he said, "you're totally right,"
Sealing forgiveness with a ghoulish smile.
We turned to catch the discomfiting sight
Of his mother now yapping on her mobile

(Being '89 a brick-sized contraption).
Clutching his stomach, he lent on a chair.
"Sorry," he belched, straightening a fraction,
"It's Edward Carver but call me Blair."

I pondered why there was no connection,
But before I'd even posed the question
He'd viced my hand, bone crunching bone,
My grunt akin to a winded groan.

A doubled-up Blair replied with brusqueness:
"Thunderbox calls," and, on taking flight,
"Chocolate thunder ahoy!" His exit's abruptness
Let my paw fade from pulse-starved white

And resume its accustomed milky pink.
However, no sooner had it come round
I was ambushed by Quinn - from Maine, I think.
Fingers re-clamped, I stood my ground

As he relayed his weekend by the sea;
Details of which, though, I could not glean,
For so strong was his twang that on TV
They would post subtitles across the screen.

As I strived for a basic translation,
He even *laughed* with an American accent.
At last tuning in to his one-way oration,
I swigged my poison as a relaxant.

It was a shame, between me and you;
Despite received opinion, I'm fond of Yanks.
Pretty controversial, I know, but it's true.
Searching for back-up from either flanks

- Salad's crimes against music trashing Dire Straits -
Quinn emptied the reserves of my sanity.
As my friend Holden succinctly states,
He sure had a lousy personality.

I trust you know who I'm talking of, yes?
You're fairly well-read, to hazard a guess.
Just to be clear, though, Holden's the guy
From J.D. Salinger's *Catcher in the Rye*.

Why, I would fret that, having read it so much,
I'd become Holden's foe - the phony, the fake.
You wouldn't think books would affect you as such
- They are only books after all, for Christ's sake -

But truly they can; it set my mind ablaze,
So much so I wound up this virtual mimic.
It riled me, though, when, damned with faint praise,
It was termed a "teen classic" by some lofty critic;

As if youth a barrier to the human condition.
I mean just because you follow what Holden is saying
And he's no dictionary-swallowing technician,
Does not infer it deserves downplaying.

As for how theorists yawningly reckon
It's fodder for a killer or suicidal loner:
Yes, it's synonymous with Chapman and Lennon
And Holden's as blue as a pheasant in October,

But does that imply that supposed sane souls
- Many as damaged as Holden in their way -
Can't relate to *Catcher*? As I rate Holden's role
Does that mean that *I'm* going to kill one day?

A snapper arrived but, supremely efficient,
Quinn was at liberty to prate once more.
A coma setting in and beer insufficient,
I devised a strategy to withdraw.

The standard, "I mustn't keep you any longer,"
Was trumped by, "You're not keeping me here."
I considered trying something stronger,
"Fuck off" maybe, but, feigning good cheer,

I listened remotely to Quinn's sermon,
Spying my olds through guests ambling by.
Words tangled with noise, I could not be certain
But there seemed to be something seriously awry.

Mother bore a look of mock composure,
Her jaw now clenched, puffed cheeks scarlet-blushed,
Helpless to prevent their spat's exposure.
Dad's brazen tones rang out as they rushed

Through raucous chatter - Salad mercifully done -
His organ stop eyes compounding my dread;
Mother's mascara was threatening to run
As she raised a hand to shield her head.

Her great friend, Sue, less than ten feet away,
Appeared concerned then more so shocked.
Biting my lip, I watched her eyes stray
Back and then forth until they were locked

On the feud behind her fellow guest's back.
She seemed so fraught for a moment I thought
She'd reveal her hand and launch an attack,
Slamming Dad's ways whilst cutting him short.

Looking on, wincing, it got so bad
That soon teary Mother was glaring at Sue,
Begging, I sensed, to be saved from Dad.
Yet before her friend could break up their blue

They'd parted ways, tensed arms flailing.
I watched Mother quit the merry-tongued din
As Dad stood muttering, balance ailing,
Attached to the bar, draining his gin.

The rumpus over but Quinn still blabbing,
I was half relieved to see Blair returning.
As he neared I could see him dabbing
His darkened crotch, his face now burning:

"Turned on the tap and watered my groin!"
As, narrow-eyed, we gauged his excuse,
A hush fell on those he'd dared to join,
The pain of which Blair sought to reduce.

"Look, here's the filly I met out in Oz."
He brandished a snap. "Six months away.
Was amazing over there, truly was.
You really should try to go one day.

And see this," he pressed, grinning a touch.
He gave an envelope a knowing pat.
"A condolence card for Rozzy Such.
You know, for her birthday. How mad is that!"

Deflecting the torment inflicted by Blair,
Dad was now stumbling from the marquee.
Scratching his pate's micro-island of hair,
He bundled past Bertie then rounded me.

I threw Blair a frown then, at the double,
Came thumped footsteps as Hell closed in.
Gilly Reeve was now taking the trouble
To say hello - or dodge talking to Quinn,

Presently juggling three pints of Guinness.
He was that guy who thinks he's your friend
After meeting you once for barely five minutes.
"One for you both. To an awesome weekend!"

It was hard to say who would most bore me,
For though I had rarely met Mrs Reeve
I actually knew half her life story
From the round-robins we would receive,

Spilling from family-snap festive cards;
An all too common habit these days
But back in the 80's the whole charade
Had yet to snowball into a craze.

This year's epitomised previous releases:
Trailing *Another year gone, how time flies!!!*
Was a warts and all four-page thesis
Listing *huge lows and* *outrageous* *highs*.

Gilly enthralled us with extensive accounts
Of her ma's incontinence/hip replacement,
Her pa's enlarged prostate, before she'd recount
Her son's *stellar year abroad, his dream placement*

With a leading bank, a most prestigious firm.
As a surprise, she and hubby Phil
Flew out to visit him, which we'd learn
Was a *roaring* *success - such a thrill!!!*

And then lastly, but by no means least
Given the details force-fed our way,
We were told that Truffles, their beast
Of a dog, had, at the very end of May,

Lost sight in one eye and, after a fall,
Had to be put down in early June.
It was a harrowing day for us all.
Batting away a sagging balloon,

Gilly sipped her fizz and turned to Blair.
"How were your travels?" "Oh, mad," he gurned.
He gabbed of Oz and his "crazy time" there.
"Though craziest of all," he discerned,

"It was truly incredible, Mrs Reeve.
I met this one chap from our hometown.
I mean fancy that, it's hard to believe,"
Swilling his plonk then slamming it down,

"Bumping into someone from round here
In some bar in Alice. Unreal, eh?"
Of course, it was no feat or even near
Given the surge in school leavers - say,

A third of the pre-matriculating mob -
Who flock to Oz to defer their studies;
Augmenting those still without a job,
Despite splurging Daddy's hard-earned money,

Maxing out cards on their *previous* gap year,
Splashing cash in beach bars in Northern Queensland.
Hell, *!WORK!* triggers such buttock-clenching fear
Most would sooner flee to goddamn Greenland

Than look for a job they can't get anyway,
Because the uni supplying the qualification
For a job in PR by reading Proust and Hemingway
Would hoof them out with no justification,

Shamefully overworking the little mites
By demanding no less than an essay a month:
"Every month? A whole one? That can't be right."
I merely let slip a disproving humph.

Blair's comments finished off Gilly Reeve.
"Oh, look, the birthday girl. Better scoot."
Excusing herself, she took her leave,
And Quinn, oddly muzzled, followed suit.

Such withdrawals I'd witness in due course
- We struck up a friendship; yes, I know -
For Blair's critiques were often the source
Of people insisting they had to go.

His "revelations" proved unbearable:
The victim of strangers' first impressions,
He emptied rooms at rates comparable
With kids fleeing class at end of lessons.

Some friendships, I guess, are in part due
To all others refusing to put up with you.
Last picks for the game, schoolyard prey,
We were The Leftovers, one might say.

In Pinteresque silence, I groped for a question.
"I was just wondering why you're called Blair
If you are Edward. What's the connection?"
"Middle name," he grouched, gasping for air.

As he dry-heaved then vom-bombed the floor,
I moonwalked outside. All the guests were gone
Save my olds on the terrace giving what for.
They froze as I loomed. "What the frick's going on?"

"We're off," Dad snapped, culling the exchange.
Thanking our hosts from the heart of my bottom,
I skulked to our Saab, and, soon out of range,
Dad whistled *Hey Jude* like all was forgotten

Whilst Mother espoused the Such family.
"So nice, aren't they, darling? Really nice lot.
So kind to each other," she murmured sadly.
Lost in her patter, she plainly forgot

That, once alone, they would probably be
Barking like drill sergeants at each other
Over what garbage to watch on TV,
Or just praying they didn't become their mother.

"About your row," I said, "it crosses the line - "
"Sonny, just leave it, for your mother's sake.
She finds driving hard at the best of times."
Whilst I pondered the pile-ups left in his wake,

We coasted as Dad urged, "Give it the gun,"
And skirted around the night's commotion.
Was it the trigger for what was to come
Or was my "fate" still a distant notion?

Melbourne Times

July 1st 2005

MOTHER AND CHILD CLUBBED BY KOOKABURRA KILLER

"Stalked by the homeless recluse, Rose Bracewell was beaten savagely over the head with a Kookaburra cricket bat, sending her and her young daughter, Mary, to their tragic deaths."

1.1

As they rowed upstairs I switched on The Band
And polished off *The Times* quick crossword,
Aping Dad's spindly, doctorly hand;
The Qwerty ink dashed, the lettering blurred,

Determined, it appeared, in its negligence.
He always said it was a sign of intelligence
And, naturally, I disagreed with him then,
But I'm drawn to that line every now and again.

Quivering, I glazed singed toast with honey.
Dad, in that most middle-class of habits,
Refused to use heating "to save some money"
Yet had just booked a week in St. Moritz.

Goosebumps rippling across sleeve-rolled arms,
I bit into the brittle, black-dappled toast.
Blighting the kitchen's momentary calm,
Came hissed voices, dampened, like demented ghosts:

My parents stuck in their age-old rut,
The height of marriage's disunity.
At one the spare room door banged shut,
The start of short-lived impunity.

For, eight days on from their grim-faced pact,
I returned from nets early - another wet weekend -
And entered the snug to catch Dad in the act:
Embracing Sue; yes, Mother's best friend.

As it replays I can hear her cries,
I dread the sight as I turn the handle,
His hands worming up her varicose thighs,
Dark mustard cords slopped about his ankle.

Set to be spared, "It's not what you think,"
He plumped instead for the last-ditch version:
"I can explain," his face fuchsia pink,
Babbled as panicked as Sue's desertion.

Mother returned home from church commitments,
Our profanities staining our Christian veneer;
Dad flogged his hole-filled, black-is-white arguments,
The extent of his lies abundantly clear.

I grimaced at Mother, she grimaced at him,
And, explanation long overdue,
I told her straight of Dad's little fling,
Countered at once with a sigh that she knew.

They'd tried, I'd hear, to resolve things at first
But were now splitting before it got worse;
Deciding that divorce was the best thing
Was the first time they'd agreed on anything.

In the throes of divide they were drawn together,
Defending each other with perverse endeavour.
"Please understand," Mother sought to explain.
"Yes, please," urged Dad, "we both feel the same."

"That's right," came Mother, "Your father and I
Have been talking of how we might begin - "
"I can't believe this. I cannot see why - "
"Listen," she maintained as Dad chipped in:

"Yes, please do, sonny. At the end of the day - "
"We knew," she took over, "you'd find this tough
But with your exams only weeks away
And Grandpa poorly, you've quite enough - "

"That's right, sonny, we didn't wish to concern - "
"Wish to 'concern', Dad? Are you kidding me?"
Frothing, I swallowed as my stomach churned.
"Do you really think that your actions be

Of someone 'concerned' with how people feel?
Do you?" I said. "Do you?" I pressed.
"Oh, please," Mother begged in frantic appeal,
"Don't you see things are already a mess

Without all this upset. Can't you just try…"
It was all too much and she began to cry.
Yet I was still gripped by the injustice,
Words spewing like lava: "No, wait, fuck this,

I'm not gonna stand here and pretend, like you,
That it's water under the bridge and life's okay."
"But it is," she whimpered, "we've talked things through
And it will be best for you both in a way."

"How can you back him when he's sunk so low?
It makes no sense at all, please tell me how.
He's been caught red-handed just moments ago
But you're acting like the whole thing is now - "

"Please!" Mother screamed. "It's all for you.
You and Lara. Always has been, always will.
Keeping you happy, that's all I want to do."
She leant, out of breath, on the window sill,

Nudging the Good Book into a rose-filled vase,
But snaring the bass as it toppled over.
Her sobs met the grumble of passing cars
And she dropped, overcome, onto the sofa.

Her impact uprooted our tabby, Nat,
Vexing Dad as ever as he scampered by.
Dad would top his wish to "drop-kick the cat"
- Ironing him out by the gate that July -

But, for now, he fled through the wedged-open door,
Pricking Dad's shin with an outstretched claw.
"Sarcastic little fuck!" Vanquished in his ruse,
Dad fled to the cellar to tend his home brews.

"We don't wish," Mother wept, "to fight all the time.
We've just grown apart, as I fear some do.
Perhaps we have come to the end of the line
But I swear we will never give up on you."

"So siding with Dad, it's all for Lara and I?"
Mother sniffled, nodding in despair.
How I rued my response, the way I'd let fly,
For thinking I was victim of Dad's affair.

***

Saying you'll split is one thing, of course,
But doing it is another thing altogether.
It was as if the spectre of divorce
Made the alternative somehow better.

And so a year on from the affair
- Or at least the one I have just described -
In resigned martyrdom Mother declared
They'd agreed to revoke the remedy prescribed;

Their plans were put on hold forever
Despite the shambles of their marriage.
One broken home that stayed together,
This uni drop-out surveyed the damage,

The vicious cycle of burning suspicion,
Exposure, outrage, frosty resentment,
Then disbelief as Dad was forgiven
And cast in the role of excused defendant.

"A slip," Mother called it for the umpteenth time,
"He said he's sorry and ashamed of himself."
She, like me, even borrowed Dad's lines:
"Infidelity's as old as marriage itself."

"Well, that makes it alright, then," I would reply.
I'd turn on Dad but it came to no good:
"Sonny, it's between your mother and I."
Hence I'd blame her - because I could –

For being too proud to concede they'd failed,
For subjecting us to their daily blue,
For thinking he'd change when that ship had sailed,
For trying to patch things up with Sue.

Anger unsated, once through with her
I'd revert to Dad but, raining "sonnys"
- And master of the non sequitur -
He'd switch our talk to my failing studies.

"What's that got to do with the price of fish?"
"Everything. Get your bloody head down," he cawed.
"You can't simply come and go as you wish."
"I'd rather work than waste three years or more

In some college of knowledge that doesn't cater - "
"Fine, then, get a job," he answered coolly.
"I'll think about it." Then seconds later:
"I've thought about it. I'll go to uni."

Yet, weeks on, all dirty washing and debt,
I'd hitchhike home to rebreak the news.
Swelling Dad's umbrage, my retreat was met
With wide-eyed revulsion at their do's.

Dismay I thought, at first, was imagined
Was proven as guests spoke like a)
I plainly needed my head examined:
"What is the boy doing? Chucking away

His life, now dogged with uncertainty."
Or b) someone died: "*Such* a waste."
Ignoring the scuzz-fest that is university
Where honours are gained in getting shitfaced.

There was the small matter of a degree
But what use was that to the budding artiste?
"If you're not going back you can work for me,"
Fuelling the fire for a year at least.

Having aired our delicious indignation,
We would briefly hold civil conversation;
Briefly, I stress, for one loaded remark
Was all that it took to relight the spark.

Take a drive that summer to Uncle Sean.
Windows were down to tame August humidity
Whilst we talked cricket and Saints' poor form,
Our banter passing with rare placidity

As, creeping, we slithered through city suburbs,
Bumper-sniffed the clogging weekend traffic.
Idling shoppers brimming at the kerbs,
We chewed the fat until - symptomatic

Of our stop-start ride - Dad voiced the injustice
Of heeding the core of The Highway Code.
"Oh, for Pete's sake, must we put up with this?
Get these bloody brownies off the damn road!"

Note at this point I thought I'd misheard,
Being, even for him, ill-timed disenchantment.
Deducing I had not, and with Dad undeterred,
I thrust my head inside the glove compartment.

Somehow we thankfully escaped unharmed;
His revving engulfed the offending phrase.
Dad, however, could not be becalmed:
"These effing camel drivers along with the gays

Are hastening our once great nation's demise!"
I retrieved my head as Dad cranked the gears,
And scanned the surroundings to gladly surmise
We were clear of "brownies" or potential queers.

"Do you really think that or is it some joke?"
He gazed, bemused, doubting my morals.
"Of course. Am I that - what do you say? - 'bloke'
Who believes in something then rests on his laurels?

Should we all now have to suffer in silence?"
"How are you suffering? If anything," I rasped,
Nostrils flaring and gushing with defiance,
"Gays are suffering from us living in the past."

Addressing my point by ignoring it entirely,
Dad turned to his former bone of contention.
"Look at the schools, the fulcrum of society,
Bursting with migrants who, with the odd exception,

Lower the whole standard of all the other - "
"Hold up," I said, "we were talking about - "
"Let me finish, you're worse than your mother."
"When was the last time you heard her out?

Maybe if you listened and applied some logic
You'd realise the grief you cause us all.
Christ, the atmosphere back home is toxic.
And you wonder why I want to leave!" I bawl.

"Oh, at last! When?" "When I've sorted - " "Some work?
Couldn't organise a piss-up in a brewery.
You think 'art' pays?" he signed off with a smirk.
"See, off you go again," and approaching fury,

"When will you *listen*?" Stealing my silence
- And as if to entirely prove my point -
He launched back into his rant on migrants.
"Who, largely speaking, are the troublesome oiks

Playing truant, coming bottom of the class,
Holding back others till their chance has gone?"
Try as I might, I could not let it pass.
"Have you lost your mind? Where's all this from?"

"From parents we know who haven't had means
To send their offspring to private school.
Who, as a result of disruptive scenes,
Watch their boys suffer. Give it time and you'll - "

"So we send them back to face more hardship,
Untold cruelty and persecution?"
"What claptrap," he pounced, spittle catching my lip,
"Some have a case and make a contribution,

But most lead us on a merry little dance
And have no reason for asylum. None."
"That's typical. We've got to give them a chance."
"At the expense of giving *our* children one?

You've had too sheltered an education
To grasp the real world...look, sponging wogs!"
Two were begging by Old Street station.
"No wonder this country's gone to the dogs.

Those coming here to get an education
Are ensuring standards take a battering,
And those who could change things, who have an education,
Don't effing know that it's even happening."

"You can't let 0.1 millimetre of skin
- The only real difference between our races -
Define - " "Oh, puh-lease, don't give me that spin.
You think they don't judge us by *our* faces?

That they give *us* the benefit of the doubt?
That's the problem with your generation,
Race is so cut and dry. If you don't spout
The joys of our multicultural nation

You're seen as a peddler of prejudice."
"Yes, but you - " "Trust me, one day you'll learn.
Boy, you want to know why I think this?
Last time I drove here I took a wrong turn

But, seeking directions, I couldn't distinguish
The writing on the signs; in Arabic, I think.
I stopped to ask but no one spoke English,
Then some buffoon started kicking up a stink,

Shouting at me - quite what I'd no idea -
But the translation of which, to put it bluntly,
Was, I've no doubt, 'Fuck off out of here'.
I was a foreigner in my own country.

Then, almost as bad, last week I'd learn
That Bertie - " "From the Such's?" "Yes, that's him.
Well, he went for a new role at his firm
- They said they were promoting from within -

But in the end they went for an outsider,
Some box-ticking blow-in fresh off the boat
Because they wished to 'cast their net wider'.
Lord, soon we won't even be able to vote.

The way things are going, in 2020
Half our jobs will be reserved for minorities
And middle-class whites will be seen as the enemy,
At the mercy of quota-centric authorities."

"Oh, that's ludicrous." "Ludicrous? And yet
Look how crazy we've become over 'race'.
So keen to be inclusive that we forget
Who in fact lives here in the first bloody place."

Under the pump, as a last resort
I revived my gripe at him changing the subject.
"Hang on, we were talking about gays I thought,
Not migrants or 'blacks'. Yes," I object,

"You've twisted the argument completely away
From my opposition to your thoughts on gay - "
"Oh, gays, blacks," he droned, "it's all the same."
"Jeeesus," I growled, "do you have no shame?"

"I do actually, from when I was at school
And some pre in my house tried to…have his way.
And you question why I'm not, in your words, 'cool'
With how they are all now flavour of the day."

"That…happened?" I stuttered, but nonetheless keen
To take advantage of his sizeable lapse:
"The main problem with your argument's been
That you can lump together gays and 'blacks'."

"I didn't mean it. My point was the lout - "
"No it was - " "Yes it - " "No it was *not*!"
Rowing over what we were rowing about,
We swerved off the road and, tied up in knots,

Continued our spat though hushed suburbia,
A world from the maelstrom moments earlier.
The residents' peace as they savoured the breeze,
House sparrows fluting in the bough-nodding trees,

Dashed by the cries spilling from the road,
Snatched with the *whouf* of our speeding car.
"…It was society…!" "…But the gays…!" "…What a load…!"
"…You said blacks…!" "…Batty boy…!" "…Touch of the tar…!"

Our feud raged till we agreed to disagree.
"Believe me," Dad sniped, "I won't say another word."
Trusting him less than a campaigning MP,
He duly reneged: "This is ab*surd*."

And, with that, our altercation rumbled on.
It was no mere matter of opinion:
We knew we were right and the other was wrong,
Spawning the slanging match's dominion.

"I feel sorry for you!" "Listen to you!" he replied.
"What about you, if you could hear your*self* speak!"
We'd desist for a second but a peeved aside
Would rekindle the bedlam, yet to peak.

"I'm shocked," Dad snarled, "by the cheek you're displaying."
Cut up by a bike, he dealt the horn two wallops.
"Look," I replied, "I appreciate what you're saying
But I just think you're talking absolute bollocks."

"Sonny, how dare you! Always thinking you're right."
"Well, I'm hardly going to think I'm always wrong."
The road had cleared and, running the lights,
Dad hit the gas as I strived to hold on.

"With the greatest respect, you just don't get - "
"The greatest respect? Now there's a fine phrase.
Since when have you shown me any respect?
That's just lip service folk employ these days

As if it's permission to say something rude."
"Wait, that's not true." "It bloody well is."
"You don't get it," I said, "you have just used
Your own experience and think that it gives - "

"If you don't be quiet…if you don't be quiet…
You can get out the car!" He elbowed my wrist.
"Jeez, psycho," I mumbled, enflaming the riot.
"How dare you," he stormed, "how dare you persist…"

Maddened by how he had "attacked" me,
I spelt out my righteous views to the letter.
Lost for words, Dad thundered, "Exactly!",
Then decried my case: "A tonk could do better."

He parodied a "black" having our barney
Which, like many such impersonation,
Dissolved into strained Welsh-Pakistani.
Incensed by his latest abomination,

I cursed then likened him to the devil,
Sinking beneath even his debased level.
"It's mad," he said as he stole through a gap,
"If blacks impersonate a Caucasian chap

It's seen as a funny, acceptable opinion.
But if whites mimic, let's say, a West Indian,
It's slammed as 'racist'. What's that about, eh?
Where is free speech? Double standards, I say."

Further incensed, my riposte could not wait.
Noting my temper, Dad slowed up his speech:
"Calm down, sonny, you must learn to debate.
Make your case, sure, but there's no need to screech - "

I finally snapped: fists tightly clenched,
I smashed them against the glove compartment.
With the door cracked and, in turn, wrenched,
I kicked the flap in sustained bombardment.

"Control yourself, boy." "I'll pay for it all."
"How exactly?" "Oh, bring it back to money."
"You've just wrecked the car! If you can't keep your cool
You'll hurt someone one day. I swear it, sonny."

"Don't be ridiculous." "I'm not having you on.
It seems minor now but these things grow - "
"Where do you think I get my anger from?"
"You can't reproach me each time that you throw - "

"Why are those who accuse others of anger
Often angry themselves?" "Stop passing the buck."
"I'm not," I seethed with vein-popping rancour.
"Don't blame others, sonny, for coming unstuck - "

"Stop calling me sonny. And yes, I do blame - "
"You're gabbling," said Dad, "sss-lll-ooo-www down."
"I am *not* gabbling." He condemned my claim
As we hung a hard left into Kentish Town.

"Anyway," he said, "thanks for the apology."
"What do you mean? When did I say sorry?"
"No, really, thank you." With wolfish ferocity,
I shrieked as we shaved a jackknifed lorry:

"You've got completely the wrong end of the stick!"
Driving the car, and me, around the bend,
Dad screamed so hard he was almost sick:
"I've discovered my own stick and found my own end!"

The tick-tock tick-tock of the indicator
Signalled our turn into Uncle Sean's drive.
Finding neutral, Dad pumped the accelerator,
A habit of his that I would revive.

We'd greet Uncle Sean as we'd always do,
Happy as sandboys, smiling on cue.
Yes, Dad praised us all, the cat - even me -
Before the ride home spelled World War Three.

And that, my loyal listener, was a good day.
Next morning I woke to cries from the hall,
Fallout from Dad's latest "playing away".
I hugged weeping Lara, slumped at the wall,

Then raced down to act out our role reversal.
Parenting - that series of bribes and threats -
Now the two weapons at their child's disposal:
"If you don't stop this.../Say sorry or I'll get..."

Parenting one's parents the final straw,
Mother begged we go back "to how it was before";
A past that never was, a dream up in smoke.
Faux nostalgia blooms when there's no hope.

Tempers tinder-dry and the outlook bleak,
It will hardly come as the greatest surprise
That I moved out the following week.
I still see the tears in dear Lara's eyes

As I waved tamely from the London train.
Clutching Strat, cricket bat and rucksack of clothes,
I was staying at Blair's just off Brick Lane
And had lined up a job - yes, one of those -

At Quills, a bookstore, in The Glade mall.
Inevitably, Mother tried to stay in touch;
The more I ignored her the more she'd call.
Although we made no plans as such

I vowed to meet "when things settled down".
On a whim one day I promised to visit
Then later agreed to lunch in town,
But I cancelled both at the last minute.

Lost to the call of artistic ambition,
Weeks grew to months, months grew to a year,
Mother stopped calling and, blind to contrition,
I had won the day, or so it would appear.

1.2

In between pruning what I deemed would be
My Booker-bagging tome, I began writing songs
For my eponymous genre-bending LP.
Assembling a band, one soon five strong,

We refined the sound that would make our name;
Penning tunes, it felt, that defied imitation,
Of which the critics would uniformly proclaim
As defining works of our generation.

A dash of The Smiths, The Who, The Stones,
A nod to The Cure, The Fab Four and Dylan;
Yet, to our ears, a sound all of our own,
One to make the world sit up and listen.

A small tour planned - and album launch to boot -
And buoyed by my novel's Bold New Voice,
It was only time before my works bore fruit;
Twin triumphs as heir to Lennon and Joyce.

Oh, what halcyon days when all seems possible;
When hope seems justified, what once seemed rash
Is viewed a masterstroke, defying improbable.
Yet greater is the pain when true hope is dashed.

There were no echoes of the late Beatle,
Or cut-and-paste reviews of his literary equal:
The *Read it in one sitting then started again/*
A book I long to press into the hands of friends.

Catchy…like the plague they tagged our single, *Yelp*,
Before my tome drew the stock thumbs-down letter:
The narrator is beyond psychiatric help.
It's safe to say things could've gone a bit better.

Each day was the morning after the night before:
Sore heads from our "show" - if the term's applicable -
Topped by the aftermath hanging onto the floor.
My uncertain career was truly predictable.

Then, small consolation, "fate" intervened.
Whole days at Quills without hope of a sale,
I could not flog or write books, it seemed,
So I reviewed them; at first to no avail,

Posting unread critiques by recommendations.
Then one day an editor came by the store
And took a liking to my pithy summations.
Taking my number, it was not long before

I was working for *Blurb*, appraising the charts;
Or "shooting the bull", as Blair would dub it.
I knew the ins and outs of commercial art,
Skirting success my specialist subject.

I begrudged releases some praise or other,
Honing the flattering, marketable quotation.
A few found their way onto a novel's back cover,
The closest I'd come to a literary sensation.

Meanwhile, I'd watch former classmates of mine
Compliantly step onto their treadmill,
The Road to The City that stood them in line
Until they retired and were over the hill.

Least that's how I saw it, young and blinkered.
As if an "artist" was all there was to be!
I pitied them once yet, as time tinkered
With dreams, pity rebounded back onto me.

To think I saw art as bypassing commerce,
Untouched by the cogs of the fiscal world!
How it stung - Dad was right - to face the reverse
As art's corporate heart was cruelly unfurled:

As much a business as spheres I'd denounce,
Most of us capitalists posing as moralists,
Denying our motives (unlike friends in accounts,
Banking, law, the signposted materialists).

Yet one bleary morning always strikes me anew.
Playing to one man minus dog at The Gate,
I'd crashed at muso friends, Sam and Drew,
With whom I'd had several over the eight.

I see myself now by the scuffed café door:
Clock nudging twelve, it's breakfast for me,
Having passed out in the bath at gone four.
Blenching, I brush breadcrumbs from my knee,

Sighing at headlines that sell my red-top,
Tongue juggling ice that was half my drink.
A dull throbbing head and teeth on edge, I slop
From my seat and, feet out of synch,

Sway round a suit, bowed like a hunchback,
Catching the rush of his lunch hour air,
His bolt of nicotine before he lumps back
To weekend-wishing from his office chair.

Stranded at a crossing as traffic pours by,
I look across to a daydreaming stranger,
A headphoned figure who's taken her eye
Off the hubbub and its dormant danger.

Though a trice away it's a distant event,
The galleries of my mind opening once more:
Frame by frame, sound on sound, time bent
And then locked, voiding all that which has gone before,

Freezing all else after, evolving again,
History scribed with a revisionist's pen;
Every sense heightened, vision like no other,
Leaden hues switching to vivid technicolour.

Adjusting her headphones, the lights are green,
But there's a gap in the traffic, the slightest gap;
She's stepping off the kerb, the white Merc unseen,
Its wide-yawning cabbie's eyes on his lap.

We're waiting, waiting, yet no one calls out,
Her blustered black locks veiling her eyes;
A Scouse is on the phone, I think a ticket tout,
As we foresee her inevitable surprise.

Three strides in, hear the click of her heel,
See her head nod to the frantic mute beat,
The walrus-tashed cabbie tapping at the wheel,
Curls wriggling, slug-like, as he champs on a sweet.

He's looking straight at her - I am at a loss:
Why the hell is he not even braking?
It's then, right then, that I'm compelled to cross,
The pending risk all of my own making.

The Merc is closing, God's will seems done
- I believed back then, a true profanity -
What use am I? I fight the urge to run,
Risk my life for an attack of humanity.

Yet that which compelled me - destiny's about! -
Sends me forth and she's alive to the danger.
It's now or never but she's stiffened by doubt:
Should she go back or head for the stranger?

I clock the *Mail* in her upturned hand:
A puff of wind swells stage left, my right,
Catches a page and, as we are fanned,
It flaps like the sail of a wavering kite,

Pulling free of her loosening fingers;
I'm four strides across, she twists to turn back,
The Merc hasn't slowed as coffee scent lingers,
Hangs on the breeze; the tout laughs in the pack

Penned in behind as her spread *Mail* falls,
Claps the tarmac, double sheet taking flight,
Soaring like the kite as the car horn bawls
In tandem with the brakes' belated bite,

Soprano screech versus droning hooter.
As its baritone bellows we meet halfway:
Against the swirling smudge of commuters
I lunge for her pea coat's gunmetal grey,

The Merc's bearing down, it's upon us - too late.
I'm thrown on the bonnet, bundling her away,
Whumping the windscreen as locked wheels skate
And, sliding, I'm flung to the ground like prey

Tossed from the mouth of a tormenting cat.
I see her, supine, arm twisted from the blows;
A dying sight, though, as seconds after that
I glimpse another world as reality slows.

I see myself fading, heading down here
- No life-flashing montage, all that crap -
But, letting go and almost free of fear,
I sense I'm entering the final lap.

Yet drifting, drifting, death is defied:
I wake to blood oozing from my skewed head,
Leaking past buffed black shoes at my side,
A blurred suit stemming the river of red.

Her *Mail*'s sundered pages waft to the ground
Like feathers floating down from burst pillows.
I feel drunk again, the street's swinging round;
Commuters leaning like falling dominoes.

At blood-gushing lips is a cigarette stub
As I writhe, gagging, on the ragged tarmac.
My ears are ringing like I've just left a club,
I hear someone yelling, "Get the fuck back!"

Siren-sped, we're dashed through the City;
Within the hour I'll be under the knife.
I loll to one side, senseless, dizzy,
At a face that will shape that and this life.

Many of those who perceive the book as a thinly-veiled autobiography have suggested that the author's alcohol-related struggles - and which culminated in his death - echo those of the protagonist's father in *Broadlake* itself; an addiction insinuated from the very first chapter. This has given rise to the notion that the author was predisposed to alcohol misuse through genetic or hereditary means, or, in psychological terms, learned behaviour.

From *The Kookaburra Killer* by Arthur Hamlin

1.3

Coming round from surgery late that evening,
She's stood at my side, her arm in a sling.
I'd suffered, it transpired, internal bleeding,
My bones now more a network of pins.

Benumbed and running on peripheral vision,
A jungle of leads sprout from the screens,
Bleeping as they track my frail condition.
"You're awake. Oh my God. If you'd not been...

Thank you, thank you from the depths of my heart.
How can I..." Moaning, I make out her face:
"Well, you can get me some tea for a start."
I try to twist round but my neck's in a brace.

"My name's - " "Sorry, can you get me some pills."
She fetches the doc: "How are you feeling?"
"How do you think? My head bloody kills."
I flick my puffed eyes up at the ceiling;

Not that I can look anywhere else.
They recheck my meds and she brings me tea.
"Got you a straw. Don't move, I'll help."
"Move? Are you kidding?" "Just leave it to me."

The injured nursing the invalid,
She contorts her left wrist - her right in the sling -
And repeatedly stabs the straw at the lid.
"Seamless," I croak as she forces it in.

"So," I say, sipping, "do you work near the road - "
"God, no, I'm Army - " "Army?" I reply.
"Do they not teach you The Green Cross Code?"
"Well, I'm on leave - " "So the rules don't apply?"

"No, I just mean...you know what I mean."
"Not sure I do." She looks at the screen.
Boy, was I being as tetchy as hell.
But she kind of liked it - you could tell.

All the same, she consults a ward nurse:
"Is he alright? He seems a bit...angry."
"With head injuries things can get worse - "
"I thought drugs would help, not make him cranky."

"Perhaps he's just like that - " "I can hear, you know."
I feel them staring then catch the nurse say,
"We phoned your friend, Blair, an hour ago.
Number was in your jeans. He's on his way

But is there family - " "God, no," I scoff.
She double-taps a screen and ambles off.
"I should go, too." Cack-handed, she scribbles.
"My phone number. If you can read it," she giggles.

She squeezes my hand and thanks me again.
"When you've recovered I'll shout you lunch.
Hopefully you can feed yourself by then."
Left to my pains and ingrained glunch,

Blair saunters in and surveys the strife.
He looks me up and down in lip-curled dismay:
"Idiot." "What? I saved a woman's life."
"I hope she's worth it." "Oh, she is," I say.

"Your doc's a fox. Looks like this girl, Carrie,
Who lived next door and I thought I would marry."
"Why didn't you?" I groan as more meds arrive.
"Well, 1. She didn't know me, and 2. I was five."

He stays by my bed all of three minutes,
Slurping my tea, eye-undressing the doc.
"Better shoot," he says, wrapping up the visit,
"Meeting our new lodger at nine o'clock."

"Huh?" "I'm letting your room whilst you're in here."
"You what?" "I could do with the extra dough
And when I dropped by the pub for a beer
I met this guy, Tom, who, whaddaya know,

Needed a bed. I thought, Why the hell not,
You won't be using yours for a while.
Gotta strike, no, whilst the iron is hot.
Laters," he chirrups, flashing a smile.

As a "welcome home" the next weekend,
Blair had made up my bed on the sofa.
"Tom's a great guy. And so are his friends.
Oh, forgot to say, they're coming over.

When you're tired I'm sure he won't mind
If you rest in his room - as a precaution."
"*His* room, Blair? Are you actually blind?"
Flapping my crutches like a novice oarsmen

- Thwacking his *Loaded* and Game Boy pen -
I hit the roof: "If you want a damn party - "
"Oh, bloody hell, is it your period again?
I know you're frail but no need to be arsey."

I stomp off - as fast as a cripple can.
"That's it, I've had it, Tom's gotta go."
"But I promised - " "I couldn't give a damn,"
Re-popping at least three ribs as I blow.

"I'll drag him to the damn station myself."
"Good luck with that." "Oh, sod off, Blair."
"I'm off to *my* room." "Please yourself."
I open the door beside the stairs.

"Hi, I'm Tom, don't mind - " "I do actually."
He clambers to his feet: "So you must be - "
"The owner of your pants." "Ah, yes.
Do you want them back? Sorry for the mess…

Good to meet you." "Pleasure's all yours."
Tom stuffs gear into a faux leather case,
Crabbing around the room on all fours.
Like parting lovers he and Blair embrace.

I hear footsteps as I close my eyes.
"Great to be home, eh? Can I do anything?"
"You can fuck off." "Gladly," Blair replies.
I long to sleep and forget everything.

1.4

Who would have thought that three months on
I would be strolling to date number five.
Swiftly falling and limp all but gone,
It felt, dare I say it, good to be alive.

Love may be pain but, in its infancy,
It seemed we were the glorious exception.
The very essence of simplicity,
From B-movie roots sprung mutual affection,

Belief - not hope - we were somehow "fated".
Maybe much of early attraction lay
In being the opposite of those we had dated.
The fey, arty types that once held sway

Traded for the straight-talking, down-to-earth girl.
The machismo sort, robust and cocksure,
Swapped for a man whose words were his world;
Like Bertie had dreamt a lifetime before.

How I felt relief that love could appear
And not always wrapped in layers of fear,
Blame, self-doubt, hurt and resentment;
Instead a warm balm of healthy contentment.

That's not to say that Desire was missing.
I recall our first lunch, eyes trained on her lips,
Then later by The Thames, the rush of us kissing,
The feeling of my hands around her hips,

The whirr of a cyclist weaving on by,
Her hair's almond scent whilst, kissing again,
The veiled sun emerged from a slate sky
As the air filled with chimes of Big Ben.

Unseasonable warmth oft-cooled by cloud
- Onion skin weather, I'd heard it said -
I shouldered her pea coat as we slipped through crowds,
My hand taking hers as we forged ahead.

We talked, I guess, of everything and nothing,
We walked - I limped - till we ran out of river.
As dusk fell we knew we had something,
And by the time we sat down to dinner

My love-fooled mind was already made up.
I had the pasta and she had the duck.
As she shaped a neat, symmetrical roll,
I chased my spaghetti around the bowl.

"Messy, aren't you?" "Hardly first date chow."
She popped in a perfect parcel of meat.
"I was hoping you could feed yourself by now."
"Okay, you got me. We are how we eat."

"It's funny, I thought we'd be done by three."
"And there was I hoping we had a connection."
Outdone this time, she rapped my knee.
"Gosh, sorry, is it sore from the infection?"

"No. But now it is," I smiled wryly.
"Good job I have a check-up on Friday."
"I'll come with you." "Are you sure?" "It's a date."
"Oh, how romantic." "I can hardly wait."

An outpatient's ward - by a bloodied stretcher -
Became the setting for "date" number two.
Any vague notion of a romantic gesture
Was blown as we claimed some seats by the loo

- The Ladies', in dirty protest, daubed *TORY SCUM* -
And a nurse was hounded, "Fat useless cow!"
I nudged her, cringing. "Pleased that you've come?"
Called to a room, the doc furrowed his brow

Then skimmed through my notes. "Still aching a bit?"
"Not really. Just the odd twinge, I suppose."
"Good, see you in June." "I'm sorry? That's *it*?"
I returned to our seats. "All okay?" "Fuck knows."

We wandered outside through taped-over doors.
"Well, there is an hour we'll never get back."
"What shall we do, then?" "Let's hit the stores
And replace your ripped clothes, your trousers and mac."

Ducking into shops, she found some grey cords.
"They're *seventy* quid. I'm not a bloody banker."
"Thank God for that." "You don't mind I can't afford - "
"My ex was in finance. Complete and utter wanker."

The shop fell silent and, together, we laughed.
"I'll get the trousers." "That's generous of you."
"Yours were wrecked in the crash, don't be so daft."
I stole a kiss as we stood in the queue:

"You free next week?" "Busy Tuesday, that's all."
"Where shall we go? I'll let you decide."
"Just somewhere without smeared shit on the wall."
"How about a film?" "Perfect," she replied.

And so it progressed as spring turned summer:
Movies, plays, picnics - hardly grand pleasures -
But who needed glamour when we had each other?
Even when our work brought added pressures

It was as if we had it all planned.
To such an extent that even our tours
- Hers with the forces, mine with the band -
Dovetailed so neatly we barely had cause

To wait for the other's return to The Smoke.
Playing the circuit, paying our dues,
We had the days free which gave me scope
To compose my quota of book reviews

And write to her of the months ahead;
Day trips to Brighton or Bexhill-on-Sea,
Then plans for our pending trek to the Med,
The Dodecanese specifically.

Booked late July, we'd fly mid-September,
First sampling Kos then island-hopping
To more locations than I can remember;
On the return leg, via Halki, stopping

At the island of her folks' former home.
We'd spend days lolling on deserted beaches,
In hilltop tavernas, often alone,
Exploring the islands' outer reaches.

We'd drink in the silence and star-pierced nights,
Get steamed on Retsina and sleep on the terrace,
Or bask in the sunsets' burnt orange delights.
Yet all was not without a whiff of menace:

Holidays prime tests of suitability,
We'd pass, not quite with flying colours,
But with a B+ in restrained hostility.
We returned faintly changed, sunburnt lovers,

Committed and still very much together,
But imperfections, once enchanting,
Now a source of suppressed displeasure.
She found my talk of love demanding

- "Why do we have to say it all the time?" -
Likewise our future - "Enjoy the moment" -
But we were just different and that was "fine".
Though her bluntness was sometimes potent,

And the neat freak in her likewise vexed
(Hatching tempers hitherto concealed),
I felt, for the most part, supremely blessed.
With her friends Hants-based and olds further afield,

We mixed with my crowd, their partners, soon wives.
Proud to be with her - and of my endeavours -
City singledom, that loneliest of lives,
Seemed to have faded then vanished forever.

And yet. The very day that I moved in
To her 60's semi off Anson Mews
Was when my pains would truly begin.
Picking through a bag of sole-worn shoes,

Thoughts turned to home, mostly to Dad,
What he'd think of my modest triumphs to date.
I wished he could see the life I now had;
Yet, just as I thought it, it was too late.

My blood runs cold as I hear the news.
I'm upstairs book-stacking - *Sophie's Choice,
Catcher*, *On The Road*, *Delta Blues* -
When, answering the phone, I hear Blair's voice,

Horseplay exchanged for a sombre air;
Darkness enshrouding that clement May day.
To think I only knew he'd died through Blair,
Who'd seen it in *The Times*, or so he'd say.

As eyes welled with tears, too shocked to speak,
Blair relayed his illness, the fine race he ran,
Before he'd slipped away the previous week.
That night, tears paused, the inquest began:

That Blair had known was odd in extreme
- He rarely browsed red-tops let alone broadsheets -
But what baffled me and was most unforeseen
Was how he had then turned up the heat

By insisting on going to the funeral himself,
Even though he had scarcely known Dad;
This in addition to not going myself.
I asked him straight up quite why he had

Taken to reading the *Announcements* section
 - It would have been slightly less unusual
Had golf, his passion, been under inspection -
And why he wished to attend the funeral.

He alleged an old friend was getting married
And he'd "strayed to *Deaths*" whilst searching his name.
Dubious as to how this account tallied,
I questioned him further but he'd merely claim

My olds had shown him kindness over the years
 - Dad had triggered his golf bug, in fact -
And Mother would like it, being one of my peers;
Yet surely there was more to it than that.

I tried to stop him - by God, I tried -
Stating he could not go when I had refused,
And, in doing so, he was taking their side.
"How callous can you be?" he said, bemused.

My pleas were in vain: he went alone, I fear.
Cue the silent treatment, a month-long dose.
Boy, when I think about it all down here
Callous, I see, doesn't even come close.

Through waves of grief, like a child I'd bawl.
Who I was crying for I could not tell:
For Dad, for Mother, for Lara, us all?
Was it just sorrow or remorse as well?

I'd cry on her shoulder, unloading my pain;
It was like grief, though, had got in our way.
Wordless, she'd sit, then, approaching disdain,
"Just what exactly do you want me to say?"

"Anything," I'd reply, "anything at all."
She'd shun a short break down by the sea,
Revisiting Brighton, or a trip to Cornwall.
I'd slouch beside her as we watched TV

And wrap my arm around her shoulder;
Statues, I swear, would show more affection.
Christ, I thought, could you be any colder?
Hiding my hurt and dreading rejection,

I channelled all my efforts into us.
And that was the problem: the more I'd fuss
The more she'd withdraw and push me away.
We would bash on, though, as if each new day

Would present a solution to our bind;
That is till, at last, The Truth hit one night.
Streetlights filtering through Venetian blinds,
I see myself there, wrestling our plight,

Tossing and turning, awake beside her:
If this, if that, why the hell can't she just...
Can't we go back to how we once were?
There must be a way, there must be, there *must*.

What could preserve us and make her stay?
It wasn't as if we had even rowed
- By recent standards we'd had a good day -
So why precisely did I feel this now?

We'd acted out the happy couple's weekend:
Park walk, window-shop, drink at The World's End,
Until, lust enkindled by Chilean red,
We'd blundered, arm in arm, back home to bed.

Hands under cheek, palm-pressed as in prayer,
She sleeps as I seek to allay the damage.
And then it occurs to me as I lie there,
The mother of solutions: of *course*, marriage.

It would surprise her, I'd bide my time,
But would our love ever then be in question?
Past midnight and with a head full of wine,
I smile to myself in addled reflection.

I stroke her hair as it drapes the pillow;
I hear her breathe gently in, gently out,
Whilst squally rain snaps at the window
And night lorries chunter on the roundabout,

Hissing through puddles to the carriageway.
Our troubles, as you see, had already started,
But that, looking back, was our D-Day.
For the next morning we would be parted

By her duties in the forces, a tour to Belfast.
We would keep in touch as best we could
Until she returned, three months having passed,
Not long but long enough to change things for good.

Now before you go getting the wrong idea
This is no lovers-split-by-wartime saga
By the no-day-goes-by-without-regret balladeer.
Step to your left if that's what you're after,

Or stand in a field somewhere in France
- Any will do - for there is a fine chance
Someone like me will be glad to provide
A fable of how love and war collide.

Please don't think ill of me - please God, no -
I'm not belittling their pain, inflating mine.
I'm just sick of love being cast as our foe,
Of how it will make us then breaks us in time.

Down here, you see, it's one familiar pattern;
In fact, you might say it's positively rife.
Past neighbour Reg Kent - who, as it happens,
Is glad to be free of his henpecking wife -

Beyond him, though, lies one Gwen Morse
Who lost her dear Francis at The Somme.
She never recovered or remarried, of course,
Dying alone at home some fifty years on.

Drina losing Albert is her comparison.
"I know how she feels," she's prone to remark.
Widowhood, not marriage, became her marathon,
One ongoing beyond life's arc.

Together nine years, Gwen regales those above
- Quite the poet - with her take on true love:
"The eternal embers of once raging fire,
All that is left of faded desire."

Why, on second thoughts, I am not sick
Of love being "our foe"; how obtuse can I be?
To shun The Endless Subject, one that has tricked
Hearts countless different ways to you or me!

Each time love finds us it redefines what love is.
I am just scarred by the Gwens of this world,
Of how love can take back all that it gives;
Of how pain, for so many, is love unfurled.

The Sydney Morning Herald

June 27ᵗʰ 2005

PROTAGONIST'S 'IMPULSIVE AND IRRATIONAL BEHAVIOUR' DRAWS ON REALITY, SAY DEFENCE

"From leaping into the road to save a fellow pedestrian to refusing to attend his father's funeral, *Broadlake*'s protagonist exhibits alarming signs of recklessness; a characteristic that some have now attributed to the author himself. By the same token, the narrator's abrupt shifts in mood, swinging from the solemn to the comical, bear the hallmarks of manic episodes; the medication for which was found beside the body."

1.5

I watch myself, adrift, a week before Christmas.
She had long returned from the front lines,
I was London-bound, brooding, listless,
The band a footnote in *The Yeovil Times*;

The sole press who'd deigned to catch our tour.
My despair was compounded by the fact
That, for now at least, she and I were no more.
We had survived the distance intact

Yet, back, this distance drew closer each day,
Spawning imitations of who we once were.
Why I wasn't sure - I'd beg her to say -
But plainly something had changed in her.

It wasn't that she tried to end us, you see,
But talk of our future she'd nigh on forbid.
She would not say she no longer loved me,
But, then again, she never said that she did.

Rarely one to "express her feelings",
She liked that control, the power it brought.
She'd drop her guard through shy revealings,
Mumbled fondness, as if she'd been caught

Dropping trade secrets, classified information.
In my denial, fears were slow to materialise
- I'd not expect sweet nothings, love's affirmation -
But then, over time, I would come to realise

That she no longer harboured affection.
Yet *still* I would not accept the rebuff,
I claimed paranoia to deny the rejection.
I would *make* it work but - ask my olds - it's not enough.

She began to ask why I loved her so,
And I would say love defied explanation.
Hence she would pester and, not letting go,
  Coax me into further justification.

"I love you, in part, for all your faults, no less.
For being so blunt, even having a temper."
"But you can't love me for all that," she'd protest.
My response one night I clearly remember:

  "I know you may think that I love you
  For reasons you see as reasons not to,
  But isn't that what love is, at heart?"
  Desperate to stop us falling apart,

I said The Words as if, each time affirmed,
They would sustain us and love would be returned.
As ever, and as you can probably see,
Saying I loved her asked if she loved me.

Weeks on, I became resigned to our "fate".
One morning events came to a head;
Probing of our "future", that buzzword of late,
Replaced by why we had split instead.

She would not specify or even wheel out,
"It's not you, it's me/I need some space."
She said her feelings were never in doubt
And that it was simply "wrong time, wrong place".

Despite our latest tour's dismal reception
- *Pillow-bitingly awful* - we were due back Sunday,
But, owing to our singer's throat infection,
We would drive back the preceding Monday.

With doddery feet on terra firma,
I pictured her family on a ski trip,
One she had mentioned a few months earlier;
Folks who, despite our long relationship,

I had not met for one reason or another;
Though these "other" reasons weren't clear to me.
I had not begged to meet her father or mother
But I was duty-bound now, to some degree.

Swapping out buses, the cramped touring kind
Exchanged for ubiquitous carmine red,
I sought something to busy my mind.
I watch myself there as, stretching, I head

Straight into town for a flick or play,
A cultured diversion before the train back.
Red hunting hat tweaked, I dream away,
Christmas lights dancing against the off-black.

Sucking lemon Lockets to repel a cough,
Drained legs entrap my rucksack and Strat.
Vox amp and pedal board dropped off at Joff's
- Our sticksman and renter of a basement flat -

We ramble through the last bastion of green
Before hitting the recycled fumes and sweat.
Entering London, though quite the scene,
It is like driving into a cigarette.

We pass some hoardings plugging two shows,
So good, in fact, that one's about to close;
Another work flunking that Test of Time.
Speaking of which, was that the clock tower chime?

As I tell listeners, we battle to hear
What with the traffic building year on year.
Eleven, you say? So good of you to stay;
I value your patience, especially today.

A 50's show at first seems suitable
But, thinking again - and alarm bells ringing -
I recall my favoured parts in musicals
Are, by and large, when they stop singing.

At a playhouse alighting, I view billboards
Hyping a production of *Richard The Third*.
Though not something I can really afford,
I seek out the box office, interest stirred.

It was a play that we had planned to see
But, with our relationship on the ropes
- And date nights dwindling - it was not to be.
Her keenness stemmed from belief that her folks

Were "distant descendants of Richard himself".
Isn't half the country? I inwardly asked.
So though not the diversion I'd promised myself,
At least I would get to see it at last.

"Any seats," I inquire, "left for tonight?"
The clerk first checks then starts to speak
But, like many these days, he cannot quite
Stop staring at the scarring on my cheek,

A C-shaped blemish from the accident.
It isn't that large, perhaps an inch long,
But ripe to draw glares - some extravagant -
And beg the question, "Where's *that* from?"

A spot secured for the evening performance
- One hour hence - I tuck the slip in my wallet.
Thanking the clerk, with job-done assurance
I stride from the foyer, iced hands in pocket.

Through double doors and into the street,
Wind beats at my face as I'm poised to flee;
I shudder as gusts bring with them sleet
Then pace down the road like I've somewhere to be.

Cinema steps form shelter from the flurry.
Boxed in by a hotchpotch - un-British - queue,
But safe from the elements and in no hurry,
I eye the billboard that governs my view.

Reverting to type, the film's band of Brits,
Two clips of whom I had seen on the box,
Are working-class geezers or upper-class twits;
Plucky northerners or bumbling toffs.

The lead, like Her - a hazel-eyed brunette,
Taut cheeks, pert nose, suitors circling -
Gave birth in one clip without breaking sweat
And out popped the bairn, spotless and gurgling.

Piqued punters condemn another farfetched scene,
Citing a pool match as I crunch a Locket.
"Yet when are such games ever lifelike on screen?
The balls *always* hang just over the pocket."

As Slade rings out from a bar-lined alley,
I unload my rucksack and, gently, my Strat.
Dropping to the step, still free to dally,
I'm drawn to a pub, The Cheshire Cat;

We'd wandered this street on our third date.
I see us now flirting outside the Empire:
Love's young dream, united by "fate",
Queuing to see *Interview with the Vampire*.

Waiting, a monocled chap, eighty-odd,
Pulls up beside me, eyeing my case.
"That a cello?" he asks. He gives it a prod.
"Guitar," I say, brightening his face.

"Ah," he chirps, "excellent, what fun."
"Just waiting," he adds, "for the other half."
He knits his brow. "Here she is, must run.
Well, good luck," he says and I almost laugh.

Below the billboard by the lobby door
I spot some posters pushing future pics:
A love story set in the Second World War
- Starring Brad Pitt's chin - and two chick flicks.

In a war tale write-up in the paper,
The hack in question, filling his boots,
Surfaced a bum-numbing three hours later.
Split lovers aside, it portrayed ten recruits

Training for the front where in days, it seemed,
The lucky had been wounded, the less so shot.
Sure enough, it featured that time-honoured scene
Where they fast-forward the creaking plot

As no-hopers, shorn of brawn or brain,
Are magicked into The Ultimate Force.
You know the ritual: the recruits take aim
And the sergeant screams until he is hoarse

Because, on firing, they can't hit a barn door.
But then roused by a stirring Hans Zimmer score,
They can suddenly split needles from half a mile
And march for five days perfectly in file.

Of course, they'll be led by a 'Nam vet
- Out of retirement *for one last mission* -
Howling "GARD BLESS AMERICA!" at stiff-lipped cadets,
Like some phony presidential audition.

It's like tales of bards fighting writer's block:
One second paper balls are strewn everywhere
As a nerd paces to a tick-heavy clock.
Then an old master appears out of nowhere

And exclaims, "Just write from the heart now, son!"
Cue Zimmer score, "That's m' boy!" (the old feller),
Pages pile up and overnight it's done,
No drafting required, a Pulitzer bestseller.

With an hour to kill I've grown complacent,
So much so I risk arriving late.
Stirring from the step, I march up the pavement,
Progress hampered by my rucksack's weight,

But otherwise aided by a keen tailwind.
Dodging the suits running for the train,
Sleet spits down as I scurry, determined,
My hat taking off as I clunk a drain.

Shunted past grey Georgian office blocks,
I catch the workers' wind-tunnelled faces;
Their flapping umbrellas and riotous locks
Flouting the finery of their coats and cases.

A lone oak signals the wind's growing force:
The branches yanked as if on puppet strings,
Stretched to the limit till, in due course,
An offshoot snaps and, catapulted, pings

Onto the pavement, bouncing as it's flung.
Skirting past, I wipe sleet from my eye,
And, though tiring, break into a run,
Seeing her face in the passers-by.

Finding the playhouse, I seek the cloakroom,
Offloading kit to fresh-faced attendants.
Allotted a ticket, I'm free to resume
My path through the foyer's wood-panelled resplendence;

Ash walls lined with sepia photographs,
Stellar productions from years gone by:
Othellos, Hamlets, Fagins, Falstaffs,
A picture of a cast of *The King and I*.

Through criss-crossing crowds I'm forced to plough
Before mounting the stairs, a protracted ascent.
I climb as briskly as spent legs allow,
Sighing as the steepening steps relent.

Checking my ticket, squeezing to my seat,
My end spot forces the row to their feet.
Panting, I settle, the house lights dim,
The blather subsides and we begin.

Richard delivers the opening soliloquy
Then enter Clarence, the Guard and Brakenbury.
Mark our young Richard, the megalomaniac;
Who can conceive he's as straight as his back?

As the scenes chart his rise to power
Thoughts of her slowly drain from my mind,
Until house lights come up upon the hour.
How she looms large as I sit, confined,

Distant punters scattered like seeds below.
The second half starts like second halves do:
Anticlimax plagues our whispering row,
Diluting the conflict they seek to renew;

Why, we must seem a flippant audience.
An act on, though, a revival of tension
Has little to do with Richard's fraudulence.
As its cause I'd barely grant it a mention,

For my weary gaze is inadvertently led
To a duo savouring their box-seat view.
I feel raged blood fast-pumping to my head;
Richard's in despair, it's act five, scene two.

Leant in, my heart punches at my chest,
A clammy hand clasps my threadbare knee.
It can't be, I think, it *can't* be, I protest,
It's just not possible...I mean how can it be?

Richard's travails are fast fading away,
Voices muffled as if from another room.
It's not her, I think, "It's not her," I say,
Gaping through the auditorium's gloom.

She is abroad for the festive season,
She's skiing in Tignes, I must be mistaken.
But I need not bother applying "reason"
For it would appear it has been forsaken.

It is her, it is, and not only her
But she and another, a suited other.
We'd said it was over, and it seemed we were,
But surely that was until she'd discover

It was simply a blip, a glitch after all.
Perhaps he's merely a friend, I deduce;
Yes, an old acquaintance - trying to recall
His tanned features - or family that she'll introduce

Once "fate" has beckoned us back together.
I console myself as the scenes progress,
Ignorant now of the company's endeavour.
Denial, though, can't contain my distress,

I can bear it no more; the end draws near,
I can't wait for scene five as Richard is slain.
One last time to their box my tired eyes veer
As around her face his neck now cranes,

And he plants his lips upon her cheek;
She eyes him like she never looked at me,
A glance that requires no words to speak,
Saying far more than The Coveted Three.

My finale is one unbearable act,
Its *desperate adventures and assur'd destruction*!
Forgoing the last throes of our hunchback,
I leave at scene four, my thoughtless disruption

Inviting dissent as I hurdle the row.
I scamper down stairs as if on the run
And, gabbling, I twitch at the cloakroom window,
Pleading for my things, wheezing as they come.

I bolt for the street: applause and cheers
Chase me through doors; whooping and clapping
Crescendos through sleet - feeling like jeers -
And I skid by a cat-curled tramp, napping.

1.6

Reliving their embrace, I make for the station,
　　Sleet turned snow now gathering pace;
Flakes sweep down to one stroller's elation,
　　But to my ire as they streak at my face.

Arriving, breathless, I am first swivelled
　　By a soft whimper then full-blown cry:
A festive-frocked lass holds tissues, shrivelled,
　　Up to her nose then dabs at her eye.

Skew-whiff brown antlers crown a drooped head,
　　Battery lights emitting a dimming gold flash.
Panda-eyed mascara apes her miniskirt's red,
　　The token sobbing girl at the end of a bash.

Over her sobs comes the announcer bleating;
　　It appears that we will be here till dawn.
"To help resume our service this evening
　　The eleven ten train is now withdrawn."

Mulling this over, travellers gaze around,
　　Chapped faces scrunched in deliberation,
Mouthing the words at gum-spotted ground;
　　A response mimicked across the station.

Questioning cedes to grumbled acceptance
　　As a rabble of students shuffle by;
The platform echoes with soused effervescence,
　　Their rush to misquote *Withnail and I.*

Trailing are three suits, followed thereafter
　　By two chortling blondes, wolfing fast food.
There's nothing quite like the sound of laughter,
　　Except, of course, when you're in a foul mood.

Drained by events and palpably shaken,
I seek out a bench to rest my feet.
Staring around, it appears they're all taken,
So, tutting, I drop to the chilled concrete.

Ditching my hat, placed down by my Strat,
I close my eyes. Yet repose is curtailed
By the jingle of coins as they drop in my hat.
"Wait up!" But my donor's too swift to be trailed.

I revert to the gods, his lips at her cheek,
The look that needed no words to speak,
His pinstripe suit, his deep bronze tan.
Spellbound, I track a spinning Coke can

As it rolls by the clock: I note the time,
Redundant though it seems to our station.
I catch someone quip about leaves on the line
Then hear it on customer information.

It strikes me then that I'll see them both here:
If crashing at hers they'll take the same route.
They'll catch me up soon, that is my fear,
I can't see them yet but I sense their pursuit.

Rushed on by the guard in tin god glee,
Morning-read papers are whipped from clicked cases;
A *Times* reader ogles a neighbour's Page Three,
Striving to maintain the most solemn of faces.

A Nokia rings two seats to my right,
Drawing the requisite contemptuous stares.
Now you'd think, down here, we'd escape such a blight
But at times it still catches us unawares.

Only last month I sensed a phone trilling
And, although close, could not gauge its source.
Just how near it was proved somewhat chilling,
Coming from the grave beside Gwen Morse.

It turns out, a stroke victim, one Zac Stone,
Who'd been interred the day before at five,
Had been buried with a mobile phone
So he could call home if he was still alive.

Three stops and our caller takes to his feet
Alighting onto the empty platform.
The train jerks forward over Yuletide streets;
A neon Santa gurns on a Vegas-lit lawn.

It's as if his seat, though, is preserve
Of The Train Journey Caricature.
His replacement is set to test our nerve:
A ceaseless natter we're forced to endure

As he yaks like a talk show interviewee
Whilst we all crave quite the opposite.
Yet, being English, we can't possibly see
He's just being friendly. Oh, come off it,

Two people meeting on public transport
And striking up conversation just like that!
He's simply one ounce shy of a quart,
Or a poor loner desperate to chat.

Or both, I discover, by the next station,
And, this being my unlucky day,
He seeks to lure me into conversation.
He clocks my guitar. "Oh, do you play?

Go on," he persists, "give us a tune."
I bat away the dreaded proposal.
If there's one thing worse than some loon
Doing his utmost to be sociable

It's him requesting a goddamn song.
He repeats his wish with a shrieked, "Go on!"
"Not now," I grimace. "Do *Everybody Hurts*!"
Thankfully his attention quickly diverts

To the slowing train as we take to our feet;
Mindful yet victims of the halting lurch.
Grabbing the headrest of the nearest seat,
I haul up my gear and, wavering, perch

Above the worn step, waiting to alight.
Yet my path is blocked by a reeling passenger.
A passing suit, on noting his plight,
Stops to consult with the weakly traveller.

The turbaned saviour sets down his case
As the passing hordes continue apace;
His deed giving substance to Mother's opinion
That the last gents left in this world are Indian.

"Are you alright there?" he kindly queries.
He's afforded a delayed, drowsy nod.
"You sure?" he asks, unsure of the series
Of languid head rolls and the glacial plod

Inching our patient away from the door.
Slothing onward, the sluggard groans
And summons the strength to rouse his jaw:
"Free bar," he slurs. "Free bar," he moans.

We slip, steps fading, into the night.
The journey's commotion has, against the odds,
Repressed The Moment - but then I catch sight
Of them in the box as I gape from the gods.

I'm heading back now, it appears to me,
To face not her but oppressive potential:
That it was going on for months maybe,
That money - who'd have thought? - was instrumental.

For now, however, those questions can keep.
I walk briskly to Blair's where I stay,
Or rather stay up, so scarce is sleep,
Sneaking out, shivering, as night sky greys;

Those questions, it transpires, cannot wait.
I see myself dash through the unhinged gate,
Snow a brown slush as I race in vain
To beat the deluge of bulleting rain.

I ask myself if I'm doing the right thing:
What if she's not there? What if she is?
What will I do if she is with him?
What if our house is where he now lives?

I stagger to our - sorry, her - front door,
Thick gravel crunched by squelching Kickers.
Seizing my key ring with a trembling paw,
I grip the spare Yale as a streetlight flickers.

I hear the faint rumble of the carriageway,
The dull chug of lorries on the roundabout,
Just as I recall them that D-Day.
The lights now dead, in virtual blackout

I fumble the lock like a bumbling janitor.
Finally in luck, I swing the door open wide.
Lights on, her pea coat sags on the banister;
A rigid line of shoes parade to one side.

I shake hair dry like a sea-drenched dog
Then sling my damp jacket over a chair.
Losing my shoes, lungs burning from the slog,
I study the - one, two, three - fourth stair.

The shadeless hall light, flagging the clue,
Reflects off the toe of a polished black shoe;
One, I notice, of a pair of Church's.
Impulsively, and in a series of lurches,

I bound up the steps and along to her door.
Gulping, I enter and feel for for the light,
Thudding into the side of an open drawer.
The switch from pitch black proves too bright

As, from cream covers, sound smothered cries.
Detecting my tones, her voice drains of fear
And, revealing her face, she rubs at her eyes,
Flicks back her hair and demands why I'm here.

"Come to collect all your crap at last?"
She sits up and leans against the headboard.
Rubbing my hip, I shun questions and cast
My eyes to the window, to my keyboard,

My Kookaburra bat, then back to the covers.
No one else present, I hobble through the door
To search the box room; we're alone, I discover.
I glower at the crudely stripped wooden floor,

Smouldering in the centre of the room.
"Whose are they?" I say. "Whose are they?" I shout.
She is nonplussed. "The damn shoes," I fume.
"What shoes?" she asks. "What are you on about?

And keep your voice down, you'll wake the neighbours."
"Wake the neighbours? They kept us up at night,
Blaring their music. Jeez, their behaviour's - "
"Okay, more for Di. It's only just light."

She'd had us over when we first moved in.
"Sure, I'll be quiet, if only for Di.
But those shoes - " "Why on earth would you bring…"
She checks her phone. "You want to know why?"

I tell her everything, just as I've told you.
"…And please don't say what I saw was nothing."
She starts to laugh, of all the things to do.
"Look at you," she mocks, "huffing and puffing.

You're so weird. And been drinking no doubt."
Her to a tee, if I was ever irate
And she couldn't see why, she'd scowl and trot out
The "weirdness" jibe. "So who was your date?

And, FYI, two months I've been dry."
She chuckles again, only raising my alarm.
"How's it amusing? Why you giggling?" I cry.
"Crikey, calm down." "Don't tell me to be calm!"

"Is this your idea of festive spirit?
Is this your big present, barging in here
Like some madman? Not the best gift, is it?
You know what I'll get you for Christmas this year:

Some fucking therapy." I glare, slack-jawed.
"Oh, is that meant to be funny?" I fizz,
My saliva flying as I applaud.
"No," she sniggers, "but it kind of is."

I'm set to let fly but she exclaims,
"Look, we have no duty towards each other
- We're not together - but if I must explain
He was no random but my half-brother.

We'd travelled down from the Lake District
And, given the two of us had time off,
He wanted to make it a proper visit."
"You expect me to believe that?" I scoff.

"I thought you were in Tignes, not spending the night - "
"We were but Mum and Dad both fell ill
- Some virus - so we managed to change our flight.
After sleeping at theirs we had time to kill

So we stayed in town for the rest of the day.
He didn't leave at five, as he intended,
And after lunch we bought tickets for the play.
He caught the train home as soon as it ended."

Sceptical, I blast the way they were,
Their wandering hands and tender embrace,
Then slam her nerve to say what occurred
Was with her half-brother. "Like there's a case

For siblings snuggling and smooching like lovers.
And still you've the cheek to concoct this whole thing,
This alibi, this most convenient of covers,
Knowing full well I won't know if it's him

As you've never had the guts to introduce us,
To show your family this doofus you're with."
Boy, was I making one hell of a fuss.
"The bottom line, whatever excuse you give,

Is the guy tonight was not your half-brother."
I'm through at last yet humbled by silence.
Her sangfroid nettles, like it did with Mother,
Restraint absorbing my rhetoric's violence.

"Have you quite finished?" she would softly say.
"Can I talk now or would you like to go on?"
Her measured response is echoed today.
"Licence to speak. Or has my chance gone?

Must I explain my parents' worries again?"
Granted, she'd relayed them many a time.
"With the pain of my sister deserting them,
Seeking security is hardly a crime."

The saga of her sister, the man she'd pursue,
Was a cautionary tale one had to endorse,
Breeding overprotection of number two.
I won't go there yet, though; all in due course.

"Shallow as it seems that's why you've not met.
You know full well how much I care for you,
But if we have a future you cannot forget
That security's not part of what you do.

And if my parents saw…" But I cannot resist
Pouncing on this "future" we might have together.
"So now you're saying that a 'we' exists?
This after the most galling night ever,

After seeing you out with this pinstriped cad
Who, silly me, is your long-lost brother.
And then you say these dreams I've always had
Would not sit well with your father and mother.

You shame my job after thinking it funny
That I've seen you dating just two months on - ''
"Do you think that if I cared about money
I'd have been with you for quite so long?"

Her rasp reflects her maddening mood.
"Back to the point. I do think it amusing,
The way you've jumped in to rashly conclude
It was a 'date'. Ever thought you're confusing

What seems to be so with what's actually true?
Surely him showing a little affection
Towards his *sister* is a nice thing to do."
"Nice?" I sizzle in default objection,

But, pausing to cough, she is free to speak.
"So you've not pecked your sister on the cheek
To show that you care?" "Not recently, no."
"What's that say about you?" "Wait, people go

Kissing their sisters to show that they - ''
"Not all of the time but sometimes they might."
"Hang on, so they do it during a play?"
"Look, I may have been watching but half the night

I was more thinking of Mum and Dad,
Who, 'FYI', are still ill. He saw me distracted
And assured me things were not that bad,
Before he kissed me - why you've overreacted.

You ditching your folks doesn't mean every bugger
Has to ditch theirs or ostracise them.
If you really want to know, it's down to my brother
That I have been thinking of us once again.

Yes, why didn't you answer my call tonight?"
I'm thrown by the sudden change of tack.
"I left a message at around midnight.
Why didn't you answer or get back?"

"What message?" I ask. "Didn't you get it?"
Phone buried in my rucksack on the train,
I had not even bothered to check it.
She harps on about her half-brother again.

"It was him who said that if I felt that bad
I should ring at once and talk things through.
Why would I call after this 'date' I've had?
And if I was looking for just a quick screw…"

She glances down at her flashing phone.
"…Why would he not be sleeping in my bed?
Why wouldn't he be here and not back home?
When're you gonna get it into your head

It's by him that I have been persuaded
To reconsider us? God knows how.
Even though I know what we had has faded,
Even though those feelings seem distant now,

For some reason," and she shakes her head,
"Life without you has been on pause.
Forget all the things I may have said,
My happiness seems to depend on yours."

She reaches across to her bedside table
And, tugging the draw, plucks out a small box.
"Happy fucking Christmas." She rips the priced label
And hands it to me, tying back her locks.

"Let me guess," I say, "therapy vouchers?"
"Just open it before I change my mind."
She flicks dried mud from off my trousers,
But as it speckles the Venetian blind

I violently sneeze: "Bit under the weather."
"A good day's rest and you'll feel much better."
"I think I'm coming down with the flu."
She sneers and warbles, "Oh, kuchikoo."

"What do you mean? I feel ill, alright."
"Come on - " "Don't give me - " "You are the worst - "
"We can't make up without having a fight."
"Open the box!" Shushed by her outburst,

I take out the gift, a silver wrist chain.
"You like it?" she asks. "I love it," I say.
A little white lie but I can hardly complain.
"No more arguing and accusing, okay."

I thank her with a kiss then step back a pace.
I lean on her dresser, pushing in the drawer,
Cringing at what I thought had taken place.
As she rises for a drink, out through the door,

I remove the chain from the tissue-lined box.
Unaccustomed to donning such a thing,
I grapple with the clasp until it locks
And wait for her to come back in.

Hearing the squeak of the bathroom taps,
I spy a snap of her folks' former villa.
At an open window her dark hair flaps
About her eyes as she stands with her sister

At the building's rear; its façade bestrewn
With creepers, bougainvillaea and grapevine.
She'd shown me The Villa from the bay's pontoon
When we had passed up the island's coastline.

We couldn't venture in - it was no longer theirs -
But she'd spied her bedroom from the beach below.
My study's cut short as she passes the stairs
And mutters something; I don't catch it, though.

"I said he probably had a spare pair for work
And, rushing for the play, left them behind."
She enters the room. "A spare pair for work?"
"Of shoes, dumbo." They'd slipped my mind.

"Pff, you really have lost it," she quips,
Moving past the bed and over to me.
"So what do you say?" Leaning in, she sips
At her tumbler. "Do you think that we

Have a future now? Can we try once more?"
To that there can only be one answer.
Embracing, it felt, like never before,
I pose one question I'm bound to ask her.

"What I still can't grasp is why your half-brother
Would badger you to get back with me.
We have not met but, for some reason or other,
You are now saying he believes that we

Should be a couple. It doesn't ring true."
Smiling to herself, she straightens the blinds.
"He understands that it's different with you.
When visiting him the last few times,

When we were together, he was always saying
How content I was: 'happiness itself'.
But then in Tignes last week, staying
With the folks, I was so clearly not myself,

And he, more than anyone, he just knew.
I brushed it off, saying it was nothing.
I tried telling myself it was all to do
With working abroad, the thought of roughing

It again. You know just how hard it can be,
Missing your friends and your life back home.
He asked if the split was getting to me,
Which I denied, saying I was best off alone.

But he soon saw it was all a sham.
So tonight he ordered me to call, more or less.
He looks past my front to how I really am,
    To how it is with us. You see that, yes?

He has not met you but he's on your side."
Her account ends and that, it seems, is it.
Yet no sooner had we appeared to turn the tide,
And just two months later once more we'd split.

The brutal manner in which Rose and Mary Bracewell were attacked with a Kookaburra cricket bat inevitably drew parallels with the narrator's ownership of such a model. It also brought into focus the protagonist's response to those claiming that *The Catcher in the Rye* is a book for murderers or suicidal loners: "As I rate Holden's role," he asks, "does that mean that *I'm* going to kill one day?" (1.0). Indeed, if the novel is taken as semi-autobiographical, some have referred to the narrator's temper in 1.1 as a precursor to future hostility:

> I finally snapped: fists tightly clenched,
> I smashed them against the glove compartment.
> With the door cracked and, in turn, wrenched,
> I kicked the flap in sustained bombardment.

Even a fairy tale character, Twain, beating a "poor Abo's matchstick frame" in 2.6 has been cited as a masked reflection of the author's aggressive tendencies. Furthermore, the narrator's passion for "all things war" and his desire to recreate "the most violent of scenes" (also 2.6) have only added to the widespread hypothesizing. Only recently has the truth behind these correlations been established.

From *The Kookaburra Killer* by Arthur Hamlin

1.7

Befitting happiness, it was a fleeting content:
We succumbed to her fickle, flighty hand;
Her nature consistent to such an extent
That permanence is ever The Promised Land.

Proven each time we'd come to an end,
Let us go back, then, or forward I guess,
To the very last act one June weekend.
Holed up at The Swan, it was no less

Than a year on from our latest demise;
Still, I was sure we would end up together.
Appealing to God - or my conscience in disguise -
I'd promised myself to never say never.

I had ventured out that muggy weekend
From the 60's semi we had once shared.
She was abroad, I'd heard, with an old friend,
So, running down the lease, I was renting there

Before moving to Blair's new pad in Bow.
I picture myself, head on the bar, alone
- Blair is out with his latest squeeze, Jo -
Wincing at the England game being shown;

The exquisite agony stirring the mob.
Our certain exit leaving pundits stewing
And remarking what thoroughly splendid jobs
The English and Scottish refs are doing.

"Good on paper, crap on grass," a sage grunts
As thick wafts of urine - misdirected piss -
Drift in from the Gents. "Entitled cunts."
Whilst stodgeball breeds contrasts with '66,

Half-time sounds and we're switched to Sky News.
There's been some dreadful airline tragedy
And, as a coiffed journo emotes her views,
They're showing grainy footage of debris

Floating about in some far-flung ocean.
Now nothing draws viewers like a plane crash
But, given the game, its rapid promotion
To headline act prompts a backlash.

The rank hostility is quick to spread.
"Get it off!" soon canons around the room
As journos assess the number of dead.
"Like there's not enough doom and gloom!

Put it fucking back!" This notion is indeed
One I'm endorsing, at first quietly,
But then with some gusto. "Come on," I plead.
"Change the channel!" I shout defiantly.

The report goes on: "Due to fog overhead
Rescue efforts are progressing woefully.
Eighty-nine people are confirmed dead
But that's sure to rise," she says hopefully.

I order a double and do the sums.
"Get it off," I bark, joining the throng
As journos discuss contacting loved ones.
"Turn it bloody over. Now! Come on!"

A scuffle ensues; a beer has been knocked.
Step forth the victim's massed entourage.
I'm set to scarper but my path is blocked,
And the melee unfolds in a montage:

Snapshots of thrashing limbs abound
As plunging ashtrays blitz the ground;
Fag butts pepper the sopping carpet,
A beer-drenched frothing, swirling scarlet.

Just one soul is yet to join or flee;
The lone punter is the perfect scapegoat,
The only catch being the loner is me.
Calls for a truce are lodged in my throat:

An ill-judged quip on Queensberry Rules
Is met with a sharp, stinging right-hander.
I hit the deck and am pelted with stools,
Unjust deserts for the innocent bystander.

I crawl to an alcove housing the phone
And see out the brawl's remaining minutes,
Pulling stools onto me until my spiked dome
Resembles a mammoth pile of Twiglets.

Scrabbling out, arms raised in surrender,
I'm shown - no, more flung - onto the street.
Reeling from the dust-up and all-day bender,
I dodder off home, my shame complete.

Yet, shambling inside, the phone is ringing
And as I pick up the room is spinning:
To think I was slumped at the bar, fuming,
Because the match was likely resuming

And we were viewing some "damn news flash".
I see myself growing more deranged
As, waiting for drinks, I rustle out cash
And implore to have the channel changed.

"Switch over!" I yell, and on a roll,
"Oh, for fuck's sake, come on!" I slur.
If only I'd known that within the death toll
They were reporting was in fact Her.

If only I'd known that among the loved ones
They were seeking to trace was me;
Or at least should've been were I not stung
By love's win-or-bust ruthless finale.

In the end it was Sam, calling from Drew's,
Who phoned to tell me that she had died,
Saying he'd seen her name on the news.
The family, he said, had been notified.

Her friend, Anne Brown, whom I vaguely knew,
She had been with her and had perished, too.
Like Dad in his pomp, I dug out the Bell's
And stared at the deepest, darkest of hells.

I passed out, sobbing, on our bed that night,
Waking in vomit as blinds fought the light.
Things are better in the morning, they say;
It was far worse in the cold light of day.

I recall thinking, Is this it, The End?
I could not conceive how far I would fall.
Perhaps my ruin began that weekend
And childhood would play no part at all.

1.8

A full year had passed since our last split
Yet what is time but a nagging bearer of grief?
If you're thinking to yourself, "Just get over it!"
Behold Gwen's woe and my blues seem brief.

My life had frozen yet was the world sorry?
At the front window summer rain still rapped;
From the road still came the chunter of lorries;
I'd still curse the squeak of the bathroom tap;

The bills kept coming, my career was still foiled;
Our home was still broken, I was still in debt;
Neighbours' music still blared, England still toiled;
The obscured sun rose and, still obscured, set.

Then three weeks later I would take a call,
Jolting me from my liquored slumber.
I was in shock: it was her mother after all,
Saying that she had come across my number

Whilst sorting through her chest of drawers.
She apologised for the private funeral
Before, trailing off, there followed a pause.
Striving to think of something suitable,

I offered soothing words - you know the score,
That hollow sympathy I craved to hear.
She said she was sorry she'd not rung before
Then, bidding goodbye, made it quite clear

That I "should call her to talk things through.
Stay in touch," she said, though that I did doubt.
I thought she was saying it, like you do,
But she really meant it, as it turned out.

I would fill my days but then, come darkness,
There was no escape or form of catharsis.
You see, until now I'd felt protected by "art",
A shield from my troubles or chastened heart.

When my career, say, induced self-pity,
Voicing despair had instilled perspective.
Take a West Bank bombing that inspired a ditty;
It helped to channel my suppressed invective.

I'm sleeping, it opened, *with a terrorist.
Okay, I'm not, I just want to get noticed.
What an age we live in when to get noticed
An artist has to say he's sleeping with a terrorist.*

Regardless of merit, I didn't need anyone
To support me, talk to me, that struck me as weak.
Yet what use was "art", seeing what God had done?
How could it ward off the abyss, so to speak?

Seeking respite that a change of scene brings,
I'd sneak off to Lord's, often by myself,
Or play golf with Blair to take my mind off things.
Driving like a learner, I can't say it helped.

The Dreaded Line trailed each boomerang slice:
"Still you," he'd laugh, his ball nestled by the pin.
He was always on hand, though, to offer advice,
Mainly mid the latter stages of my swing.

At last on the dance floor at the sixth attempt
- Reaching for more balls than an overworked hooker -
Blair ranked my putts with joyful contempt:
A "Maradona" (a nasty little five-footer)

Or a "Salman Rushdie" (an impossible read),
And I'd duly four-putt as he downed in two.
My irons were twenty years old, I believed,
And yet the sweet spots were still brand new.

A professional amateur in every sense,
Let us just say things got a bit tense;
Like Dad, not covering myself in glory.
Why, I told old Blair Mother's favourite story,

Walking the course with him as a young lad
(Before my defection to rock 'n' roll),
And on leaving the ninth I said to Dad,
"Why mustn't the ball go in the hole?"

I began taking drives into the night.
Boombox perched on the passenger seat
- The stereo shot, like the inside light -
I'd leave the anonymous car-lined street

And visualise a tranquil refuge of mine,
A hilltop an hour from our family home;
A spot I would visit from time to time
Whose peace I would seek to make my own.

Now if that sounds quaint or mawkish dross
It is: I sought a place as unreal as possible,
A place that it seemed had never felt loss;
Unchanged a thousand years and, though improbable,

Would stay unchanged a thousand years hence.
As hoped, those trips would repress events
Until I wound back and, soon after arriving,
I would nod off and dream of the plane diving.

Yet the next sleepless night I would be gone:
Leaving London behind, I'd happen upon
An enticing straight and put my foot down,
Free of the fraught stop-and-go of town.

Through blanket darkness lights would appear,
Steadily closing, dipping on approach;
Flashing my full-beam as they neared,
An unknowing car, lorry or coach.

I watch myself nudge the vibrating wheel,
Drifting us onto a collision course,
Foreseeing my End in a crumple of steel.
Veering across like a loose race horse,

I hear the revs peaking as the engine roars,
The chassis trembling like it's having a fit;
I see her face, my foot's to the floor,
They're hooting, we're meeting, this is It;

I hard-swerve left and they sail on by,
Their tepid horn wailing as I careen.
I ease off the gas, trying not to cry,
As drizzle specks the dusty windscreen.

It is the first rain for over a week
Following a sultry Saharan spell.
Through the spent seals plump raindrops leak,
Dripping down slowly to the footwell.

A cow-quaker brewing, in sudden assault
Rain becomes hail as it rattles the screen.
Off condensated glass pellets somersault
Whilst over fresh tarmac torrents stream.

Shredded wipers swipe with scant effect
Until their workload lessens as day breaks;
The frenzy subsides and the pools collect,
Roadside puddles more miniature lakes.

Water streaks past as I creep up the hill,
Gutters overrun by the cloudburst.
Spluttering, I change down the gears until,
Nearing its brow, I'm forced into first.

Arriving at dawn - or during day, sunset -
It felt like that place the world had forgotten,
A world which, when there, I would forget.
The mossed window seals and footwell sodden,

I park on the verge at the hillside's peak.
Up and out, I jink through elm trees,
My talking shoes beginning to leak.
Petrichor rising, pitter-pattering leaves

Announce my arrival above the valley.
I survey the forest, its lone spectator,
Then, past a pine bench, one sunlit alley:
Flora brimming, inspired mother nature

Has woven a tangled, anarchic wall.
An arrow, besieged by rampant brambles,
Pokes through the thorny free-for-all.
As the sun climbs and through verdure angles,

The alley breathes in the ribbons of light:
Spasmodic shafts lend the wet leaves
A motley sheen, bottle greens turning lucent white
And golden yellow. Beneath glistening trees,

I cast my eyes down the sun-dappled track
And imagine what could lie at its end.
Spying the sign, the name in faint black,
Flaking from the grooves, I descend

Into daydream as I paint the scene
That the name and its morning splendour promise.
My vision's so perfect, so serene,
I scarcely wish to perceive the bliss

For fear it is not the envisaged gem.
Every so often I'd glimpse the sign
But, set to explore, I'd think again,
Potential victorious every time.

Homeward bound, joining rush hour queues,
I'd catch The Gloom; Dad's term for the news.
First up recession then Afghan earthquake,
I'd switch to the strains of early Nick Drake.

I see myself now, forsaking back routes
For one more direct as fatigue kicks in.
Not once but twice I almost overshoot,
Nausea building as the snarl-ups begin.

I long to be home but as I enter
A three-lane section one careless manoeuvre
Has me heading for *City Centre*.
Set to turn, almost clipped by a scooter,

The first sign's *No Entry*, the next *One Way*;
For my blunder I'll be made to pay.
The City nears: "For Christ's sake," I explode.
Slowing down, I recognise the road,

The café to my left, the bars to my right;
Or maybe I'm simply too dazed to tell.
Guzzling water, I approach the lights.
As green turns amber déjà vu swells

And with it the return of infinite loss.
It is no longer some vague remembrance:
Looking ahead, she is striding across.
This a road of more than passing resemblance

- Why, that which I can't remember to forget -
Because, my friend, it's the very same one,
Where we collided, where we first met,
Were united by my kamikaze run

Before she was savagely snatched in her prime;
The curtest meeting yet Our Start all the same.
I'm lost in the moment that fragments time,
I'm clocking each movement, frame by frame,

I'm bounding out, the Merc hasn't slowed,
I hear the tout in brazen conversation;
Nausea peaking, I pull off the road
Into the exit of a petrol station.

At the forecourt's edge I cut the engine.
In gear, I pitch forward, dashboard red.
I pant and try to stem the adrenaline
As blood pumps at the base of my head.

I grip the wheel, thick sweat now pouring,
Vision blurring, my heartbeat soaring.
The driver behind is honking his horn;
He's mouthing abuse, his stream of scorn

Reflecting in my mirror's dusky glass.
I switch on the engine, thrust into gear,
And scram to the exit as cars hare past.
I sit and pray for a gap to appear,

Scanning the moving wall of traffic.
The guy behind rolls down his window.
"Come on," I urge. "Come *on!*" I panic.
He's rapping his wheel but still I can't go.

"Move, ya tosser!" I hear him imploring.
"I can't, I can't, I *can't*, for God's sake!"
But then I can and, almost stalling,
I wheel-spin away and, screeching, make

For the snaked surge of northbound traffic.
Heartbeat falling, even breaths returning,
I find the road back and away floats panic,
Recovering to grief and restless yearning.

Sometimes not making it home till ten,
I'd fight exhaustion, but, sleep overdue,
I'd crash in my chair, denial doomed again.
I didn't want to dream of you-know-who

In all that detail, that reviving clarity.
They say that they last mere seconds, dreams,
But we all know there's a glaring disparity
Between how long they are and how long they seem.

The Northern Territory News

June 19th 2005

GUILT-STRICKEN POET DRIVEN TO SUICIDE

"Overcome by events, the wannabe poet returned to
38 Larapinta Drive and took his own life."

1.9

Hold on, will you, for two ticks, my friend.
Honestly, Gwen, can your venting not wait?
It's not only you facing The End.
If ever I start to forget our fate

I hear you damning the council again.
And you wonder where your listeners went!
I do apologise, it's just that Gwen,
The lovelorn lass beside Reg Kent,

She's finding things quite hard at present
What with all the "developments" of late.
Anyway, moving on, although not pleasant
I should expound on my depressed state.

Now in my line of unemployment
Black Dog, to quote Winston, was not rare.
Our calling extended beyond enjoyment:
"Art" was a vehicle to convey despair

Through verse or scripts, a song or score.
"Victims" rescued by ingenuity,
We had been dealt, it felt, the short straw;
Penury and pain borne like it a duty.

Frustrated failures, we bitterly discussed
The "jammy" minority who had made it.
As our creations gathered digital dust,
We'd claim Dylan or Shakespeare were "overrated".

Like a losers' convention we'd move to our woes,
Taking in themes of unrequited love
Or broken homes - "Any tragedy goes!" -
So long as it chimed with the above.

Yet, with her death, this role-play was dropped:
I was who I'd long thought myself to be.
Despair was for real, mourning never stopped,
Her death felt like the death of me.

Sometimes I'd see a way out, of course,
But, lacking even cowardice to top myself,
Each night I was taking to the old sauce,
And, ever dependent, I went to seek help.

First stop was Doc Hendrix, my GP,
Who put me on antidepressant pills,
Which was pretty depressing, naturally.
He upped the dose - I was struggling still -

But that didn't work so he upped it some more.
When that didn't work I thought to myself,
I swear I will have to overdose before
These wretched things even start to help.

He assured me: "It takes time, you know."
"But didn't you say that two weeks ago?"
I was referred to a psychiatrist:
"I'm not seeing some damn trick cyclist."

He said, "Okay." I said, "Thanks for your help."
As I left he intoned, "Take care of yourself."
I thanked him again, ignoring that Hendrix
Had been as useful as an appendix.

Full out of options, I called a shrink,
Recommended by a number of friends.
Loathed though I was, I could not sink
Any lower. Facing constant dead ends,

I booked a session with one Felix Cadiz
Who practised from his home, 60 Mills Street.
One dank morning I drew up to his:
With bilious head and hesitant feet,

I grouched up the cobbled path to his door.
Several rings of the brass-nubbed bell
Brought no reply, so checking once more
The number of the house - to dispel

Any error - I moved across to the bay window,
Seeking signs of life in the cramped front room.
Beside a round mirror with sideboard below,
Displaying purple lilies in full bloom,

Shelves rose, file-rammed, up to the ceiling.
By a pedestal desk hung a vast cabinet
Which lent the room a claustrophobic feeling,
Coated as it was in coal-black laminate.

My thief-like snooping now ill-advised,
I returned to ring the bell once more.
Having waited so long I was almost surprised
When a bearded figure came to the door.

"Oof," the beard gasped, "weeding out back."
He led me to his study: "Please, take a pew."
He bade me to start as he removed his mac,
And I regaled the heartache relayed to you.

"I see," he drawled, dabbing damp beard hair
Whilst he worked his sympathy-frown.
"It's only natural you feel this despair."
Fumbling his desk, he plomped himself down.

"This pain at present, it will fade away.
I know it feels now that it's forever - "
"Yes, but it seems to gets worse each day.
I'm starting to believe that I will never - "

"Oh, you will - " "Can I just say how I feel - "
"Oh, don't worry," he said, "I really do see.
I have helped many who struggle to deal - "
"But I haven't explained what is for me - "

"We've quite enough for us to get going.
I have a system that's sure to win through."
Twirling his beard and cheeks aglowing,
He gassed like he had more weeding to do.

"Any questions?" he said after "reason three".
"Er, I don't think so. But could I just say - "
"Let's just get through these now, shall we?
It's crucial we cover these topics today."

He was soon touting "theme number nine",
The phase of emotions I would encounter,
The standard scenario and recovery time,
The measures to cope if ever I'd flounder.

Rare comments were met with pseudo concern
- "I know what you mean/I quite understand" -
Before his case points made their return.
With every line meticulously planned,

I simmered, trembling, fists clenched in unrest.
Why, I pictured a scene exposing his capers:
I dreamt of opening the cabinet above his desk
And being hit by a volley of papers.

I flick through them (Cadiz tending roses),
Guessing the files to be patient records
Or professors' notes on psychosis
During case studies on headcase wards.

Yet, thumbing through, there descends a fear
As I sense something truly astray.
These papers, or scripts, date back years;
The top one, however, is for today.

Scanning down, eyes flicker to the door.
Rise at 6, don gown and sheepskin slippers.
Proceed to bathroom (3 minutes/4).
Advance downstairs and fry 2 kippers.

As wife enters room smile at her nicely.
Dr C BSc PhD:
I wonder, my dear, if you could slice me
Two pieces of wholemeal and make the tea.

Mrs C: Oh yes, no trouble at all.
Dr C BSc PhD: Thank you, dear.
Consume the kippers then make lab call
(8 minutes/9 if findings unclear).

Dress, comb beard, dampen if unruly.
I flip through the script - doorstop fat -
To find directions for yours truly.
No. 5 takes chair and removes red hat.

Patient: I'm depressed and always feel...
Interrupt 5 and give him The Spiel.
Dr C BSc PhD:
The root of your grief is plain to see...

His talk is the model of ambivalence,
Indifference enforced with each rehearsed line,
His stock replies the shrink equivalents
Of "Take some aspirin and things will be fine."

The truth barely differed: "In such cases, I fear,
Certain patterns emerge and what is quite clear..."
His words rang a bell as he branded my plight,
The reason for which I'd discover that night.

For capping preplanning, here was that guy
Who'd offer his views on, say, current affairs,
Or advice on what property one should buy,
Or when to invest in stocks and shares.

And you'd say to yourself, thinking it through,
Well, that makes sense - in fact, that's kinda smart.
Until, back home, unwinding with a brew,
You browse the paper and sit up with a start

As you read a piece by some highbrow mind:
Wait up, you think, this all seems familiar.
Lo and behold its views are wholly aligned
With those of a walking encyclopaedia

- Namely our panjandrum Felix Cadiz -
Who has conspired to lift, word for word,
Every single idea and claim them as his.
"Quite simply," he said, "from what I've heard,"

Delving into his desk's top left-hand draw,
"It would help if you took a look at these.
They're leaflets I've written and given before
To patients of mine. If you would please

Take them back home and we can take care
Of any queries you have next time we meet."
And so that evening, leant back in my chair,
I'd read "his" tips then put down the sheet

And read them again in a guide I had bought,
Fifth-hand Advice from Arsehole Shrinks.
Okay, not exactly, but the truth in short.
As I cursed, the swindle drew me to think

Of his likeness to one "author" friend of mine;
Nigel was his name, Nigel Dytors.
From his notebooks he'd recite the odd line,
Performing his work to fellow "writers".

One summer's night around he came
To offer up his latest pearler;
Home-Thoughts, from Abroad was the piece's name.
"I only composed the passage earlier

But I think it's up there with Hughes, for sure."
Such crass remarks he'd provide on tap,
Exposed in his verse that also bore
An uncanny resemblance to a pile of crap.

"And though the fields look rough with hoary dew,
All will be gay when moontide wakes anew
The buttercups, the little children's dower
- Far brighter than this gaudy melon-flower!"

I was shocked. That's nice - twee but nice,
Umming my approval across the table.
My respect faded upon hearing it twice
When I realised I was now unable

To distinguish these lines from those by Browning
In a piece also called *Home-Thoughts, from Abroad*,
Which, for my mind, was somehow sounding
An awful lot like *Home-Thoughts, from Abroad*

By Nigel Dytors of Angel Lane
The utter fraudster and arch-mimic.
He was even outraged at my claim
And declared I was "a pedantic prick".

I cited Browning but he reasoned regardless:
"When I read it last night," he took the view,
"It mirrored my thoughts, so it seemed harmless
To say it was actually my poem, too."

And it was Nigel's poem - if "my" meant "his",
"Dytors" meant "Browning", Angel Lane was a coffin,
He was two hundred years old, and if "fraudster" is
A perfect synonym for "literary boffin".

Cursing friends' advice, I quickly moved on
To once "relationship expert" (thrice divorced),
Now bereavement councillor. I went along,
Fretting the Cadiz method would be endorsed.

This John Lear, though, withheld his theories,
Preferring to heed what I had to say,
Only responding with occasional queries.
The only snag came as we closed the first day.

"You know," he said, concluding the visit,
"I like my patients to chart how they're feeling
In notes or a poem. Perchance, is it
Something you'd consider or find appealing?"

Blind faith in my writing starting to sag,
I pondered Nigel's ploy, between me and you.
I presumed that verse would not be his bag,
That those in the mind games took a dim view

Of such a whimsical means of expression;
"Show me a poet and I'll show you a shit,"
The quotation I assumed would, in his profession,
Portray his approach - but no, not a bit.

Opting to give his therapy a chance,
I rapped at his door just five days later,
Waving some verse eked out in advance.
I watched him read from the piece of paper,

Lightly nodding, reciting each line,
Waving in four-four orchestration.
*"Every second is hell, every moment I pine;
I'm lost,"* he flinched, *"in lamentation.*

*Do you hear my helpless cry for you?
I long to escape, flee from reality,
With each passing day I'm drifting into
The heady realms of eternal insanity.*

*I neither sleep nor eat but yearn for when
We were together, living our dreams.
Oh Lord, I'm a lovesick youth again;
Where the heart's concerned we all are, it seems!*

*Will I be with you one day up above,
Or will I always search oblivion
For the inestimable one true love?"*
Clearly, I now dreaded his opinion.

You truly realise the state you're in
When someone's telling you, in your own words,
That you can't utter two thoughts on the spin,
Never mind that colossus of a third,

Without spouting some pubescent drivel
About star-crossed lovers and the sands of time.
Lear looked away and out at the mizzle;
As if it diseased, poking back my rhyme.

"My main concern is whether you feel
A constant pain, or if there are days
When you are balanced and can deal
With the grief." Averting my gaze,

I took a moment to word my reply.
Despite my lows, I could sometimes be strong,
I could feel the hurt passing me by,
And at long last the will to move on.

"I guess keeping busy dulls the sensation."
"Well, there's a start. Nothing feeds grief
Like inactivity and isolation.
Just getting out can bring one relief.

What's up with work?" "Ah, good question.
I can't seem to get back in the swing.
My boss has given me deadline extensions
But his patience, I sense, is wearing thin."

I mentioned my drinking and late-night drives
Then alluded to Dad under my breath.
"Do you think that some of this grief derives
From delayed reaction to your father's death?

What was your relationship like to boot?"
"Oh Christ," I griped, "please let's not go down
The I-haven't-got-over-my-childhood route."
"Few of us do," he said, shrinking my frown.

He posed several more father-focussed questions,
Circling estrangement, our perceived contributions,
Which we'd return to in future sessions.
He'd close the chat, though, with practical solutions.

"Now then, exercise. Are you up to much?"
"Er, does golf count?" "For sure," he opined.
"Having said that, if you're not in good touch
It's hardly a sport to calm the mind.

If the whole world played golf for a living
All us shrinks would be billionaires."
He pursed his lips. "The advice I'll be giving
Won't bring an end to your despair,

But it will grant you a fighting chance
Of riding out dark times when they come."
Looking up, I offered a grateful glance,
My misery face now merely glum.

Discerning progress with each session,
I felt myself rising from my depression.
I could see a life beyond her, I guess;
The Unacceptable accepted, no less.

Then one balmy night just after supper
Came that promised call from her mother.
She inquired if I would like to attend
The scattering of her ashes at the end

Of August, the 29th the mooted day.
"Very low-key, just family and friends."
Its location, though, would betray
Her disclaimer, for it would send

Me, if agreed, abroad to the Med,
To the island of their former home.
Her daughter's one wish, her mother said
- And which for some years I had known -

Was for her ashes to be scattered in the bay,
That fronting The Villa's private waterway.
Initially, I would politely say no,
But, the next session, Lear urged me to go.

He deemed it the chance I had longed for
To process my anguish and disbelief.
My wounds now healing but still sore,
I sought to curb the bounds of grief;

Cold-hearted as that may first appear.
Ultimately, however, I agreed to go.
Sometimes I'm glad I listened to Lear,
But often I wish I'd stuck with no.

1.10

With the service date duly confirmed,
I'd nigh on three weeks to ready myself.
As far as logistics were concerned,
The most pressing issue had resolved itself:

"Released", alas, from my reviewer role,
I'd no need to ask for time off work.
The trip to finance and on the dole,
I swallowed pride, taking shifts at Kirk's,

A tea room battling against the chains
Eight stops away, south of Pimlico,
Cover for a worker's jolly in Spain.
Then one fine morning, six days to go,

Twiddling a broom, sizing up a scone,
Blair maundered in, happy as Larry.
"Why are you here? What's going on?"
A mistrust that he would choose to parry.

"Lovely day, eh? They say it's set fair."
I withheld response, plucking a splinter,
Naturally as suspicious of old Blair
As of an ice cream van in winter.

He eyed my frilled apron: "Love the new look.
For a fledgling rock star pretty unique."
He flicked the peeled paint beside the coat hook.
"It's shabby," I murmured, "without the chic."

His smile matured to a monstrous grin:
"So then, do you still wanna kill yourself?"
Stunned at first, I took it on the chin.
"Wow, you really are such a great help."

"You know, if you died you might sell more books."
"Generally works best if famous first," I said,
"And if your novel's not shit." My voice now shook.
"You don't exactly reap rewards, being dead."

"What if you *nearly* died? It's worth a go."
"Jesus, Blair, there's suffering for your art
And there's uneclipsed madness. The answer's 'no'."
"God, touchy, aren't you. Don't take it to heart."

Blair's flawed literary concepts were rife:
He'd once proposed that, with writer's block lingering,
My next book should be based on his love life,
To be entitled *The Lost Art of Fingering*.

My travails were nothing new: at eleven,
I'd penned a two-volume autobiography,
My Tragic Life - Pain Since The Age of Seven,
Breaking new ground in snot-nosed monotony.

"I wrote a book once. Mum loved it," Blair purred.
"Bet she did. Did she even read it?" "Uh, no."
"Was it long?" "Two hundred." "Pages?" "Words."
"A sort of non-book, then, as books go."

Sniffing his armpit, Blair took a stool:
"You're happy to see me, are you not?"
"That depends," I said, playing it cool.
He feigned bemusement. "Depends on what?"

"On what you say and why you are here.
For one thing, why are you so upbeat?"
"Oh, I lost my job." "Well, that makes it clear.
You're unemployed and almost on the street.

Call me a dunce but how does that work?"
"Loathed it, didn't I? Fuck, it was bleak.
Can't shelf-stack forever and the one perk - "
"Forever? You only did it for a week.

The lemons had been there longer than you."
Daisy, the owner, peered up from her knitting
Before attacking her purl stitch anew.
"Outlasted by a fruit. How very fitting."

Cackling to myself, I pressed a stumped Blair.
"So what, may I ask, are you going to do?"
Shrugging his shoulders, he seemed not to care.
"I mean you can't *not* stack shelves if you

Have nothing else on. It's real work you should find…"
I paused: a temp in a tumbleweed tea room,
A large pot and kettle sprung to mind.
"Yes, boss," he sniggered, stroking my broom.

He had really done no worse than me
In acquiring employment and decent pay.
Within two weeks he'd dropped out of uni
- Well, The University of Luton anyway -

And, flunking his internship at Jackson Staff,
A gig his old man had blagged him in the City
- "General incompetence"/ "Couldn't run a bath" -
Was only working once he'd drained the kitty.

Spending days surfing the Web at his flat,
Quite oblivious to the mounting debt,
Blair became such a mouse potato, in fact,
He was on course to complete the Net.

Cramming down scones, career advice adjourned,
I braced myself for retaliation.
As luck would have it, Blair seemed more concerned
With his own feelings than my crass observation.

"Dad's quite a hard act to follow, I'm afraid."
"Christ, he's hardly Murdoch or Branson, Blair.
Try going on after Queen at Live Aid,
That's a tough act to follow right there."

"Jeez, if it's not Lennon it's that pompous bugger."
"You're joking? Freddie held a mic in one hand
And seventy thousand people in the other.
But back to your dad," I said, taking a stand,

"Instead of submissively shadowing him
Why don't you try to just do your own thing?"
"What, like you?" he laughed. "How's that working out?"
I polished a teapot's already clean spout.

"But what's the point of me earning money
When I have no time to enjoy it?" he said.
"Hang on," I choked, "I don't mean to be funny,"
Clearing my throat where a clump was wedged,

"But being a probationary Tesco stacker
Is hardly a step up the career ladder.
You're talking like you earn a 100k
And can't enjoy it for working night and day."

"But I do work nights, I'm up at four - "
"But that's *all* you work. *If* you turn up."
A silence fell, during which at the door
I spied an old dear coming in for a cup.

Yet it grew clear she was just stopping by
To let her black Lab squit on the doorstep.
"So then," I whispered to Blair with a sigh,
"Why have you come here? Let's not sidestep

The matter." "Okay," he contorted,
"You know your...er..." "Why you being so coy?"
"Coy? Well, the Greece trip..." "Ye-e-s," I retorted,
Tutting as I sought to expose his ploy.

"Yes," he spluttered, "how are you with...stuff?"
"Oh, thank you for asking," I spiked in rebuff.
"Well, I never know whether to ask straight away
Or avoid it completely. Just the other day - "

"It's alright," I said. "Appreciate the thought."
Needles like daggers, Daisy shot me a look.
"Anyway," Blair burbled, "I was thinking that I ought
Ask you before we completely overlook...

And please do say if you're really not sure,
But I was wondering if there is a slight chance - "
"You're like a kid buttering up his olds before
Asking for pocket money a month in advance.

Stop talking froth and just spit it out.
Frick, listen to me, I'm sounding like Dad."
A comment that I could have done without,
For it not only delayed the question he had,

It also raised a topic I sought to avoid.
"Talking of parents - and don't get annoyed -
Do you not think it would be the perfect time
To contact your mum? With your dad gone, I'm

Certain it would help you both a great deal - "
"Help?" I replied, shifting in my chair.
"Can you, for once, respect how I feel.
You know I have cut all ties with her, Blair.

How many times do I have to say that?"
"I'm just trying to help as best I can."
"Stay in your lane. I thought I smelt a rat.
If that's all you're here for, you can damn - "

"It's not why I came." "So tell me or go..."
Another Daisy glare gagged my reply.
"Look," Blair whispered, "I have some spare dough,
Money Dad sent me to get me by.

And you'll need some, well, moral support."
"You want to come out to Greece with me?
It's not Shagaluf, a chance to cavort
Round the island. It's not gonna be - "

"Yeah, I know. But at the end of the day
Things won't be easy, and as it stands - "
"It's not an excuse to just get away?"
From bitter experience, I quizzed Blair's plans.

"Look," he said, "I need to get out of town
But I realise the importance of the trip
And that you'll be feeling pretty down.
So it seems daft to let the chance slip.

It can help you whilst giving me a break."
"I hope you've thought this through and that it's quite clear - "
"Of course I bloody have, for goodness' sake.
You think I'd be arsed to come all the way here?"

He had a point: Blair was often so lazy
He couldn't even be bothered to yawn.
"Sleep on it." He rose and, winking at Daisy,
Strolled off as if to the manner born.

Set to depart, he stopped and U-turned.
"You're alright, though, aren't you?" he solemnly asked.
"About the trip and that." Touched, I returned
A somnolent nod, still somewhat downcast.

He spun to reach for the glass-panelled door.
"Where you going?" I said as he clutched the handle.
"A date," he glowed, and I nodded once more,
Digesting his words as the bronze bell jangled.

"Wait, you're going to meet a girl?" I scoffed.
"It's eleven o'clock on a Friday morning."
"Yeah, a hussy at work had the day off
And asked me to brunch with no warning."

The outlandish nature of his tale grew.
"I begged for time out but too late, they said.
You didn't think I'd quit for nothing, did you?"
He swanned out, whistling, as I shook my head,

My skull working loose from disbelief.
I mulled over Blair's iffy proposal,
Whether he'd be more a pain than relief,
And the next morning I made the phone call.

On the fourth redial Blair drawled, "H-i-i-i."
Exhaling slowly, I guessed he'd been sleeping.
"It's me, lazybones." Forsaking a reply,
Blair reprised the Darth Vaderesque breathing.

"I've thought through what we discussed yesterday.
I'd like you to come with me out to the Med."
He answered as if he cared not either way,
Drawing up mucus as the line went dead.

Another redial, another seismic wait.
I heard a scream then a burst of chuckling;
I surmised he was with his latest date.
"You there?" I snarled, frayed patience buckling

As I considered changing my mind.
At length, he gave me his half attention.
"Yes, I heard you, that's great," he chimed,
Hardly relieving my apprehension.

"We're off on the 27th, as you know.
Now as far as all the arrangements go,
I'm looking for a cheap place to stay,
But I booked a flight the other day

So if you want to come then you should try - "
"Don't fret," he chuckles, "did it last night.
Same flight as yours. Gotta go now, bye!"
"You what? Hello? Presumptuous shite."

How he'd known my flight I was unsure;
I guessed he had peeked my travel documents
When he dropped in a few days before.
"Effing typical," the embodiment

Of rage, I unleashed a murderous groan.
I felt compelled to pick up the phone
And retract my words, but, grabbing the receiver,
Laughter came over me; I could see the

Funny side. I collapsed down into my chair
And tittered over the cheek of it all;
Carefree, for a moment, as old Blair
Until I saw our picture up on the wall.

We looked so happy in windswept embrace,
Grins like shot foxes on Brighton Pier;
Erasing the row that had just taken place.
Nothing lies quite like a photo, I fear.

Part 2 Introduction

Background to the Bracewell case

At times it seems inconceivable that a novel comprising such jocular exchanges as 1.10 would ever become pivotal to a murder trial. And yet we are constantly provided with intimations of the legal wrangling that would beset the novel, raising suggestions that *Broadlake* may well be a fusion of fact and fiction. This is, at first glance at least, exemplified by the narrator's erratic behaviour and his references to several objects found in the basement of 38 Larapinta Drive and 60 Mills Apartments; the latter property shared by Bracewell and Damascus. Quite how the author acquired knowledge of the apartment's contents would only become apparent during the Damascus trial. In view of the author's probable cause of death, the issues of suicide and alcoholism are also prevalent examples of the text drawing on reality. The novel's more nefarious subtext becomes increasingly apparent during the latter stages, notably Parts 4 and 5, but it is worth prefacing this entanglement with further study of events that sparked the revelations.

As has been well documented, the trial of Ivan Damascus began on 3rd January 2005 at the Alice Springs Law Court Building. The case had taken over two years to come to court. Damascus was accused in the first instance of the murder of his partner, Rose Bracewell, and her twenty-month-old daughter, Mary Bracewell. However, following the fatalities on 10th August 2002, it was found that Rose Bracewell had been four months pregnant at the time of her death, making Damascus also potentially responsible for the killing of her unborn child. (For the record, Rose had borne Mary by a previous relationship which had ended in April 2001.)

It was first believed that Bracewell's heavy drinking had resulted in her accidentally falling from the balcony of the third-floor apartment on Barrett Drive whilst holding her daughter. Yet the autopsy showed that, alongside a cracked skull, shattered spine, fractured collarbone and abrasions to her left wrist, Bracewell had been struck on the temple by a blunt object. The weapon, police ascertained, was most probably a Kookaburra cricket bat that was found beside some black leather gloves in the Frances Smith Memorial Park on 11th August 2002. Partially buried in scrubland behind the children's play area, both the bat and gloves had sustained fire damage, indicating that the perpetrator had attempted to burn the evidence. Damascus would later admit to keeping the bat beside an unstable and crooked MDF bookcase that contained Bracewell's collection of novels. This bookcase was situated behind the living room door of their home, 60 Mills Apartments, and the Kookaburra bat was stored beside other sports equipment, namely a set of Bobby Locke Vintage Slazenger golf clubs and a fluorescent yellow Mitre football.

Although Damascus owned the Kookaburra bat and was its principal user, his fingerprints being found on the handle was not incriminating evidence as such. There were a number of other fingerprints on the object, including those of Bracewell herself, members of the Rovers Cricket Club where Damascus played, and several that were unaccounted for. Accordingly, the bat could not conclusively prove the culprit's identity. To compound the uncertainty, at 9:38 p.m. on 10th August the emergency services received an incoherent telephone call from a male, notifying them of the bodies' whereabouts. The individual spoke with an English, Home Counties accent but his name was not given and is still unknown to this day. Was this, we have come to ask, *Broadlake*'s author?

Bracewell's long-term boyfriend, Ivan Damascus, with whom she had a reportedly tempestuous relationship, was immediately suspected. According to testimony provided by their neighbour, Sarah Ainsworth, Bracewell had broken up with Damascus following a heated exchange at The Golden Inn on Undoolya Road on the evening of 9th August 2002. Ainsworth rarely spoke to the couple following a series of disputes over loud music - the residents already had to contend with the notoriously noisy Legend's Nightclub next door and the Lear Haulage lorry depot seventy yards away - but she had witnessed the confrontation whilst dining out with friends. Damascus was subsequently seen by another witness,

Brendan Robbins, entering the couple's Mills Apartment block at 8:15 p.m. on the night of the 10th. Incensed by Bracewell ending their relationship, Damascus was lumbered with a clear motive. Given the additional circumstantial evidence, a warrant was issued for his arrest and his abscondment from Alice Springs only reinforced claims that he was guilty.

Then on 28th August 2002 the body of *Broadlake*'s author was discovered in the basement of 38 Larapinta Drive. As previously noted, the autopsy revealed that the man had drunk himself to death, choking on his own vomit, whilst also suffering arsenic poisoning. Vomit was found not only on the victim and the surrounding area, but also on a painting propped up against the basement wall. The partly ripped watercolour depicted a yacht, The Lady Mo, a vessel once owned by the grandparents of the proprietor, Rupert Tome. Initially, there appeared to be no connection between the two cases or between Damascus and the author, but three suspicious deaths occurring inside a month in Alice Springs could not be reasonably attributed to mere coincidence.

Although theft is common in the town and there had been an unprecedented number of burglaries and attempted burglaries during the second half of 2002, Alice Springs averages just one murder every three years.

Despite the case against Damascus, it was originally thought that *Broadlake*'s author may also have been involved in the murders of Rose and Mary Bracewell. Having been discovered on 28th August 2002, some 18 days after the Bracewell murders, it was plausible that he had committed the crime before he died. Rumours circulated that he had taken his own life as a consequence of his actions. Yet, according to the pathologist, Dr James Radcliffe, the author had been dead for "between 21 and 22 days", contradicting any theories regarding his potential guilt and quashing any case against him. It was therefore deemed likely that Damascus had played a role in all three deaths and, following his escape from Alice Springs, the search for him began.

These events were the start of what was to be an arduous and lengthy pursuit of justice. As I shall explain in Part 3's

Introduction, merely bringing Damascus to trial was the first obstacle to this being realised. For now, though, let us return to *Broadlake* as the narrator and Blair prepare to fly out to the Greek islands.

2.0

11:36 a.m.

Loading up the car as the clock struck four,
Streets silent beneath the moon's misty glare,
I climbed in the boot - the last working door -
And made the short drive to pick up Blair.

Inside, packing was almost underway.
"Jesus," I gasped, "Don't tell me you've just - "
"Chill your boots, we'll be delayed anyway."
Stropping to the car, I revved my disgust

Until marvelling at the street's early rise
- What's with the waving and the V-signs? -
And grasped to persist would be unwise;
The budding fist-shakers parting their blinds,

Especially one feral-maned, cussing pop,
Were hardly crooning, "Howdy, lovely morning!"
Tapping the wheel, quietly blowing my top,
Blair snailed out and I heard the boot wauling,

Then his ballast-weight bag thudding the floor.
Followed by two more, landing with a judder.
"How many - " Muting me, he slammed the door.
Unconsciously headbanging to the shudder,

I could smell Blair behind, his morning breath cough.
Clocking the neighbours, he grunted, settled in:
"Boy, you really know how to piss people off."
"Are you having a giraffe?" Noting his grin,

I sensed the futility of further riposte,
And, bonnet pointing skyward, we scraped away.
Muttering bitterly at the time we'd lost,
I see us now creeping up the carriageway

Through the ashen light, unimpeded as yet;
The road eerily empty, not a car in sight,
As if it has been closed for a film set.
We pass mainly lorries driving through the night,

Or, more truthfully, they mainly pass us;
My car a box on wheels essentially.
As aerodynamic as a pre-war bus,
It did 0-30, well, eventually.

Blair scrolls the radio, finding Busta Rhymes.
"Love this," he drools as he chants the refrain.
"How am I not bored hearing it thousands of times?"
"I believe it's called having shit for brains."

On the news they talk of famine on the rise.
Blair clicks his fingers, slowly counting to ten:
"They say each time I click another child dies."
"May I suggest you stop doing it, then."

The final insult, a scooter trundles past
As we arrive, to Blair's glee, with time on our side.
Lamenting that with more planning at the last
We could in fact have been taken for a ride

By a kind friend, not the parking authority,
We shell out for a spot in the Long Stay.
With more kit than the Queen, our priority
Is to check in before the trolley gives way;

For the ill-equipped a source of annual fear.
My rickety case and ancient apparel
Stir visions of loosened wears rolling clear,
Like museum exhibits, up the carousel.

As we enter the mall Blair stops me short.
Spinning, I blanch as a flash illuminates
On his new camera, a disposable he's bought.
"What *are* you doing?" "Just testing," he states.

He bolts his first breakfast, a Barbie iced bun.
"Off to buy a hat. Back in a while."
Yet, spying Wetherspoon, he breaks into a run.
"It's five o'clock somewhere," he says with a smile.

As he sprints bar-bound I recall we need booze.
Spotting Duty Free between Smith's and Gap,
I bag some Bell's then grump at the queues
As a teen hovers by the Durex rack.

Paid up and a belching Blair at my side,
I see our flight's boarding at gate 28.
A semi-brisk walk then travelator ride
Has passengers gathered and I contemplate

The pending journey, this final goodbye
To the life envisaged for she and I.
Amongst the revelry of holiday goers,
We board the jetway: the temperature lowers

As make-up-caked crew, one Estelle and Jewel,
Jazz-hand directions to our wing-side spot.
Intercom glitching, Estelle asks us all
To heed safety measures; the longest long shot,

Our blanket snub punished with looped Kenny G.
A groin-glaring steward asks the lard in 6a
(And, despite its occupant, much of 6b)
To fasten her seatbelt without delay.

He finds another in whose faults he can revel,
A mother whose row was inspected twice
Yet whose handbag is now at the wrong level.
It's whisked from beneath her on his advice

And is stowed overhead, "it's proper place",
Perfectly poised so that when the hatch opens
Down it will plunge into her neighbour's face.
The steward persists in flaunting slogans:

"It's for security's sake, if you don't mind…"
The captain, meanwhile, over the engine's grind
Relays those essentials preceding a flight,
The precise wind direction and cruising height.

Airborne and out over a steely sea,
Turbulence ensures rest remains elusive.
Mid plummet, we're thanked for choosing *Flybe*
Despite many opting for the all-inclusive.

Clearing skies signal much-needed food,
Yielding, sadly, short-lived elation.
Dry melon, squashed croissant, cold tea - over-stewed -
More than live up to their reputation.

As Blair hoovers up my tray is taken
And I feel spent senses fading fast.
Our early start telling, words are forsaken
As sleep begets an ever-present past.

I see her plane ailing, first signs of trouble,
Port engine smoking, smouldering, alight;
Crazed, bug-eyed panic as, at the double,
Stewards rush by and the fire burns bright.

The faux calm captain swiftly comes on,
Trying to dispel the passengers' alarm,
Informing them over the intercom
Of the engine shut-down, the need to stay calm;

Unsettling in its bid to reassure.
9:12 reads the aviation report.
9:13 it's the captain once more,
Any action now a last resort

As they tumble through cyanic skies.
I see her snatching her oxygen mask,
Terror in her glistening, hazel-brown eyes,
Hot tears at the captain's hopeless ask;

Mechanical malfunction, the report said,
Turbine and fuel pump failing together.
It's *9:15*: there's one minute of dread
Before they'll vanish from radar forever.

Locker-stashed luggage cascades to the floor,
The starboard engine erupts with flames,
A drinks trolley slides to the cockpit door;
Fact or fiction, it's my truth all the same.

The aisle lights flicker then begin to blow,
Each snap for a life and demise apiece.
The children now sense, the parents know,
Know full well this descent will cease

With savage meeting of metal and ocean,
So brutal, so quick, they'll not feel a thing.
I feel their oblivion, their futures stolen,
As they nosedive, an infernal din,

A thunder climaxed as, like a bomb,
The plane hammers down and detonates.
It's over at last but the carnage goes on
As the fuselage fractures and disintegrates;

Crumpling, splintering, wings disengage,
The severed tail vaulting into burning air.
Spiralling, it falls in degenerating rage,
Splicing the water's phosphorous glare.

There are no survivors, no desperate cries,
Just flotsam clunking, hissing as it chars.
A stillness descends, in the wash she lies,
Islands of fire drift like fallen stars;

The perpendicular tail, a momentary cross,
    A fleeting shrine to the floating dead.
    Fizzling swell is all that's left of the loss
As the shattered beast sinks to the seabed.

    Waking, I flicker into consciousness,
    Like an ageing strip light coming to life.
I look back, squinting, at the boisterousness,
    A husband bickering with his son and wife.

The latter through with keeping her Timmy amused,
She ribs her husband. "Play some cards," she pleads,
"A quick game of Snap." Though less than enthused,
    "A quick game's a good game," he concedes.

    Dazed, I see us here just three years before.
    She's talking of her sister, her former home,
    A small flat she rented down by the shore,
    Ten miles from the villa they used to own.

    As I reminisce Blair bestrides the gangway.
"Where are we?" I groan. "On a plane," he quips.
    He clocks his fake Tag. "Few minutes away."
    No sooner have the words left his lips

    Than the landing gear is whining below.
    Portholers coo in raised expectation,
Glimpsing waves gleaming at their window;
    I see them only as her final destination.

2.1

Growing worlds below are flattered from the air.
Warehouses attain a symmetrical beauty,
Sheer mountain roads appear a tame affair;
Lorries, in holy silence, cruise about their duty.

As if the land itself is gathering pace,
Villas hurtle by - as we slow they quicken -
Until we jolt down and the sun hits my face.
On landing it's like we've completed a mission

In a Hollywood take on World War Two:
Half the passengers are whooping and clapping.
Blair leads the way, high-fiving the crew,
Blended with clicks of hasty unstrapping.

Our bodies are struck by ravenous heat
As we gingerly descend the aircraft steps.
Saving the use of our swollen feet,
We're bussed to the terminal where bronzed reps

Ape the strained smiles of our cabin crew.
I spy SunDayz, our travel firm's name,
And our bags - intact - are first to pass through.
Stifling smugness, we leave Baggage Reclaim

For a driverless coach by the car park gate.
Our smugness fades as, powerless, we wait.
Sweating like sprinklers, peeling shorts from derrières,
Kaz, our preened rep, cares to join us and dares

A joke on lateness being "a Greek thing!"
She's met by looks often given by my father
On declaring that for a job I would sing
Or, failing that, I'd be applying to RADA.

Our driver in situ, we pull away,
Twisting through wasteland that enfolds the road.
The occasional villa that lines the way
Expands in accordance with Greek code.

The town betrays all the classic quirks:
Brilliant white structures beside those part built,
All structural poles and cubist frameworks.
Faulty fans overhead, we collectively wilt

As we push on beyond the last dwellings;
Waves of olive trees herald their suspension.
The perfect alignment is strangely compelling,
Like endless brigades stood at attention.

We meander through a comparable town,
A mix of pristine and shell-only abodes.
We pass by one "street" which, as I look down,
Sports a house either side before, ceasing the road,

The tarmac dissolves into tyre-rutted track.
It seems works commenced but, needing a break,
The builders downed tools and never came back;
A postman's paradise left in their wake.

Ahead, our port appears and we join the melee
Of yelling drivers and honking automobiles
Jostling to embark - or disembark, who's to say -
Until the ramp clacks under our wheels

As we mole into the throat of the ferry.
As if a school trip, we're warned, "Back by two!"
Alighting into the cavernous belly,
The deep growl of engines is cut through

By the sequent hiss of brakes, exhaling,
And the clank of cars mounting the ramp.
Seeking deck air, I spot the stair railing,
The iron clanging as up it we stamp,

Engines muffling to a lo-fi hum.
The long flight of steps prompt swift ascent
And, head of the pack, I boyishly run
Until the breeze catches and I relent.

"Okay?" Blair asks. I drop the tell-tale line,
The one she'd employ. "Sure, I'm fine."
I break into whistling to further my case
But, quickly fading, he sees in my face

That I am lost in a bout of solemnity.
Clearly concerned, Blair probes once more,
But the stoked ferry, with timely lenity,
Saves my pretence as we watch her draw

Slowly away from the lulling quay,
Checking his words with the grace of her motion.
Turning about, we make out to sea
Across the white horses whisking the ocean.

I dig out some smokes and, downwind, turn away.
Lighting up at last, I take a deep drag.
"What're they?" Blair asks. "Er, cigarettes," I say.
"Yeah, I know *that*," clicking the dial on his Tag,

"But you don't even smoke." "Well, I do now."
He tries to pinch them. "Leave off," I grumble.
"Jesus, Blair, what's it to you anyhow?"
As I twist round he reflectively mumbles,

"Actually, I fancy one here in the sun.
I know I gave up but, damn it, we're abroad."
I extend my hand but, instead of taking one,
He swipes the packet and hurls it overboard.

Agape, I scowl at him, lost for words.
"What the hell?" I say, deepening my stare.
"They're bad for you. As you may have heard."
"What are you, the fun police? You're hardly, Blair,

Testament to clean living and early nights."
He unleashes a grin. "Come on, it's funny."
"Funny? You've lost nineteen Marlboro Lights.
It's just 'hilarious' blowing money."

Blair regards me as my anger grows
And the coming days fill me with dread.
"You know," he says, "you've got a really big nose."
"Well, it's not as big as the dick on your head."

Though Blair had sunk much of our air food,
Not shy of the trough, he ends our banter
And seeks the café as I stand subdued,
Catching the waves as they rhythmically canter

Into the bow beneath my position;
Like years before on our isle-hopping rides.
Why, noting the coastline that's crept into vision,
I turn to my left and she's stood at my side.

She flicks tousled hair from narrowed eyes
And vacantly hums as she leans on the rails.
She looks to the bow as through billows it scythes,
Then to a yacht as it regally sails,

Spinnaker ballooned, up the craggy shore;
Burnished hull knifing through white-tipped seas.
Stretched above the breakers, cream sails soar,
Harnessing the might of the strengthening breeze,

The verve of the now burgeoning meltemi.
It rivals the yacht once owned by her olds
Before events, disastrous and many,
Ensured such luxuries had to be sold.

We pass her sister's former beachfront home
Before she moved across to neighbouring Kos.
There she met a Perthling, one Rupert Tome,
Before they moved to Alice Springs in Oz.

On a bolted-down bench, I ponder this tale,
Tasting the salt that has settled on my lip.
The horizon climbs and falls beneath the rail,
Charting the tip and slide of the ship.

At my ear, Blair chews with a caveman's finesse.
I do not recall acknowledging his presence
But, midst daydreaming, I must have, I guess.
Largely detached, soon our port's entrance

Is not the docking that we now undergo
But that which we'd shared three years before.
I'm watching her viewing crowds flocking below
As we bob quaywards to a docker's roar.

A giant starting grid, cars line the dock,
Windscreens blinking in the sun-bleached light;
Wayfarers clustered amid the gridlock
Gawk at the beguiling, imposing sight.

Just as I do, watching her watching them.
Though my timing is spectacularly out,
Given the imminent offloading mayhem,
I let slip a line that leaves her no doubt

As to my affections and hopes years from now.
She returns my pledge as only she knows how.
She does not blush or shyly glance the ground;
She is quite accustomed to the stuttered sound

Of smitten fools and their helpless flattery.
She humours me, nigh on spurning my words,
Leaving exposed my sentimentality;
I start to wonder if I've even been heard.

I caress her hair but, ignored, pull away.
She eyes me like Nat, our tabby, would do,
When you'd quit stroking, as if to say,
"Why are you stopping? Where are you off to?"

Po-faced, she looks blankly across the port
Like she is tired of what my vow infers.
Then comes unease of a different sort
As she drops a conundrum, a trait of hers.

"How I so wish we could choose who we…"
She tails off. "Never mind, no matter."
But I can't let it rest. "No, please tell me.
Say what you mean. Please, it *does* matter."

She begins afresh. "I so wish we could…
Oh, leave it," she snaps and, through with delaying,
I ask her again, as you well would,
But I know exactly what she is saying.

Below is a transcription of one of several messages discovered beneath the floorboards of 60 Mills Apartments on 4th February 2002:

You have been in my thoughts all day. I know it's complicated and you don't feel the same way yet, but just give it time. You may not believe in fate but I swear we are meant to grow old together.

All my love,

L x

From *The Kookaburra Killer* by Arthur Hamlin

2.2

Fighting sickness from a pick n' mix,
Blair mines his shorts' left-hand pocket.
"Hey," he gulps, "got your cancer sticks.
You were right to give me a rocket.

Chucking them overboard was a bad call."
"Well, here's not something you see every day.
You do have a conscience after all."
I take the packet. "Thanks a lot," I say,

Then sling them joyfully into the sea.
"Are you nuts? Why on earth would you throw - "
"It's funny. Besides, they're bad for me."
"Okay, touché." "Come on, let's go."

Edging from our berth, we clatter the ramp
Then, jostling through anarchy, slowly decamp,
Past rattling cases on the coarse tarmac,
And a ghostly taverna, more glorified shack.

Airless, musty seats meet pungent sweat,
Now capped by the rasp of a toddler's wail
And Blair's frog-faced, "Are we nearly there yet?"
Turning, and noting the coach on our tail,

The town appears, sooner than I recall.
The road is peppered with set-back villas
Before enter high-rise hotels and tall
Apartment blocks, not dissimilar

To those once reserve of southern Spain.
Promptly swallowed by the concrete jungle,
A couple in front voice their disdain,
Backed by their neighbours, likewise disgruntled,

As we fight to quell the peaking depression.
The gates of hell a comparable entrance
- Prisons could offer better first impressions -
We stop and, like a judge passing sentence,

Kaz scans her list and plucks out a name.
Rising, we peruse the crane-blocked skies
Then hang our dripping heads in shame.
We scavenge for bags and, as tempers rise,

I sense the feeling from the tinted window:
Rather you than us. Very best of luck.
Our thoughts as we snare our luggage, though,
Are something more along the lines of: Fuck.

Branching off the street, we enter an alleyway
Which leads to a breeze-blocked flight of steps.
Dragging Blair's excess, Kaz shows us the way
Then, at the third floor, she first of all checks

The air con's still broken and that the main room
Has not expanded since she last passed through.
At least that is what we are led to assume
As she tries to enter, only for her shoe

To become lodged against the opposing wall.
Oh, alright, my friend, I'm joshing again
- We were lucky to have found a room at all -
But it was more fit for mice than men.

Shorn of adornments to lift the gloom,
The monastic emptiness finds us subdued.
It felt like standing in a familiar room
When the festive décor has just been removed.

The glossy blurb had sold it, of course,
As a *bijou flat in a stunning location;*
So central promised the Photoshopped source
You won't miss a thing! A declaration

That we'd find was true to its word.
For, barring the use of industrial earplugs,
You could not miss the racket that would be heard
Throbbing below from the two nightclubs;

Bodies rocking to the bass till it - and we -
Came to a standstill at gone half three.
As the room quakes from a bus on the drag,
Blair drops his rucksack and grabs a taupe bag.

"I've been meaning to give you...actually, no,
Leave it for now." He sinks to a chair.
"Give me what? You can't say that and then go,
'Hang on, let's leave it'. How is that fair?"

"Fair point, I shouldn't have said it, sorry.
You'll get it after the service, okay."
"Whatever," I mutter, drowned out by a lorry.
But I'm not done: "What is it anyway?"

"Just leave it till Sunday, as I have said."
Waiving a follow-up, I finish unpacking.
As Blair hits the hay, dry-humping the bed,
I'm keen for a stroll so at once get cracking,

Heading past the clubs, JUICE and Tide's Reach.
I step unexpectedly onto a pavement
Which now runs along behind the town beach.
The tarmac is fringed by an adjacent

Wall that divides the shore from the above land;
Preventing sunseekers, as they once could do,
From dropping straight down onto the sand.
Greige steps earmark the assigned walk-through.

Joining the beach, I pace to the water.
Wash slurps at my feet as I rove the shore.
Almost jovial, I casually saunter
Until, having covered fifty yards, no more,

It suddenly looms high above the bay,
Peering out behind a tall band of trees;
A verdancy that, needless to say,
Is rare for these parts - the bountiful leaves

Incongruous with the xeric landscape.
The Villa's facade is dotted with shutters;
Turquoise flecks pierce the greenery's drape.
As, hovering above, a box kite flutters

I re-engage my study and look closer still,
Counting the shutters along the first floor
To the one where she's stood at the window sill;
Her bedside picture alive once more.

I recall the photo taken from the lawn,
As she stands with her sister inside her room;
The Constable clouds in the left corner torn
By years of reliving that fine afternoon.

Such reverie is bluntly put in check
By the rap of a ball at my neck.
Searching its origins, I quietly curse
- Everyone equally a culprit at first -

Until I round upon a likely buff Greek,
Waving as I screen my eyes from the glare.
As he calls out I'm too stunned to speak;
I think he's saying sorry but, in his stare,

I see he just wants me to boot the thing back.
I unduly oblige and, grinding my teeth,
Pelt the Mitre with a venomous thwack,
My right foot snagging on a jizz-filled sheath.

I plan my route as the beach arcs round,
Casting my eyes up the steepening hill
Until settling upon The Villa's grounds;
The chalk-white pillars, as they spill

Through trees, basking in the gilded sunbeams.
Foreseeing the sight, I slalom through bathers,
Many now dozing or applying sun creams.
A stretch-marked mother browses Tuesday's papers;

Her spouse scans *Ulysses*, chaining away
On a fast-shrinking pack of Embassy;
The esteemed front cover on full display,
Held on high to claim cultural supremacy.

Why, seeking betterment in every way,
I spot **SECOND IS NOWHERE**'s bold typeface.
No doubt he's that guy who, come sports day,
Slips on his spikes for the father's race.

Taking the route that retreats from the beach,
I sight the tiered hill's uppermost shelf.
Often, when The Villa seems within reach,
The hairpinned road winds back on itself.

Tempting though it is to forge through trees,
Up through the hill's sun-flecked farmland,
I follow the spiral until, on my knees,
I clock the town beach, its bather-specked sand.

I approach The Villa's striped landscaped grounds,
Cascading down to the improbable blue.
As if the resplendent vista astounds,
I gasp up the stretch and, as I do,

Surroundings grow with each stride greener.
The tree-lined avenue and spring-lush lawns
Usurp aridity; the air, too, feels cleaner.
Then, as through the emerald The Villa dawns,

Its pillared frontage nudging through the green,
I'm struck by a figure by the black gates, pacing;
Wishing to observe but not to be seen,
Veiled by a scarf, sage with grey lacing.

She flits to and fro in quick succession,
Occasionally resting her head on a stanchion.
She's too absorbed to notice my progression
And I'm just seconds from the gates to the mansion

When a deft breeze flicks the scarf from her face.
Rumbled, she stumbles and, plainly crotchety,
She glowers and pulls her scarf into place
Before resuming her gaze of the property.

Sensing my intent to make conversation,
She bolts from her position by the gate,
Stealing several yards before I hasten
To make up ground and ask her straight

What business she might have way up here.
"Excuse me," I appeal, but her wish is clear.
Alone I stand in the shade's honey glow,
The cooled air hushed, like falling snow.

Shifting closer, a buzz from above me
Curtails my thoughts on the fleeing figure.
Seeking its cause, I look up to study
The limestone gateposts with growing rigour,

Their Romanesque grandeur marking the entrance.
Above the bricked drive and formal garden
A security camera detects my presence.
Like a target lined up by a marksman,

Its silver barrel hones in on my person,
Whirring shrilly like a dentist drill,
Dipping to focus on the incursion.
Unnerved by the security overkill,

And clearly not wishing to cause a stir,
I retreat from the gates and start the walk back.
From the farmland grows an engine's purr,
Powering a vehicle up an off-road track.

It ascends to a chug as I shamble on
Until, almost upon me, the revving slows
And the plucked strains of traditional Greek song
Flood through the van's open windows.

Beside me, the rusting Ford pulls up
And out pops a plump, shaven head.
"Is hot, yeah?" I'm asked. I manage a "Yup".
Drawn to reinforce what I have said,

I oscillate my arm as if it were a fan.
"You want go down? Me give you ride."
He eyes the space at the back of the van.
I'm struggling to cast my fears aside.

"Come on, my friend, me take you down now.
Is no problem," he says, tapping the key.
He lights a fag and scratches his brow.
I begin to conceive that I am maybe

Overcooking the risk so, indulging his nod,
I wander round to the back of the van,
Crawl in then shift up until I am lodged
Between a beer crate and a petrol can.

I hear Mother's voice as I nestle aboard:
"Why's it acceptable," she'd say to herself,
"To shun seatbelts in taxis or when you're abroad?"
No taxi in sight, let alone a belt,

"Hold on!" I hear as the horn is pounded.
We pitch down the road and bear sharply right.
My caution, I discover, is well-founded
As the first hairpin veers into sight.

The cornering is, to put it kindly, unsound,
And I'm left clinging to the side of the van.
My lower back thumps against the surround
As we rally on down, the petrol can

And Amstel crate knocking at my knees.
Despite the incline we persist in this fashion,
The engine and music smothering my pleas,
   Prompting the same preventative action

Until, at the hill's base, we skid to a halt.
I wait, expecting us to finally shift,
Then, without wishing to in any way insult
The driver's kindness for the impromptu lift,

I ask - the song over - why we've stopped dead.
"Not going into town?" There follows a silence.
"No-no, my friend," he says, shaking his head,
   "Me go no further. Me no licence."

"Ahhh," I neigh, keeping as calm as I can.
"Out now. Have goats. Must kill." "Oh...sure."
I slide up the boot and drop down from the van.
"Efharisto," I say, padding round to his door.

"No problem. Have nice stay." Reversing back,
He crunches the gears, slams his foot down,
   And hares up a road, or more dirt track,
   That I presume ring-roads the town.

As the van shrinks into the distance,
Heat-shimmers set outlying buildings ablur.
My pins feel revived from the Greek's assistance,
My heart, though, is heavy with thoughts of her.

2.3

Is that the clock tower striking twelve noon?
It's hard to tell above Reg's sour drone.
Like many here, he rarely changes his tune,
Slating his wife then plying Zac Stone

- Interred with the phone the other weekend -
With tales of what the council have planned.
Simmer down, Reg! (excuse me, my friend)
Between you and Gwen all my efforts are damned!

Wearied by the slog of our lengthy trip,
We have our hearts set on an early night;
Even Blair, at first revived by his kip,
Can't shake the effects of ferry and flight.

Yet, below, the bass is cranked up at ten
To an ear-flapping, floor-bouncing volume,
And, in minutes, he is up once again,
Swaying like a hippie in a 60's commune.

As he slips out I feel the surge of noise,
And, through paper-thin blinds, the frenzy of light.
As the bass bulges, glints of turquoise,
Purple and ruby, almost as bright

As the strip's, swirl around my eyelid.
I believe insomnia cannot be broken,
That I'll never sleep; but like you do, I did.
For next thing I know I am gently woken

By the buzz of a speedboat crossing the bay.
Hearing a snuffle, I turn to face Blair,
Fully clothed and hugging a Smirnoff tray.
He feels for a tumbler on the bedside chair

And garbles gibberish as I lean closer;
Although "sod" and "off" feature for sure.
With a sleep deficit and acute hangover,
I leave him to his wind and ogreish snore.

Wrenching belongings from the under the chair
- Towel and *Catcher* - I'm set for the beach.
Before I depart, though, I stop to ask Blair,
Taking great care to soften my speech:

"Shall we meet up when you're feeling better?
There's a quiet place off the main street.
Serves souvlaki, dolmades, feta.
Not that fast food crap you're forced to eat

In those so-called tavernas on the front."
I assume he's game by his tone-raised grunt.
"It's up in the hills, has views of the bay.
I went there years ago with…anyway,

I'm writing its name on this luggage tag here,"
A touch vague now as to what I am doing.
"I'll sketch you directions for when you get near."
Keen to guard against the gusts now cooing

Around the building, flurrying through doors,
I trap the tag under his Game Boy wallet.
"You're coming?" I ask to be totally sure,
Tipping some shrapnel into my pocket.

"I'll be there," he groans, "unless I'm not."
"Well, thanks for that, Blair. Shall we say one?
Did you hear me?" "Yes, one…on the dot."
"Pigs might fly," and I squint at the sun.

I had offered guidance as, the week she died,
Blair got lost when meeting by Camden Lock.
I sourced an *A-Z* but he simply replied,
"Who needs a map when you've got a cock?"

As if an octopus had given directions,
He'd tried every road within a square mile,
Sampling en route umpteen ale selections,
Spawning an excuse list as long as The Nile.

Water aboard, I bag a spot by the shore,
My cream-slathered skin like buttered white toast.
A good hour's peace precedes the uproar
As trippers, like ants, pour off the boats.

Yet the onslaught all but passes me by,
Lost as I am in *The Catcher in the Rye*.
Why, it's not until I glance up at the sea
That I conceive the numbers encircling me.

Perma-tanned natives flank pallid-skinned Scots,
Entwined newlyweds border bickering lovers,
Disturbed nappers tut at sand-kicking tots,
Narked sisters bark at towel-hogging brothers.

A mum thumbs picture books, son smearing ice cream.
"What are these?" he's asked of a leggy pink bird.
"Mflingoes." "And this fruit?" "Strawglies," he beams.
"And these insects?" "Flutterbies." "Wow, what big words!"

As a vamp struts by, though, in a fuck-me dress,
She elbows her husband: "Eyes off the floozy."
He ogles the caption on the belle's breasts:
Area of Outstanding Natural Beauty.

Medium rare and parched, I exit the beach.
Rambling, the fierce sun saps my strength.
Glugging tepid water, I jadedly reach
The end of the strip then scan the short length

Of twisting road up to the taverna.
Rounding the bend, I'm picturing the view
That I'd sold to Blair just two hours earlier;
The seclusion that greets the precious few

Who happen upon this serene backwater.
My outlook, though, is somewhat less picturesque:
For it is as if the UK headquarters
Of, say, Arriva or National Express

Have been transferred to the Aegean.
An armada of coaches greet my arrival
As the hordes flock into Trish & Ian's.
Too hot to care - and of our meeting mindful -

I haul myself up the Disney-themed steps.
More room in a phone box, I am first squeezed
Onto a bench of *Hokey Cokeying* reps;
Their heaped charred toasties a mass grave of cheese.

Waiting, the staff seem blind to our corner
And, hangry, I'm waving in a diva-like strop.
Tended to in alphabetical order
I sense I'd be down there with ZZ Top.

A familiar face, though, diverts my attention;
Rotating, I sense her glancing at me.
Relooking, though, it's of my own invention:
Her eyes are transfixed on the shallow sea,

Or more vast reef that spreads like a map
A stone's throw away from the swarming shore.
A third glimpse, eyelines appear to overlap
But this time I'm less convinced than before.

Ordering at last, I rack my brain
Until just one possibility remains.
Of course - of *course* - by The Villa we'd "met";
My God, they look so alike, I fret.

She reads *Saving Agnes* with steadfast endeavour
Until the reps launch into *YMCA*.
Clapping the covers of her book together,
She springs from her seat and scuttles away.

Gradually crushed and starved of air,
I wonder if I should've ordered for Blair,
Or at least waited for him to arrive.
Then again, since I may not be alive

When the food appears - given the NHS wait -
And doubtless afterwards - seeing neighbours' plates -
I'm consoled by thoughts of an evening Scotch.
I round on one family as I people-watch:

In the finest tradition of The Holiday
The idea has far outstripped reality.
Lobstered mother slams the heat they
Had come for, whilst Dad, a model of vitality,

Is slumped to the table and, suffice to say,
Will return more pooped than when he went;
In dire need of, well, some time away.
Despite all this, when they return to Kent

(Their home I gather) they'll tell a friend
- Who'll have had "a fab time" in, say, Rome -
Of their fabulous week, when in the end
They'd all have sooner stayed at home

Waiting for sun under overcast skies
Whilst dreaming of jetting off to the Med.
Batting away the dive-bombing flies,
I observe their abandoned mains with dread.

Past the seat our vexed lass had forsaken,
I pick out Blair, his usual panicked self,
Lively as a mannequin and soon overtaken
By a grave-dodging relic, tottering herself,

But a true Olympian by comparison.
A full sitting later, Blair staggers in
As if he's just run The London Marathon.
"So peaceful," he pants with signature grin.

"Have you been dressing in the dark?" I snort.
He's clothed in what can be best described
As a vomit green shirt and rainbow shorts;
The former, in flame-orange letters, inscribed

Tug On My Fuel Pump. Above blinding red shoes
His knee-high white socks read *Born To Relax.*
It's as if he has covered himself in glue
And jumped in the bargain bin at TK Maxx.

We sit conjoined, hermetically sealed.
"If there is one thing I can rely upon
It's you being - " "Horny." Clunge-eyes peeled,
Blair wolf whistles a rep in a sheer sarong.

"Blair, you really shouldn't - " "Oh, listen to you.
The only people offended by wolf whistling
Are the very women it never happens to."
He headcounts briefly as I chunter, bristling.

"There must only be about two hundred - "
"I know," I spark, "think I didn't notice?"
As I massage a warm sachet of mustard
Some food arrives which, on diagnosis,

And much evidence to the contrary,
Is my BLT - carefully disguised
As an impenetrable slab of granary,
So out of date it has all but fossilised;

The sandwich world's equivalent to Fort Knox
Complete without its Cola and fries.
Levering it open, Blair tardily clocks
The sinew of bacon - unseen to most eyes -

Which, it appears, they've neglected to cook;
On review I detect the proverbial pulse.
In gastronomic hell, a nose-turned look,
During which I am set to convulse,

Reveals the soggy light brown lettuce.
Then I spot, soaked in bubbling phlegm,
A breeding splat of tomato. Other than this,
    I'd be delighted to have it again.

Quite the sea change from our trip years before.
"Is the squid fresh?" she asked the owner that day.
He seemed averse to state when it came ashore:
"Was caught…ten this morning. Sorry, that okay?"

    Attacking the crust, I peek a tickled Blair.
    "Took the liberty of not ordering you one."
    I fish out a complimentary pubic hair.
    "I'd rather have a bowl of Pedigree Chum."

    Dabbing oil, Blair joins the excavation:
    "That worth getting fat for?" "Fat?" I say,
    "I'll lose half a stone from mastication."
    I drain out the oil slick onto a tray.

Slit-eyed, Blair pokes the crust, limp-wristed:
"Didn't know bread was grey. It's just so…old."
    "If it was a building it would be listed."
I nip at the lettuce, circumventing the mould.

"You should watch your weight, pal." "Fuck off, Blair.
    You put pounds on just *looking* at a cake.
    You seem permanently pregnant, I swear."
He gives his six-rolls a belly dancer's shake.

    Still a drink down, I alert a boy waiter,
    And a surprisingly short time later
    It crash-lands the table; the pleasant surprise
    Dampened by it spilling over the sides

As gum-propelled Kian drops a fork in Blair's lap,
Our server's name flashing on his Mickey Mouse cap.
"Good to see you," I say, "in a hurry back there."
Blair dings the fork. "What do you mean, back where?

You know, I think I might be a bit concussed."
"Don't you need a brain for concussion, Blair?"
He ignores me. "I slipped last night and must
Have banged my head against the stair.

I was rushing back to this scrubber, Kim,
Who I'd been fondling on the terrace sofa.
Flat as an ironing board but gorgeous quim,"
Reprising his role as The Gentlemen Groper.

"If you really think you're concussed," I say,
Try out this test I was given the day…
The morning after…the crash…" Losing track,
Language fails me as it floods back.

I see myself charging, her face as she froze.
"Yes," I continue in faint affirmation,
"If you raise your hand to touch the nose
It's a good test of your co-ordination."

Slightly puzzled, Blair heeds my request.
He proceeds to lift his hirsute left hand
Until the place where it comes to rest
Tells me he does not quite understand.

"Not *my* nose," I shriek as he fondles my flesh,
His rhino-knee fingers stroking my beak.
"Not just an ugly face, then." He starts afresh.
"You'll live," I snicker, pinching his cheek.

Blair's unconvinced: "My head's been thumping.
What if it winds up far more serious?"
"Calm down, Blair, we're all dying of something."
As end-of-world hysteria turns him delirious,

I swiftly move on. "By the way, minutes ago
There was this woman reading at a table
Who looked almost exactly like…you know…"
"Oh, really?" he wavers, flagrantly unable

To hide the inner cynic. "Truly," I say,
"You didn't see her descending the hill?"
"I had my head down most of the way.
I was more concerned with not being ill."

Praying there's a dentist in the vicinity,
I recommence chiselling into the bread;
But after only a few seconds' futility
I sense I would have more luck with lead.

Giving the crust a valedictory stab,
I chase the bill, catching the eye of Kian.
Moments later, as I'm handed the tab
- Signed *With love from Trish & Ian xxx* -

I ponder how good the meal could have been
If they were as focussed on food as billing.
But then, seeing two fathers venting spleen
Over a late bill and them making a killing,

I sense their promptness must be some mistake.
Leaving as the reps bludgeon *Oklahoma*,
We're hurried by the hill until, dizzy, we flake
Onto the drag, sniffing chargrilled aroma,

Tugging Blair across the coach-locked street.
He halts by The Vine to watch diners eat.
"Is this," he calls out, "a 'so-called taverna'?
You know, the type you were talking of earlier?

Their 'fast food crap' looks pretty ace."
Still tasting regret, a five-minute wait
And I'm viewing Blair as, with the grace
Of a pig, he wolfs a belt-popping plate

Of succulent chicken and sauté potato,
Washed down in one with an ice-cold Sol.
Moaning like he's being given fellatio,
I long to climb into the nearest hole.

"All this," he says, "and baklava to follow,"
Swamping his food in a sea of gravy.
"Got enough there?" "I've got a dry swallow."
"You'd see less ocean in the damn navy."

Mooching home, stomach still rumbling,
We stop for hop juice, iced tea and Red Bull.
Blair trousers my change then utters, mumbling,
"You'll have to carry it, I'm just so full."

Back at the flat, I hear curse-laced muttering
As he braves the shower's Baltic trickle.
Pipework groaning, I catch the spluttering
Until it's reduced to a torturous dribble.

As I read *Catcher*, Blair gruffly emerges
With fevered shivers through the chipboard door.
Modelling a tea towel, he sustains the curses,
Mincing across the square inch of floor.

"All I could find." He stoops to a boombox,
Dust-sprinkled by the chair between our beds.
He flicks the *ON* switch cloaked under his socks
Which, to our surprise, triggers Grateful Dead.

He screws up his eyes, revealing two red spots.
"Do that again," I say, flicking the lights.
"Well, I'll be damned," probing the dots,
"You have a matching pair of eyelid bites."

Dropping his tea towel, cussing as I cower,
Blair checks the mirror as I spy more disaster:
His joystick has shrunk so much in the shower
You can barely tell if he's Arthur or Martha.

Chipolata clutched, though, he turns cheery:
"You know, I was blessed with a nine-inch dick.
Problem was, it belonged to Father O'Leary."
Giggling, he slips a sock on his prick.

Covering himself, he crouches down,
Vile grin exposing his pearly whites.
"I see a little smile coming," he clowns.
I curb my mirth but, re-clocking the bites,

Can't help but release a strangled titter.
"Could you be any more annoying," I roar.
My chuckles subside to a light snigger,
Then to a sigh as I remember once more.

"I'll stay in tonight." "No need, I'm fine."
"I'm just concerned - " "Blair, please don't dwell."
I punch his arm. "Go and have a good time."
Grabbing some tumblers, I open the Bell's.

"I know you're tired from being out in the sun
But sitting here on your own won't be much fun.
All you'll do is read J.D. Slazenger."
"Blair, it's *Sal*inger, not effing Slazenger."

"Slazenger, Salinger. Who cares, whatever.
You're always reading that book for some reason."
"I'm *re*reading the thing. A great novel never
Loses its appeal. God, you're a heathen."

He cackles, rising, then drops back down.
"Whoa, I feel really giddy," he winces.
"Well, what the hell did you expect?" I frown.
He moves to stand up and, at first, flinches,

Then straightens his back. "I'll take it down a peg."
Yet, before moving, he says with a start,
"Hold your horses," and, cocking his leg,
Lets rip with this quite tremendous fart.

"For Christ's sake," I squeal, "have you got the runs?"
I squirm at his belter. "Flip me," I guffaw.
The stench circulates. "Fuck a duck, that hums."
"Brace yourself, mate," and he trumpets once more.

As I wretch out the window, Blair's quick to dress.
"I'm off," he cries, sniffing, moments later.
"Good luck tomorrow, are you sure - " "Yes!
Just bugger off, will you. If you wait a

Second longer I've a damn good mind - "
"I'm gone!" he shouts, skiing through the door.
I listen to his footsteps as they wind
Down the steps, slowly fading, before

They become those of strollers below.
I watch the JUICE sign's strobing light show,
Skipping above the street as the clammy air
Crackles with traffic and the undefined blare

Of maxed bar music competing to be heard,
The cryptic clamour of carousing voices.
I graze on some bread, stumped by a crossword,
Then head in to rest as the town rejoices.

Yet lain down, eyes closed, all I see is her face.
Catching her breath, her eye pricks with a tear.
"I'm so sorry," she sobs as we embrace,
"It's just when we make love we disappear."

I escape to shower then, knelt mid-thawing,
Dig out my tie and turn in for the night.
Tossing and turning with thoughts of the morning,
I drop off at two but wake at first light.

The Australian

June 19ᵗʰ 2005

BITTER AUTHOR'S RECLUSIVE LIFE UNVEILED BY DAMASCUS

"Ivan Damascus revealed that the author never once received visitors and left his room solely to buy provisions. When asked whether he would describe the man as a loner, Damascus emphatically affirmed this to be the case."

2.4

I see that dawn, not like it were yesterday,
But as if it's still breaking and is yet to pass.
I wake for the first time to the drowsing bay
As the morn catches our pane's cracked glass.

Pulse at once racing, the world's in no rush
As the whine of a moped breaches the hush.
The ocean lies still, its waves barely break,
Our centrepiece taking the form of a lake.

The sky is a cirrus-plumed purple-pink,
Awaiting its master; still biding his time.
Pale yellows diffuse before a scythed chink
Of crystal white light hails the climb.

Rays spill forth through the fleeing cloud,
Daubing the welkin in powdery blues.
Dark shadows on the headland, dawn's parting shroud,
Descend and release the water's hues;

Like jewels, silvers and greens flicker below,
Under the torch of the clearing heavens.
A squadron of pedalos reflect in the glow;
Lounging in light, their cherry gloss reddens.

Dubstep pounds from a passing Clio
As the nectarine sun rises slowly;
Its splendour wasted on the chanting trio
- "FUCK THE IRA!"- on the road below me.

Neon is submitting to the lustre of day,
Beats are usurped by the chirr of cicadas;
A zephyr is ushering the clouds away,
Bringing to my nose the stench of lager.

Onto the balcony, I pull up a seat,
Resting my calves on the rust-flaked rail.
Looking to sea through outstretched feet,
The celestial sight is to no avail:

I rewind to her mother's kind invitation,
Sam calling to say that she'd been killed,
The theatre mix-up, her explanation,
Us together, apart, my racing mind filled

With our detritus, playing over and over:
I can hear the tout laughing at my back,
I can smell the coffee as I draw closer,
I can see my blood, lain on the tarmac;

Life turning on one revolving blur.
Oh, to move on and just accept my lot!
Yet my own shadow is cast by her;
How do you let go when it's all you've got?

Shaken from musing by a bleeping truck
Reversing the side street behind our room,
I await renewed peace but, no such luck,
I retreat inside to the relative gloom.

Immersed in what the coming hours hold,
Blair's absence has been quite forgotten.
His sheets still bear my clean-up's folds;
Beer-marked shorts crown threadbare cotton.

I turn to the wardrobe, backless and listing,
And seize my travel-creased suit and shirt.
With hours to kill and the noise persisting,
I check in with Holden then, faint with thirst,

Pluck iced tea from our fridgeful of beer.
I brave the shower but, on dressing for the day,
My cufflinks are missing so I raid Blair's gear,
His month's worth of clothes for our one-week stay.

Taming my locks with an unused comb,
Each follicle, it seems, has a mind of its own;
A barber's worst nightmare, as Blair would joke,
I could ruin wedding portraits at a stroke.

Resting, my shirt is plastered to my back
As I glug a vat's worth of chilled water.
Half nine and it's time to hit the track.
Heart now galloping and each breath shorter,

I don suit jacket and retrieve the key.
As a conquering sun creeps on by
To my unmade bed from the balcony,
I tweak a kinked flap of black tie

Then slowstep, twitching, to the front door
And into the heat that's building outside.
Yawning nerves and surveying the shore,
I join the calmed drag and quicken my stride.

Stray sand and chippings tarnish my shoes,
A trip on one stone scuffing the leather.
The breeze holds its breath, the sky's cobalt blue,
This feted morning not even a feather

Would flutter from the bay's loftiest spire;
Nothing can distil the heat's oppression.
No wonder a bronzer can't grasp my attire
As, with a quizzical, are-you-mad expression,

He gawks, lime parasol slung over his shoulder,
And makes for the beach like a marching soldier.
Each time I undertake that morning's hike
I recall it differently, reworked, if you like.

A stumble one day is forgotten the next;
The towel-cloaked dame sporting two gold brooches,
Singing to herself, book clutched at her breast,
I see her face sometimes as she approaches,

Double-taking at my inappropriate dress.
Then sometimes she blurs as she maunders by;
The past is dead but it breathes nonetheless.
Yet, without fail, I see this one guy

Dressed in beige slacks and light blue shirt
- Public school uniform - ten yards ahead;
Beaver brown deck shoes kick up the dirt
As he limps on, clasping paper-wrapped bread.

Hobbling, though, does not hamper progress;
He matches me every step of the way.
I'm kept in his wake much like, I guess,
The woman by The Villa on the first day.

I tease out her mother's list of directions
And hunt the turn to the next bay along.
Ahead, I spot the sea path she mentions
Then picture The Villa as I press on.

As the beach morphs from sand to stone,
That is where the limping soul is heading,
Twisting up the hill to their former home,
Steering round the road's crumbled edging.

As he moves off and away from the sea,
I take the path beside the poppling surf.
Sheltered by boughs of a lone Chaste tree,
I inhale crisp air and smell the warm earth,

Pausing beneath the bower, glad of shade.
On past swathes of yellow flowering gorse,
I catch something glinting through the glade.
Maintaining my speed, I hunt its source

Then land upon the most likely of matches.
Through the foliage of a cypress tree
I glimpse the hobbler: the snatches
Of light I presume to be

Those of a watch face, though I can't be sure.
I maintain my stare and again it winks,
But I'm able to hold my gaze no more
For I'm switched to the path as it jinks

Round the broad face of a lichened rock
Then passes, sloping, under olive trees.
Hastening now at the call of the clock,
I follow the path till, emerging, I see

A throng on the beach that fronts The Villa.
A bobbing Kaiki adorns the stretch:
The captain, I presume, stands over the tiller
Whilst, centre stage, a muted crowd etch

Latent unease into sand with their feet,
Raking its surface then kneading once more.
Leaving the bower, panting in the heat,
I shyly trudge up the sequestered shore.

As I progress in my Sunday best
The engines' start-up dispels the malaise,
Summoning the attention of the guests
Who, in unison, divert their gaze

Towards the captain of the lolling boat.
Above the canopy an ensign flies
But it hangs limp like a hung-up coat.
As snarls from the outboard engines rise

My belated advance is quite unnoticed;
Met as I am by a blockade of backs.
I hope the lizard-skinned gent standing closest
Might hear my pocket's chinking drachs,

The loose change that I'd scraped together,
But it seems the years have stolen his senses.
My toes curl against my shoes' hard leather,
Carving cooled sand into six-inch trenches.

Above the bay we hear church bells peal
And, turning round, guests spy the sanctuary.
I'm in full view but, overlooked, I feel
As welcome as Christmas songs in January.

With no end to my exclusion in sight
A scurrying figure lays fears to rest.
Her mother, I deduce, relieves my plight,
Rescuing me, her floundering guest.

"You must be..." and, in counterfeit cheer,
We hug as I thank her for the invitation.
"No, thank *you* for coming all the way here."
Then she adds in nerve-laced elation,

"So pleased you made it. What a day for it.
I think you can see why she used to adore it.
I really hope it's nice where you're staying?"
Spotting the urn, I find myself saying,

"Oh, yes...it's lovely," my senses on strike.
Her fervent blitheness is unstinting:
"In spite of things, I hope today feels like
- And do forgive the wishful thinking -

A true thanksgiving and not too rueful.
Not like at the church, that I could not bare."
I blanch as, for me, this is her funeral,
That event being a private affair.

"Rev Keats has promised nothing heavy,
Just prayers between words from her father and I.
We'd not planned for a priest but up stepped Sebby.
He's a dear friend and days after she died

He said he'd be honoured to officiate.
He's retired but does the odd service or other."
As if he can hear his name under debate,
Rev Keats looks over and beckons her mother.

His summons cuts short our conversation
And, excusing herself, she turns away,
Passing her husband, deep in contemplation,
Clutching the urn as he savours the bay.

Her mother mounts the barrel-buoyed pontoon
And converses briefly with Rev Keats.
Her husband joins them, urn in hand, and soon
We are invited to take our seats.

Eyeing varnished pews set into ribbed flanks,
We walk the pontoon and take the captain's hand,
Stepping aboard the deck's mellowed planks.
From an aft spot, I look past the fine sand

To the towering trees, The Villa's guard.
Ruling the skyline, an arboreal Manhattan,
We can scarcely discern The Villa's façade;
Noting the treescape, the stud-lined pattern

Forged by the run of turquoise shutters
Is now reduced to an artist's impression.
We're jounced by the engine as it splutters,
But a quartet of flashes in quick succession

Seize my attention, then a fifth, no less,
The cause of which I cannot detect.
Their source at this stage I can only guess,
But as the boat drifts a touch to the left

The Villa's balcony is partly revealed.
A blue-shirted soul stands alone and stooped.
Leant on the rails, his face is concealed:
Binoculars hide he who'd earlier trooped

Up the hill then who I'd tailed on the road.
The flickers now emanate from his lenses,
Flashing towards us as if in Morse code.
The boat swings back and my body tenses:

I can hardly bare to look him in the eye.
I note his wrist chain, like that given to me.
I scan up from his Church's to his Paisley tie
 Which, for all the world, appears to be

The very one he wore that night of the play;
Likewise his sharp suit and year-round tan,
 Reviving the fright of that December day.
Or perhaps I see him the only way that I can,

As the man who on that bitter winter's night
Gave me the shock from which we'd never recover.
The trust went, you see, not believing her outright.
Who would have thought it was her half-brother?

Now united in loss, we pull out to sea.
The pontoon recedes, loosening grip on the wake,
 Until from our roots the wake is free.
I watch, shock-haired, as churned trails snake

Whilst her grandfather recalls, many moons ago,
 Skippering across these once remote waters.
 He talks of their yacht, The Lady Mo,
Of times spent aboard with his granddaughters.

Her mother takes his hand, smiling dutifully.
 The engine slows then gurgles to a stop.
 Her father regards the captain approvingly
 As against our hull the timid waves slop.

Carefully rising from his seat at the bow,
Rev Keats opens then promptly gives way.
 Her father steps up, wiping his brow,
 And begins his reflections on the day.

 "Like all of us here have been doing
 Since our girl left us seven weeks ago,
 I've been trying to find comfort, pursuing
Some good, that may have come from this dreadful blow.

And it's been hard, so incredibly hard,
Almost impossible you might even say.
Our lives appear irrevocably scarred.
But one comfort we can take from today

Is that this spot which means so much to me
And to my wife - indeed, the whole family -
Is where she would choose as her resting place.
Back in the day, when the village was our base

And we would relish the joys of The Villa,
I thought I derived most pleasure from being here.
Yet, reflecting now, I'd beg to differ.
Although she was young it has become clear

She loved this spot more than I ever knew.
As some have remarked, she was in heaven.
She would ask us to return, she begged us to,
Even when we sold The Villa in '87.

When I'd point out we'd have nowhere to stay
She didn't care, she'd return, ending our chat.
And so though the circumstances we face today
Are tragic beyond words, at least she's done that."

He nods at this feat and, dwelling upon it,
"Your absence is filled with our love," he sighs.
His words are followed by those of a sonnet.
Pensive, we watch her mother's slow rise:

She steadies herself then, like her husband before,
Mops her brow as a calmness descends.
"Like as the waves make towards the pebbled shore,
So do our minutes hasten to their end;

Each changing place with that which goes before,
In sequent toil all forwards do contend.
Nativity, once in the main of light,
Crawls to maturity, wherewith being crown'd,

Crooked eclipses 'gainst his glory fight,
And Time that gave doth now his gift confound.
Time doth transfix the flourish set on youth,
And delves the parallels in beauty's brow,

Feeds on the rarities of nature's truth,
And nothing stands but for his scythe to mow.
And yet to times in hope my verse shall stand,
Praising thy worth, despite his cruel hand."

Her words are done but, pervading the lull,
A speeding gin palace appears in the distance.
Engines full throttle, its pufferfish hull
Cudgels the water, testing the persistence

Of Rev Keats who begins the ceremony.
He turns to her father and procures the urn,
The sun glancing off what looks like ebony.
One hand deployed, the other he upturns

As he recites a prayer, trembling slightly.
The gin palace rumble continues to swell,
And as it rips past bathers wave excitedly,
Speakers pulsating with *Highway to Hell.*

Wash jabbing our hull as their strains collide,
Unsteady Rev Keats steps back from the side,
A canopy stanchion grabbed for support.
Restarting, though, the boat is then caught

By two surfer's waves, one after another,
Almost upending her stranded mother,
Backwash from the gin palace speeding away.
I twist to Rev Keats who, fighting the sway,

Recalls a pre-walker clinging to furniture.
The surge unlocks his hand from the stanchion;
Regripping but foiled by the slippery curvature,
He is forced to take alternative action.

His right hand stretches for the side of the boat,
His left, urn-clasped, he strives to hold off,
But the chances of that are less than remote.
The jolt of the drop into one last trough

Compels his left hand to check the stumble.
He contorts it so as to protect the urn:
It raps the gunwale, preventing a tumble,
But then it buckles and his grip, in turn,

Is cruelly severed and the urn falls free,
Clunking polished wood, bouncing off the side,
And plopping, spewing ash, into the sea.
Floating a second, it's engulfed by the tide

As a wrist-clenched Keats looks on, aghast.
Her father scrambles up from his bow seat
To where her ashes were set to be cast.
Knees locked to the side, he begins to beat

At the thick froth as we rise together,
One dismayed eye fixed on her father,
The other on swell by the portside propeller.
As we stare down into the lather

The boat's sharp pitching begins to subside.
Though hopeless the cause, he cannot surrender.
He hangs, a trapezist, over the side;
The urn may be worthless but the slender

Chance of rescue only ramps up the search.
He slashes at the water with karate strokes
Until, following one near fatal lurch,
His wife crawls over as, weeping, he chokes,

And at his shoulder implores him to stop.
"It's where she wanted to be," she entreats.
Her father lets his dripping chin flop
Then submits beside a spent Rev Keats.

I fight layer upon layer of disbelief:
That it is over when we've barely begun,
Shock at the mishap, sidelining our grief,
That I'm here and she's not, disbelief done

Every which way and yet, still in its thrall,
The service is somehow, absurdly, resumed.
The final prayer is lost on us all,
For how can we not still be consumed

In the calamity of minutes before.
Stuttering upon the concluding Amen,
Rev Keats shuts his book and looks to the shore.
The engines splutter to life once again

And the captain, taking his place at the tiller,
Brings us round gently to face the beach.
We move off as the bow points to The Villa,
Curbing the remnants of whispered speech.

Spray flicks our cheeks as the revving soars,
And our bungled memorial is complete.
We're fanned by the draft, making for shore,
A short-lived succour from rabid heat;

Almost half ten, it may as well be noon.
We reach the shallows to the mew of a gull.
Engines idling, we clip the pontoon,
Cushioning tyres nudging our hull.

As The Villa's figure charts events below,
Her mother, disembarking, bids our attention.
"Sorry, everyone, in all the…you know…
I fear I totally forgot to mention.

We've had a plaque made, as you may've guessed,
Which will soon be placed in St Martin's graveyard,
Where many of our lot are laid to rest.
Seeking a memorial, it has been hard

To find something apt, but I hope you'll agree
That such a gesture will be quite fitting."
Heeding widespread nods of approval, she
Spins and strides on, pace unremitting.

We shelter from the sun beneath olive trees.
I exchange pleasantries with her half-brother
Then, snacking on grape juice and pastries,
Swap tales with her strain-faced father and mother.

On the periphery, I say my farewells,
Slipping up the sand and down the glade path.
Jacket whipped off but, in the hottest of hells,
I join the packed drag dreaming of a chilled bath,

Even hankering for our polar trickle.
Once back - past the beach's barbecuing skin -
I enter, mid undress, the shower cubicle.
Drenched, I sink Bell's as sleep pulls me in.

2.5

I come to with the crack of gust-slapped shutter,
Squinting, dry-mouthed, at my tumbler's chip.
Catcher's on the floor: its yellowed pages flutter
Like a humming bird or loose sails on a ship.

How the wind's risen since I beat my retreat.
Approaching half five, I lean on the headboard.
A soreness at my heels, I look to my feet
Where the hard leather has nibbled and gnawed.

I sit and palpate my chest's rippled skin,
Branded by the hardened sheets as I'd slept.
Blair trumping outside, I slope off to join him
And slump in the bow-legged chair to his left.

Supping Red Bull, "You okay?" asks Blair.
"Yep," I snap like a bottle-popped cork,
Running my hands through electrocuted hair.
Taking bluntness as not wishing to talk,

We dwell in silence as eve capes the bay:
Stragglers are withdrawing from the town beach
As deserted sunbeds are packed away,
Stacked in bulked piles of nine or ten each.

Two islanders, perhaps mother and daughter,
Settle their towels down by the shore.
The dwindling sun glisters in the water
As the waves break with a gentle roar.

Blair seems keen to avoid talk of the service.
"Good kip?" he asks as the shutter re-slams.
I nod as two snorkelers rise to the surface.
"I think you were talking in your sleep to Sam."

"Was I? Oh God, what was I mumbling?"
"Stuff about your family, your mum and dad.
It was like you were on the phone or something.
You wanted to meet them or maybe you had."

"Good job, then, that it was just a dream.
To quote - well, myself - I've cut all ties."
"Come on," says Blair, "you don't actually mean - "
"Oh, don't I?" I thunder and I rise,

Then get to work fastening the shutter
Whose clanging is driving me mildly insane.
Using luggage tag string from the gutter,
I spot a rusted latch beneath the pane.

I stomp back inside, pour an oversized drink
- Plonk from the kitchenette's cobwebbed rack -
Then rejoin Blair, a bubble gum pink,
And find a new bite to itch on my back.

Whilst most visitors like spending their days
Reading Archer or King, or even Tolstoy,
Blair - the cultured adult he is - plays
Bionic Commando on his Game Boy.

I watch darting figures burst into flames
But, within seconds, my attention's straying;
There's one thing duller than computer games,
Namely, of course, watching someone else playing.

A frustrated "Bugger!" follows *Game Over*.
"So then," he murmurs, his speech unhurried.
I'm dreading questions on grief or closure
But, as it happens, I needn't have worried.

"Last night had a schlong like Nelson's Column,
So took a bird to the beach and had it away.
Hardly knew what hit her. Shagged her rotten."
"Jeez, you should be careful. There will come a day

When you make a move and they won't be sure."
Blair smiles: "He who dares, Rodney. In any case,
   It's not rape if you shout 'Surprise!' before."
I nearly explode as he straightens his face.

   "Chill out, will you, you bloody bedwetter."
   "Blair, I just think that a couple of checks - "
   "Next you'll say I should write her a letter
   Thanking her for the 'unscheduled sex':

   My dearest Slapper,/I'm writing clearly
   To express gratitude for the unplanned act...
   ...Oh, I might have the clap.../Yours sincerely...
   Grace she was called. How priceless is that?

   Thick as a brick and been round the block,
   But peachy arse, great rack and all on show.
   Cleavage like two baldies in a headlock.
   Wasn't too keen on Dirty Sanchez, though.

   She fled so I tried Tide's Reach for a beer
Where I was getting these looks - and not just a few.
   I thought, I'm the daddy, I'm really in here.
But glimpsing the mirror when I went to the loo,

   The reason I thought I was king of Tide's Reach
   Was because half my face, and most of my hair,
   Was covered in sand from lying on the beach."
   "A village has lost its idiot, I swear."

   I give in to his folly and we titter as one.
   Blair's rapture fades as cloud hides the sun.
   "So how was it, then? Wasn't sure how to ask."
   "Oh, you know," I say, struggling to unmask

   The injustice of events out on the boat.
   Naturally, he's shocked when I mention the urn;
   His words momentarily stuck in his throat.
   He gathers himself and tries to overturn

My hurt by viewing things another way.
"She's at peace now," he says, arranging his balls.
"Really, you think so? I'm not sure," I say.
Blair goes again before his pep-talk stalls:

"You must be pleased it's all over, though?"
"Over? How's it over? Don't be dumb,
I have my whole life without her, no?"
"But aren't you relieved that today is done?"

"Well, on a scale of 1-10," I beef,
"It's hardly a cured-of-cancer relief.
I really hoped it would help, this visit."
Boy, was I being a laugh a minute.

"Know what I do when a girl I want to bone
Is out of the picture, giving me the hump?"
"No, but I think you're gonna tell me," I groan.
"I imagine her taking a massive dump.

Full-on arsequake, puts you right off the mare."
I almost projectile my gulp of wine.
"You missed your calling as a counsellor, Blair.
Seriously, though," extending my spine,

"You say she's 'at peace' - I don't think so."
My cynical response thwarts a reply.
Wordless, we watch the choked street below,
Appraising the beach-weary passers-by,

A silence to which Blair seems to object.
Seeking to comfort, he's lured to wonder
About the other Mighty Endless Subject
Through whose proofs we can but blunder.

"There must be a place we go, don't you think?"
"Look," I say, double-swigging my drink,
"It's not the best time to debate God, is it?
I mean it's never ideal but to visit

That beast now..." I let my face do the talking.
Blair is unmoved. "There is a place we go."
I urge him to tell his story walking
But he perseveres. "I only want to show - "

"Listen, if you want to talk God," I say,
"There's nothing to state that's not been said before,
And I *truly* have nothing to add today."
"I understand that but I want to make sure - "

"Blair, it's really lovely to hear your voice
But could I just have a minute to myself?"
Blind to my protest, it seems I've no choice.
"I'm trying to say this as I think it will help - "

"Please," I butt in, "I know that you're trying,
But saying she's with God, which you're implying,
It won't bring her back or lessen my grief."
I kick the duff latch and stare out at the reef.

Guilt slowly builds. "I'm sorry," I refrain.
"No need to apologise." "No, I'm a pain."
"I thought you'd feel better knowing she's at peace,
Now that you've scattered her ashes in Greece.

Just 'cos she wasn't, shall we say, kept safe,
Does not mean you should abandon beliefs.
I know her death is a huge test of faith
But I guess it's all part of facing your grief."

Unforeseen compassion at once outweighs
My wrath at the timing of his theories.
"Because of what's happened and events today
Do you not believe in God?" he queries.

Rolling sore eyes, a wearied objector,
I dread doomed debate on the Lord's existence,
Yet another airing of borrowed conjecture
To which, in life, we show scant resistance.

"There's a God," I drone, ever predictable,
"If we want to believe or are raised to think so."
I try to halt there with the damage minimal
But, this being religion, I can't let it go.

"God gives us hope when we're counting the cost,
When our means to cope are ineffectual,
When we're in need or are feeling lost."
Channelling my inner pseudointellectual,

Blair's efforts to muscle in are in vain
As my misgivings persist unabated.
"Imagine a world without death or pain,
Would we need the God that for this we've created?

Christ, even the most ardent atheists,
When push comes to shove they fervently pray,
As if the God they otherwise deny exists
Will suddenly appear and save the day.

So, yes, we turn to Him when in despair
Or turn against Him when life's so unfair,
When x wouldn't happen if He existed."
Lost in my pitch, how I wish I'd resisted:

Smugly wheeling out the layman's answer,
Ignoring the clichés informing my views.
I was like some guy who tours the Sahara
And cries, "Gee, it's hot!" like it's breaking news.

"But isn't that," Blair asks, "the problem now?
You think God can't exist if he 'let' her die?"
"Not at all," I say. "Nothing like it," I vow.
"Sure," says Blair. "Sorry, don't mean to pry."

Even Reg laughs at The Living's dilemma,
The centuries of rumour and endless wonder;
Hearsay we thought would endure forever
Until we came to be six feet under.

Blair's tangoed cheeks now seem oddly pale.
"Whoa, I'm so dizzy. Even sitting down."
"How about a few nights off the old ale?"
He nods as a busker serenades the town,

Her opener *Girls Just Want to Have Fun*.
So much fun, in fact, as a hen do pass,
The bride - a plastic penis weaved into her bun -
Bawls "Let's 'ave it!" then spews in a glass.

Temporarily shunning the stock singalong,
Our busker opts for Soleá flamenco;
The kind of track Dad sometimes had on,
Inspired by a trip he took out to Mexico

When fancy-free in his early twenties.
With donations, though, becoming infrequent
Our busker trawls the early seventies,
Don McLean this time, his classic *Vincent*;

Again, Dad's pick on the odd car ride.
Why, I think, noting the shift in style,
Much of the set - Cyndi Lauper aside -
Dad would put on every once in a while.

Music a time machine, he shunts through gears:
"If this track is not playing at my funeral
Then I'm not coming. Chocolate for the ears."
I picture his send-off, my snub inexcusable.

Our busker then drops a folky original,
Dispersing her crowd in the blink of an eye.
She curses off-mic; I suppose quite typical
Of folkies being hotheads and metallers shy.

Striving to hear above the roisterous throng,
Blair hustles in to drown out the song.
"Permission to bore," he says, de-gunking toes,
"My second cousin's friend's friend knows

Don McLean's brother." I look Blair's way.
"Really?" I reply, considering his claim.
"This friend of your second cousin's friend," I say,
"Who is he exactly? What's his name?"

"Mmm, not sure. Pete…Paul," as if it's irrelevant.
"So, hang on, do you actually know him at all?"
"Look," he retorts, blind to impediment,
"All I know is that he's called Pete or Paul

And that he once knew Don McLean's brother."
"Oh, so now it's *once* knew?" I dig in.
"He no longer knows him, we now discover."
"How do I know? I don't even know him."

"Alright," I respond to the claim's implosion,
"Say the friend once knew, or knows, his bro.
I don't want to be petty but quite what notion
Are we employing of the verb 'to know'?

At first we were talking a real close buddy,
Now we're contemplating a one-off meeting
Watching Don with a field of muddy
Fans one year. Frankly, and not beating

About the bush, I don't think *he* knows him at all."
As with the God-talk, I simply can't stop.
"Are you sure the bloke in question, Pete or Paul,
Doesn't work in some scummy guitar shop,

And is a bitter 'n' twisted failed musician
Who, as you're sampling an overpriced Strat,
Reels off blurb to which you're forced to listen:
'She's got treble-bleed volume and, not only that,

A slim maple neck and, if you want my advice…'
Which of course you don't, and next thing you know
He is saying you won't find a better price
- 'I must be damn crazy to have it that low' -

'Cos folks, as we speak, are bidding on the phones.
Before you can say knife, he starts ranting about
How he was once chief roadie for The Stones
And wrote *Paint It, Black* years before it came out,

But Jagger, the bastard, nicked it off him."
"Well, that's taking it to an extreme level."
"Extreme? You're joking?" I incredulously grin.
"I've seen closer links between God and the devil.

What you've suggested, Blair, is like saying,
My great aunt's friend had a pair of dogs
Who shared some fleas with an ass, which was braying
In some nearby fields, which Joe Bloggs

Happened to pass through one afternoon,
The same day that Joe's fourth cousin's maid
Brushed past Don's resentful brother." The tune
From below at last supplants my tirade.

"Not really," he responds. "Yes, really," I mutter.
A question enters my head as he sighs.
"Tell me, does Don McLean *have* a brother?"
"Er, no, I don't think so," he replies.

Clouds roll in as the mob flock through.
"Turn," says Blair and I grudgingly comply.
He takes my picture. "What is it with you?"
He darts off to dress, grabbing beer on the sly.

"Thought you were staying off the booze tonight."
"Just the one," he writhes, "need the dunny."
He nukes the bowl: "Like the bird I mentioned, right?
Fuck, I'm back! I'm like the Duracell Bunny."

As Blair departs, beer necked, I head in,
Unfold on the bed and kick-shut the door.
Predictably, though, I can't block out the din
And, owlishly alert, I make for the shore.

I pass the stoners perched on the brick wall
That divides the beach from the bar-lit street.
I'm forced to pause by a ram-packed stall
Flogging novelty gifts and copies of *heat*.

Swarmed hands, like tentacles, grab at wares
As the vendor eyes suspicious sifters.
A plethora of accents pervade the air;
An international mix of shoplifters.

One flame-haired boy, despite pa's arm-twisting,
Recites a mug's slogan as I linger behind:
"*Nothing Says I Love You Like A Good Fisting*."
"What's fisting?" asks the boy. "Never you mind."

Our tumblers chipped, I spot a new pair,
Unfazed by the *I LOVE GREECE* tag line.
I turn to the vendor, smoking in his chair.
"You didn't know you needed these," he chimes.

British tabloids for sale, I evade a biker
And pluck a ripped *Sun* from off the rack:
Saints have signed a journeyman striker
To bolster our newly extinct attack.

I pass Bargain Basement, an Aladdin's cave,
Spilling its bric-a-brac onto the pavement.
Their neighbour lobs me a cheeky wave,
Befitting <u>Even Better</u> Than Bargain Basement.

I step over four mousers - Mother's term -
Caterwauling, marble-eyed, up at a table,
Pestering a diner with an eighties perm.
Past the clowder of cats, I am able

To spot the last bar's jade palm tree motif.
The bright lights fade and the thick crowds thin.
Yet, approaching the sign, my mounting relief
Is undone by a look from the tables within.

For I'm spied, or so it seems, by that face,
Eyes meeting twice as I bumble by.
She forfeits her gaze as I feel my heart race
And coyly gape up at the starless sky.

With adrenalined strides I forge up the street
As I try so hard, too hard, to stay calm.
Dust clouds around my two scuffing left feet;
I wish it would hide me as in my alarm

I turn back, head bowed, forgetting till I reach
A pounding Yanni's Bar halfway down
That I had sought to walk up the beach.
Deranged, I battle on back through town

Then bound up the steps to our empty room.
Crashing to the bed, my mind is flooding,
Firing out questions, mute bullets in the gloom;
As I think of her the music's thudding,

A dissonant symphony of clashing keys,
The mad orchestra from *A Day in the Life,*
An endless crescendo carried on the breeze,
In through the window, feeding my strife.

The Northern Territory News

June 21st 2005

AUTHOR'S DOOMED LOVE AFFAIR PORTRAYED IN 'BROADLAKE'

"Estranged from his family and starved of the artistic success he craved, the alcoholic author embarked upon a secret love affair that would end in tragedy."

2.6

Head full to bursting, I still cannot sleep
So I opt to return to the beach after all.
Just minutes on from collapsing in a heap,
I'm met by the fallout from a nightclub brawl.

A JUICE punter blots the freshly-paved ground,
Besieged by onlookers below the club steps.
Catching the dialogue as I steer round,
It appears that he fell in a scuffle with reps

And cracked his temple on the way down.
Medics on the scene, I sharply change tack,
Crossing the main road then forging through town.
The sequence of events takes me right back

To a fall of my own aged nine years old.
I tripped on the stairs, rapping my head,
And, like the clubber, I, too, was out cold;
In fact - I shit you not - they thought I was dead.

Seriously, my olds were having kittens,
They truly believed I'd *died* from the blow.
You see, I had one of those rare conditions
- I hate saying that, it sounds phony, I know -

A form of Locked-in Syndrome, or so they said.
For some the condition triggers collapse,
For others it's sparked if they knock their head;
It strikes ten in a million, even less perhaps.

Sufferers enter this state akin to a coma:
Breathing desists and your pulse drops as low
As twelve beats per minute, sometimes lower.
Despite all this, you can still hear, and though

Vision is blurred, make out people's faces;
I still detect Mother's tears of dread.
With vital signs weak, there have been cases
Where so-called victims are declared dead

Before, in the morgue, they finally come round.
One instance Stateside - where else, of course -
A passing porter was disturbed by the sound
Of knocking from a chamber, a waking corpse.

Spying the steps, and with traffic slowed,
I skitter across the bottle-strewn road.
Traipsing down to the slumbered shore,
A single light shines from The Villa's top floor.

I take my grain-filled shoes in hand
And paddle through the shushing water;
Tumult ebbing, I stroll up the sand.
I hear her father as he honours his daughter

And relays her last wish earlier that day.
I try to make out the Kaiki's position
When the urn toppled into the bay.
I ponder Rev Keats' fateful decision

To persist when we first came under threat.
I hold these thoughts just a short while
For I'm sidetracked as ahead I am met
By a couple going at it, doggy style.

Swerving briskly, I take to my toes
And detour round them then scamper on,
Past the massed ranks of parked pedalos
To a sheltered spot eighty yards along.

Yet no sooner do I find private terrain
Than a bickering family are closing in.
I think it's the boisterous dad from the plane,
Scolding his kids before his wife scolds him;

An ill-timed echo of our family quarrels.
I see Dad storming off, attacking my morals,
Down to the cellar to tend his home-brews,
Hollow Legs Scrumpy *and* You Gin You Lose.

Why, his stints below lasted so long
It seemed way beyond just "tending cider".
Sometimes I'd hear the faint hum of a song
But, Dad no Dylan, I was none the wiser.

Sure enough, in time he padlocked the door
To prevent us stealing in, which, by nature,
Heightened curiosity even more.
I was still in the dark all these years later.

Gripped by these thoughts, I'm slow to react
To the freak rush of surf invading my spot.
I rein in my instinct to abruptly retract
And my world is again a melting pot

Of family feuds, ones I thought left behind,
And visions of the service off the coast.
I guess my folks weigh heavy on my mind
Since this is a time when I need them most.

Perhaps Blair's right but surely it's too late.
With Dad now gone and bridges long burnt,
I am, for good reason, resigned to our "fate".
Yet, from nowhere, come memories unlearnt:

I see Mother, frazzled, knelt by my bed,
Reading to me, Lara clamped to her side.
I'm propelled, years on, to her stroking my head
Soon after the Such do when Grandpa died;

Then Lara, that day, playing at mum,
Telling me that Pops "put up a good fight".
Who would have thought that at twenty-one
She would be a mother in her own right,

To a girl, Mia, and a boy, Saul.
How distant a brother can one be
Only learning such things on a pub crawl;
Strangers knowing more about her than me.

I'd been drinking with Drew in the West End
And had mentioned my name to some gin-soaked girl,
Who had known Lara through a school friend.
All I could muster was, "Christ, small world."

The only trace of her was a Post-it note,
Scribbled, aged six, in the wake of a blue:
I hate you today. Love Lara she wrote.
God, I miss her so much, I really do.

We strove to be the family dreamt by Mother,
Loving, forgiving, patient, like her;
We were good people, just not good for each other.
Always picking up the pieces, as it were,

I see Mother hug me one December night
When I had split from my first love, Maisie.
"Love is a leap," she said, holding me tight,
"And I'm afraid you rarely land safely."

Vowing I prized her more than anything,
She replied whilst lighting an Advent candle
- She had a godly saying for everything -
"The Lord gives you what He thinks you can handle."

Back I flit again - I must be seven or eight -
To those bedside tales that portrayed her ethics.
One in particular that she liked to relate
Described a race between three eccentrics.

Her yarn was set on the Isle of Good,
A land of every nation, colour and creed,
Where beside past foes comrades stood,
Where charity ruled in place of greed.

Every year three souls were selected
To contest an event, The Desert Trail.
The chosen few would be subjected
To a fortnight's hike from Peace's Vale

To the isle's capital, one Sand's End,
Where they'd receive a hero's reception.
To mirror the isle's eclectic trend,
The fields were diverse without exception.

One year, Mother said, the race was between
Twain, an Abo, elder statesmen at seventy,
Whose knowledge of the land's every ravine
And desolate bush was wisdom aplenty

To contend with the drive of Jake, a Yank,
Former marine (now church official),
And Klaus, a German, who, if we're frank,
Was so off his chump that only by miracle

Would he complete the trip to Sand's End.
For, and Mother chuckled, within his rucksack
Was contained the most impractical blend
Of objects ever taken to the outback.

Augmenting a stove, food rations and tent,
Fundamentals for the day-to-day,
Was a box of black fireworks, a wodge of cement,
Two fishing rods and a Noel Edmonds tray;

This to supplement an inflatable raft,
Complete with life jacket and flask of beer.
And, just to add to the already hard graft,
A fur-lined coat from whose pockets would appear

A free copy of the world's quickest read,
The Best German Jokes Since 1901.
So they set off at variable speeds:
A staff-twirling Jake dashed as he sung

Star-Spangled Banner, soaking up the applause.
Klaus was behind, giggling heartily away
At the one about Brits being humourless bores,
Thus leaving Twain to gently make his way

Across stony flats through the arid air.
At nightfall Klaus and Jake would rest,
Lain under stars, yet whose guiding glare
Twain would exploit until night regressed,

By which time he'd caught the snoozing pair.
As the sun rose on those blazing days
Twain slept on whilst the others despaired
At the long slog towards the rippling haze.

A fortnight on, Twain assumed the lead
Whilst Jake flagged behind even Klaus.
At dawn our Twain, still at the same speed,
Was sighted from a Sand's End clifftop house,

Making for the capital over barren ground.
A message was swiftly sent to the bell tower,
And soon Sand's End awoke to the sound
Of brisk chimes that meant within the hour

This year's winner would pass through the gates.
Huge crowds gathered to greet his victory,
Cheering Twain's trudge up the final straight.
But then, just yards from his place in history,

Twain pulled up and the crowd fell silent,
Flummoxed beneath the sun's morning glaze.
Twain eyed the crowds, hitherto so vibrant
And chanting his name in fulsome praise,

But now flaunting the same bewildered expression.
Twain spied the earth with a knowing frown
And, entitled to act at his discretion,
He removed his baggage and sat down.

The multitudes, like me as Mother spoke,
Were truly bemused yet, likewise, fixated.
They questioned his health or if it a joke,
Just two of the theories that had filtrated

Through the gathered crowds by the time
His Royal Goodness had rushed out to Twain.
Yet soon the bell tower began to chime,
And it was announced he was neither in pain

From the outback's insufferable conditions
Nor had thought it a fine prank to dally.
Instead - and Mother smiled at the tale's fruition -
He was waiting till, from the bowels of the valley,

His fellow walkers appeared and, in time,
Crossed the expanse approaching Sand's End,
Where they'd embrace and, as one, cross the line.
All things war my passion, I would pretend

- Following the ending's neat resolution -
That Mother's conclusion possessed a twist.
I'd salivate at the end's dissolution
And replace it with one less idealist.

Jake and Klaus would be savaged in the bush,
Shredded by a nine-headed, fire-breathing beast;
Or perhaps Jake, second after one last push,
Would reject Twain's plan - Jake an arriviste -

And beat the poor Abo's matchstick frame,
Stirring up riots, the most violent of scenes.
The city would burn and things would never be the same.
Klaus would reach where Sand's End had been

And, finding ruins, would live out his days
(All two of them) floating, or so he thought,
On his inflatable raft in a forlorn malaise
Till his hours were numbered, all of them nought.

Sadly, I was assured this never occurred:
Twain always waited, the other two always came,
The city celebrated a tale thence referred
To in Sand's End lore as that of *Jake, Klaus & Twain.*

2.7

Rising late the next morning, I slip away
And head for brunch in a café on the front.
Blair out for the count, I plan a quiet day.
I potter up the drag and, taking a punt,

Spot a gold sign for Jewel of The Aegean,
Nestled at the end of the beachside wall.
In contrast to the farce at Trish & Ian's,
I take a seat, order, and in no time at all

Food arrives, as if fresh from the bakers.
Devouring two pastries and sipping green tea,
I notice a figure rising from the breakers;
Tracked, too, by the diner opposite me,

Gawping from behind his week-old *Mail*.
I watch, peeking over the brim of my cup,
As she leaves a tapering footprint trail
To a beige towel about thirty yards up.

Her beauty triggers a bewitched expression
But protraction is due - not to the onset
Of some oversexed, carnal obsession -
But as she's the lookalike that I had met,

Or more stumbled upon, at every turn.
I place my drained cup onto a coaster.
Intro planned and feigning unconcern,
I pay the bill then wander over.

The polished banter rehearsed in my head
Is reduced to the bunkum that you dread.
"I'm sorry?" she rebuts, ringing her hair.
"What is it you want?" Fully aware

I'm faffing, I pursue the task at hand.
I ask, though certain, if she was the soul
I had seen by The Villa, then crammed
On the terrace, and then on my stroll

Up the chocker drag late last night.
She shakes her towel. "Who knows? Maybe."
Striving to not be thrown by her slight,
I itch non-existent bites on my knee

As she opens a cellophaned pack of dates.
At the risk of sounding rather curt,
I query her actions by The Villa's gates.
"Forgive me for asking," I add to avert

Any charge of rudeness at quizzing events.
Replying, she seems a touch ruffled, I sense.
"Oh, that. Just someone I used to know,
Someone who lived there a long time ago."

I ignore she'd tell me if she so wished.
"Really?" I push. "Who was this 'someone'?"
She glowers, her face scrunched like fist,
And deduces I must be from London,

Given my penchant for being so frank.
"You think so?" I smirk. "Maybe," I say.
"Well," she counters, "you're hardly a Manc
Or Scouser, not with that accent anyway.

I bet you work in the City or in law,
Something like that." Kneeling on her towel,
She pecks at a date as I guffaw,
"Not exactly!" "Well," she snipes with a scowl,

"If you're not 'exactly' a City high-flyer
What is it you do?" "I'm in a band."
She replies with the scorn that this inspires.
"Oh, right, have I heard of you?" she asks, offhand.

She has refrained longer than most
But I can feel her staring at my scar.
"From a car crash," I drawl. She's still engrossed.
"I wasn't looking," "Yeah, right," I spar.

I brashly laugh. "That's what they all say."
She discards her caution. "So, what happened?"
"Oh, I once pushed someone out of harm's way
But, in the process, got half flattened."

"Sounds like a B-movie," a dig I defuse.
"I know, when I tell people that's my line."
Feet now sweating in heavy deck shoes,
I ditch them as she asks whether we're signed.

Diverting her less hostile inquiry,
I release a squawked, effeminate howl:
My feet are being singed by the sand's fiery
Top and I hotfoot to her dampened towel,

Knocking her knee in making my ground.
"Mind if I join you?" I ask from above her.
She looks up, snorting, her dark skin frowned,
And I exhale as my hooves recover.

" 'Mind if I join you?' Gone polite, have we?
What happened to your surly City-speak?"
"What is all this, 'Londoners are pushy'?"
She drumrolls her towel. "Bloody cheek.

So you're in a band." She straightens her bob.
"I've always thought that being a musician
Is just an excuse for not having a job."
Torn between chuckling and voicing opposition,

I playfully cock my left eyebrow.
"I'm so glad I came over to talk to you."
"Fluent in sarcasm, are we now?
Come on," she argues, "it's largely true.

Most artists, if you can call them that,
Do anything not to work, it's so old hat.
Next you'll say you've written a novel."
I blush as she sips from her water bottle.

"You on your hols?" "Hols? God, no.
That woman I saved - came to scatter her ashes.
Like you, just someone from a long time ago."
Duly startled and, twitching eyelashes,

She aborts her study of a tacking yacht.
"Gosh, I'm so sorry, I'd no idea when…"
My divulgence has unnerved her somewhat.
"I didn't mean to be blunt back then."

"It's alright," I say, waiving her faux pas.
"No, but I - " "Don't be silly," I insist.
"Look who has gone all polite now, huh!"
My crosstalk is met with a clipped wrist.

"It sounds like she was pretty close to you."
I um as the yacht disappears from view,
Then sense our talk is growing austere.
"This is crazy," I say, "look at us here,

Bogged down in matters of life and death.
Actually, not even that, merely death."
My protest draws a nervous laughter.
"I mean we've just met and, Jeez, after

Scarcely two minutes I'm pouring out my heart.
It's all a bit much to put you through."
We have role reversal down to an art.
"It's fine," she says, "what else could you do?

I simply asked why you were here
And you, straightforwardly, filled me in.
I'd like to think a sympathetic ear
Would greet me as well. I mean that's the thing,

You never know when it might happen to you.
Lose someone close that is, someone dear.
It strikes when we least expect it to."
Her reflections are over, it would appear,

But she rallies: "What's Lennon's famous quote?
'Life's what happens to you...' What's the last part?"
"While you're busy making other plans," I gloat.
"That's it. You can't take life quotes to heart

But that one there is especially good.
So good I can barely recall it," she chortles.
She tugs a straw bag, leant on some driftwood,
Revealing the tip of a purple snorkel.

Sharing her towel, I feel her body's weight.
"Yes," I say, nodding, "all of this happening
Makes you want to act before it's too late."
"I know what you mean," she says, slackening

Her bob. "Oh, really, how so?" I sharply reply.
"You've had experience of this kind of thing?"
She takes out a peach and says with a sigh,
"I guess your story has a familiar ring.

Mine's not the same but something similar.
Though I've not had it, I'm having it now."
She shields her face like she did by The Villa
As I flick sweat from my moistened brow.

"So what happened to you?" I warily ask.
Yet this time my prying is taken to task.
"You're right," she says, "this is ridiculous.
We've only just met and, well, look at us:

It's a bit OTT, don't you think?"
"I guess," I recoil, "I just thought you would be - "
"You thought wrong," she bites, now on the brink,
Looking over my shoulder and out to sea.

"I'm sorry," I murmur, "won't say any more."
I try to curb my frank strategy:
"We're talking of things that, for sure,
Are only for the ears of your family."

"Well, if I'd family perhaps I'd do that."
"Sorry?" I say, my approach falling flat.
"What the hell, I might as well tell you now.
We have not spoken for goodness knows how - "

"We?" "My parents. I want to heal things before…"
Her words peter out, their inference clear.
She nips at her peach and looks up the shore.
"Each summer, pretty much, we would fly out here.

I guess it was something of a pilgrimage.
Right now I'm over for a few days,
Staying in a villa here in the village.
Apologies, resort, I should now say."

"Talking villas," risking being cut down,
"You still haven't said why you were outside
The one on the hill high above the town."
She takes the question in her stride.

"That's where we would stay as a family."
I feel my heart thud. "God, there's no way it…
Christ, you're not…no-no, you can't be."
"Please, if you're gonna say something say it."

"Are you…" I can barely utter their name.
She gasps and spits out a chunk of peach.
"How do you know? It's not possible," she claims.
Her shock is shared as, in broken speech,

I try to clarify the how and why.
"Listen, do you - did you - have a sister?"
I say her name, stunting her reply,
And, trawling memory, I recall the picture,

The one of them posing at The Villa;
Yes, she had changed but it's her, no question.
"I used to...know her," trying to deliver
The tragic news with utmost discretion.

In a fog, the salience is beyond her.
I cannot bear to look her in the eye,
I cannot tell her or keep it from her.
I stutter again: "Years ago I - "

"How is she?" she cries, setting neighbours astir.
"Why won't you say? Don't just sit there, speak!"
The moment upon me, I'm compelled to tell her,
Unable to refute the irrefutably bleak.

Despite evidence suggesting that the author could not have played a part in the Bracewell deaths, much has been made of the narrator's constant referrals to *The Catcher in the Rye* - a novel synonymous with several homicides and attempted murders. Whether donning a red hunting hat, drinking Scotch or simply quoting Holden Caulfield, by idolising '*Catcher*' the author inadvertently laid himself open to comparisons with others who possessed the book and subsequently committed crimes. Some, such as Trudy Allenby, have maintained that many of these supposed allusions are purely coincidental - "Can no one mention golf or the movies without being accused of plagiarising Salinger?" - but nevertheless the author has been added to the role of dishonour associated with the text.

Some have aligned him with John Lennon's killer, Mark Chapman, who, as the narrator refers to in 1.0, was found with a copy of the novel on the night of the shooting. Within the opening pages of the book Chapman wrote, "This is my statement", before signing Holden's name. Despite the narrator's attempt to distance himself from Chapman's actions, the mere mention of the murderer (and Lennon himself on several occasions), seems to have only worked against the author and generated a whole host of conspiracy theories.

Others have compared him to John Hinckley, whose copy of *The Catcher in the Rye* was found in his hotel room following a failed assassination attempt on Ronald Regan on 30th March 1981. Similarly, Robert John Bardo, who stalked Rebecca Schaeffer for three years before murdering her on 18th July 1989, was in possession of the book when he visited Schaeffer's apartment in Hollywood and proceeded to shoot her in the chest.

From a victim's perspective, Peter Falcanio, a British tourist who disappeared in a remote part of the Stuart Highway in the Northern Territory on 14th July 2001, was reportedly seen reading *The Catcher in the Rye* at Threeways Roadhouse in Tennant Creek two days before he vanished. A number of acquaintances described him as a "depressive" and a "recluse", in keeping with the perceived profile of the author and his protagonist. Falcanio's body was never found and several conspiracy theorists have since contended that the writer may even have been Falcanio himself; advocating that the manuscript was stolen from him following his death and, through reasons yet to be established, ended up in the hands of the unnamed author at 38 Larapinta Drive. Despite the alarming lack of evidence, Falcanio had been a gifted student at the UK's University of Brighton - a city mentioned on three occasions in Part 1 - and was believed to be redrafting a work of fiction, lending some credibility to the growing speculation.

From *The Kookaburra Killer* by Arthur Hamlin

Gwen often asks why I'd not twigged before
That she was no mere double but something more.
I mean witnessing someone quite so similar
Pacing outside the former family villa

- When knowing her sister had moved to Kos -
Must have, at first sight, seemed suggestive.
But she said her sister had then moved to Oz
(Joining Alice Springs Tours), so irrespective

Of the pointers I'd discounted the idea
Of them being related on its conception.
She returned two years on, I'd later hear.
What's more, I had dismissed a connection

For since the snap of the sisters was taken
She'd changed appearance, growing her hair long,
Swapping specs for contacts - a transformation.
So I promise, my friend, I wasn't having you on.

Her focus strays to the scar on my cheek,
The tale of its origin, the hurt it now wreaks.
It is the butt of her ridicule no more;
Why, the tacit trigger of a quivering jaw.

We're languished there still, some minutes later,
Trying to tell ourselves it cannot be.
I reach out my hand to comfort this stranger,
I guess in the hope that she'll comfort me.

She looks down sombrely at my hand on hers
And shapes to withdraw but allows it to rest.
Yet, on tightening my grip, she demurs.
"I really should go. I think it is best."

She gathers up her bag, takes to her feet,
And tosses her dates and peach core inside.
Her towel next in line, I vacate my seat,
Wriggle on my shoes and stand aside.

She checks that nothing is left in the sand.
"Look," she says, trying not to break down,
"I'm staying at Villa Daglas near Casinoland
And the new high-rise on the edge of town."

"Ah," I dither, "I don't mean to be difficult
But which new high-rise might that be?"
"Oh, yes," she concedes, "alright, my fault.
Let's think...you know Europcar? You see

It entering town, the rentals in a line.
It's just up from there." I dubiously nod.
"On the front gate there's a makeshift sign.
Come round at, say, I don't know...oh God..."

The distress that she is fighting to conceal
Is meddling with her train of thought.
"Yes, if you want to come over...if you feel
Like coming...then I suppose that you ought...

No, scrap that, you must come over tomorrow.
You'll come, won't you?" "Of course I will."
"Elevenish?" "Sure thing." Owned by sorrow,
She about-turns and scurries off until

She melts into the massing stew of bodies.
Seeking some shade, I follow her lead.
I join the drag and bag a seat at Molly's
- An expat haunt - where, without my read,

I sip a Scotch and watch droves on the gad.
I piece together their family history,
Putting a face to the sister whose actions had
Hastened their fall yet who'd stayed a mystery.

Although averse to my meeting relations,
She'd relay their endeavours every now and again.
Her father, for one, was in communications
And, during the late seventies, his acumen

Earned him a fortune and many a home.
Their portfolio stretched from The Scottish Highlands
To - wait for it - Salcombe, Chester and Rome,
To the cherished villa in the Greek islands;

The firmest of favourites with the two girls.
They were among few Brits on the island,
Unknown as it was to the wider world.
But one compatriot was Al Streisand,

A property mogul who lived up the shore.
Over the years they'd become firm friends
And he would often make visits next door.
Through July and August they would spend

Long and lazy days by the tiered pool,
Dining on the terrace overlooking the bay.
The daughters, at this point still at school,
Warmed to Al's charms almost straight away.

With family members otherwise engaged,
Al would take them out on The Lady Mo,
Or on his cruiser, The Golden Age.
After dinner, over a port or Ouzo,

Her father and Al would chat into the night,
And throughout '83 and '4, I'd learn,
Their terrace confabs were a common sight.
But, due to expansion in her father's firm,

They steadily lessened - he'd visit only briefly -
Then, with the firm struggling, they ceased completely.
The troubles' roots had a familiar ring:
The company had committed the cardinal sin

Of striving to become too big too quickly.
They borrowed what they could not pay back
And the venture would end fairly typically,
　　With many employees taking the track.

The expansion was curtailed by spiralling cost
　　And the withdrawal of the chief investor.
The bank pulled the plug which, in turn, lost
The family their home on the edge of Chester.

Despite all this, they seemed over the worst.
　　Yet, after selling up their pad in Devon,
They would soon feel nothing short of cursed.
　　For, flying to Greece in October '87,

There came some news from the outside world
　　That plunged them further into adversity.
I picture her father as events unfurled:
　　Taking a call one day at two thirty,

He was relayed first reports of The Crash.
Their losses were nothing less than gargantuan,
　　And put alongside the amount of cash
Still owed from borrowing under expansion,

Their fortune was on the steepest of slides.
Clearly, they'd have to sell further commodities,
　　The Villa included, to stem the tide.
　　Their friend, Al, though, being in property,

Stepped up and dealt with the solitary bidder.
　　Alas the one offer would not suffice:
Al conveyed news of the "paltry" figure
　　Which fell well below the asking price.

Yet Al, who'd long admired the property,
　　Then made an offer they could not refuse.
Her father felt blessed by his generosity
　　And, revived by the unexpected news,

Believed their troubles could be overcome;
The Villa's loss one they would have to bear.
Conveyancing in hand, the deal was done,
And, relieved to have Al to manage affairs,

A completion date was set for spring.
As a last hurrah, the family flew in,
And, packing complete, their final night's stay
Would end with a dinner out by the bay;

A twelve-minute stroll from their hilltop home.
So family, minus their youngest daughter
Who had fallen ill and wished to rest up alone,
Left for the village's ancient quarter,

Winding slowly down the hairpinned hill;
Al sadly absent on an urgent call.
With their mother, though, also feeling ill,
Dinner ended early before nightfall.

Muted by the grievous state of affairs,
They returned home in the gathering gloom.
Music could be heard as it spilled from upstairs,
Echoing down from their daughter's room.

Muffled voices sounding at the ceiling,
Her father wandered up and glanced round the door.
Yet instead of asking how his daughter was feeling,
Of whether her head and throat were still sore,

He stood there speechless, beyond appalled:
She was neither unwell nor was she alone.
Viewing tangled limbs, her father bawled,
Cries of anguish, intense and full-blown.

To his daughter's partner it mattered not.
He - and I do not mean to be patronising,
But that's Al if you've yet to join the dots -
Barely tried to defend his fraternising.

He sloped out of bed, oblivious to the tension,
Kissed their daughter and dressed at his leisure.
Her father looked on in incomprehension,
Reproving them there and then for good measure.

The two men approached her mother and sister
Who had rushed up on hearing the commotion.
Both were now forced against the banister
As Al and her father, devoid of emotion,

Swept down past them into the hall,
A sea of stacked boxes and refuse sacks.
Her father, apparently, said nothing at all
Whilst Al tucked his shirt into his slacks;

The very same outfit that he had worn
When I'd trailed him up the beachside road,
And later to the service when he had torn
Left up the hill to this very abode.

Al, she recalled, lingered by the stairs
And snapped up an object, dropping a knee;
Binoculars he'd left by the terrace chairs
And which he'd employed from the balcony.

Tempting though it may have been to wallow,
Her father made for Al's later that night,
Unaware that his eldest daughter had followed
And would hear the full extent of their plight.

Incensed, her father forged straight ahead.
"Why her?" he pleaded. "She's eighteen years old."
Al, though, looked quite shameless, she said,
An icy-veined coolness taking hold.

"Do you not fathom you've broken our trust?
She's eighteen, for Pete's sake, not twenty-eight.
My youngest daughter, too. How is that just?
How does that not carry the slightest weight?"

His staccato speech crackled with rage.
"Lord, my own flesh and blood," he cried.
"In our own home and with someone that age."
Al merely shrugged and faintly replied,

"Barely, if we're doing things by the book."
"Barely? What the hell do you mean by 'barely'?"
"Well, in truth," said Al, as if off the hook,
"You have got - let's do the maths - scarcely

Twelve hours till the place is no longer yours."
"Oh my God, Al, you're not sorry at all.
You can't see our pain, of which you are the cause."
He looked in disgust at the man he would call

The closest of friends, a rock through the years.
"You've betrayed us in the worst possible way
And all you can think of now, it appears,
Is stealing our home so you own half the bay."

Al, unruffled, viewed the moonlit water.
"Was that a sham, too, the whole operation,
Like how you've played around with our daughter?"
More flippant riposte than accusation;

One that, even given the latest finding,
He did not believe could actually be true,
Only spilling forth in his blinding
Fury, in the light of this ballyhoo.

His claim was more valid than he hoped.
For the very first time Al seemed uneasy.
"Oh Lord, don't tell me," her father choked.
"Don't tell me you've capped your sleazy

Games by doing us over with the sale as well."
"Calm down, you'll get your cash," Al smirked.
"But there's something else, something more to tell."
"Don't be silly," Al laughed, but increasingly irked,

Her father was by now having none of it.
"Let me see the sale papers, every file,
No matter how trivial, every single bit."
Reserved, Al returned a derisory smile

As her father strained to contain his dismay.
"We've been through the papers," Al retorted,
"Only last week," trying to steer away
From the great sham her father purported.

"Your lawyers vetted them," he continued.
"How could I be at fault with the dealings?"
The question rendered her father subdued,
Yet still he could not ward off the feeling

That something had been amiss all along.
"You see, that's just it," replied her father,
"How could there possibly be something wrong?
You're quite the expert at playing the martyr,

At making things seem all above board,
At not even rousing the slightest suspicion,
When really a liar and out-and-out fraud,
Your charms concealing a shady disposition.

So, yes," he said with growing assurance,
"How *could* there be anything untoward?"
At last Al dropped his detached performance.
"You make a fool of yourself saying I'm a fraud - "

"I'm making no more of a fool of myself
Than you've made me look already today.
If you will not show me to the study shelf
Where I know all the files are stored away,

I will go there myself. Do you understand?"
He started to shift towards the slide door
- One that fed the terrace - but he felt a hand
Paw at his shoulder as he crossed the floor,

Unbalancing him as he turned about.
"Wait, you can't do that," Al cried out.
"Really? Can't I? Well, you just watch me."
He threw off Al. "This is private property!"

Her father made another lunge for the door.
"Since when exactly did you care about that?"
Al grabbed ahold of his shoulder once more.
"Listen," barked her father, as good as trapped,

"If there's nothing to hide then show me the file."
For a few seconds Al maintained his resistance
But, conceiving such actions to be futile,
Grudgingly bowed to her father's insistence.

Her daughter, now installed by an ajar window
- Lit by the banker's lamp's tawny glow -
Listened, half-knelt on the slate-paved ground.
As minutes passed by she could hear the sound

Of files thumping, one by one, to the desk,
Followed by the rustle of scrutinised pages.
Stood perfectly still, almost statuesque,
She spied her father as, in measured stages,

He sifted through the sheets laid before him.
At times, he'd request Al to step his way
And query a detail; then, briefly sanguine,
He'd turn the page and, sensing foul play,

Dig ever deeper into the ream of paper.
The process continued until a while later
He perused the last sheet, closed the file,
And, rubbing his eyes, looked down at the pile.

"There seems," he declared, quietly perplexed,
"There seems nothing wrong with what you have here."
As he rose to consider what to do next,
Al waded in. "Well, I'm glad that's all clear."

"Yet I'm not so concerned with what is here
But more with what *isn't*, if you get my drift."
"God, you really have lost the plot, I fear,"
Giving her father, once again, short shrift.

"You've filed every contract, letter and fax?"
"Look, I don't know what you are getting at
But I'm extremely tired and I've got stacks - "
"Tell me the truth, Al. Why can't you do that?"

Al's self-imposed innocence seemed premature.
"Forgive me, but you said the files contained
Every sale detail, from when the deal was secure
All the way back to when the sale was arranged?"

"That's right," said Al, now himself perplexed.
"Every correspondence, every bit of text?"
"Every single thing from when the bidding started
Right to when The Villa was taken off the market."

"What about when you got that 'paltry' offer,
As I believe you called it some months ago.
Where's it registered? Or did you not bother?
Did you say it was faxed?" "Oh, I don't know - "

"You don't know?" her father gulped. "You don't *know*.
It was a bid that could've saved us this bother
And now you're saying, 'I don't effing know'!"
"Heavens," Al replied, "it was a miserly offer,

Well below asking. Not worth registering."
"But you said *all* the correspondence was filed."
"All the relevant stuff - " " 'Scuse me, but anything
Offered is fairly 'relevant'!" He was so riled

That he cracked his fist down onto the table.
The release served to calm him somewhat,
Effecting a hush in which he was able
To discern a picture of their former yacht,

Al and the girls posed at the helm. "Relevant...
Unless the offer was never actually made."
It was only a mumbled amendment
Yet it spoke volumes above his tirade.

Al responded as calmly as he could,
Inhaling then planting an eccentric frown
On the chair by which her father was stood.
Her father peered up as Al looked down,

Gazing at the chevron parquet floor.
"Is that what happened?" her father resumed,
A question that Al would try to ignore.
"At least speak to me, Al," her father fumed.

"Did you hear what I said? I think," he proposed,
"The reason the offer was in no way 'relevant',
Even though you said all the facts were disclosed,
And there is no mention of the development,

Is because there was no offer. It was never made."
Al replied as if *he* had been betrayed:
"I have done your family an enormous favour - "
"Don't give me that, save the rhetoric for later.

Just tell me what happened. Why's that so hard?"
Al looked up from the floor, where his focus had been,
And, reviving his smirk, he would discard
His crumbling defence and finally come clean.

"So what if there was no 'paltry' bid.
You've got your money." "That's not the point."
"It is the point, you've made a few quid.
Money's always the motherfucking point."

Her father threw back his head in despair.
"Let me ask, did you ever *get* an offer?"
"I may have, yes." "Then why isn't it there,
Listed in the files, good and proper,

Like I - foolishly - trusted you to do?
Wait, no, let me guess, you had a high bid
But kept mum so, at the last minute, *you*
Could make a lower one and therefore rid

Us of this mess, and still be the hero. Right?"
Al's silence said everything. Well, almost everything.
The most rankling news had yet come to light.
For now, he was happy not saying anything.

"We thought you were doing this 'enormous favour',
We felt fortunate to have you as a neighbour
And yet you've..." he faltered, now tongue-tied,
"You've been messing with our...and you've lied..."

He rapped the desk, harder than before.
This time, though, it could not stem his rage.
"Stay away from us, Al. And, what's more,
Stay away from my daughter!" Yet by this stage

Such full-blooded threats could do no good.
"That might be tricky," Al sedately replied,
Glad it seemed of the unlikelihood.
Her father, unsure as to what he implied,

Puckered his forehead and leant on a chair.
"Tricky? What do you mean that it might be - "
"You'd better ask her. Go on, she's there,
In your nice villa. I mean mine, forgive me."

His daughter's answer came as no surprise;
He'd second-guess what Al had dared to infer.
Though being the man they'd come to despise,
In the summer of '88 Al married her.

It was a union as good as his word,
Just three years later ending in divorce.
She moved to Kos then Oz, as you have heard,
Until that marriage, too, had run its course.

Part 3 Introduction

The Damascus search and the disputed manuscript

Following the Bracewell deaths and with the author's role still unknown, Damascus' capture proved to be a laborious and time-consuming task. Three weeks after he absconded from Alice Springs, he was thought to have been spotted in Western Australia heading towards The Kimberly; yet extensive searches yielded no trace of the suspect. Between August 2002 and September 2004 there were many supposed sightings but he remained at large, and it was only by chance that Damascus was eventually seized. On 1st October 2004, his silver Honda hatchback was pursued by Western Australia Police for the comparatively minor offence of speeding. Damascus attempted to outrun the vehicle but, in doing so, he spun off the road down a grass embankment, thwarting any possibility of escape. Amongst property found in the boot of the car was a plastic carrier bag containing a copy of Rachel Cusk's *Saving Agnes,* a dust jacket for *The Temporary* (also by Cusk), and an unopened box of disposable contact lenses; all of which had belonged to Rose Bracewell. Having been apprehended for speeding and resisting arrest, Damascus was charged with not only the murder of Rose and Mary Bracewell, but also with the killing of Rose's unborn child, for which he was brought to trial on 3rd January 2005.

Meanwhile, as the search for the killer continued in 2002, the book's champion, David Balkan, began editing the disorderly manuscript found beside the author's corpse at 38 Larapinta Drive. The meticulous work required to transcribe the text is apparent by examining the numerous photographs taken by the Northern Territory Police. Despite the author appearing to keep and date all of his work, thus enabling him - and Balkan - to track the most recent draft, one can only imagine the lengthy process of deciphering the cramped handwriting and endless corrections that were symptomatic of the author's writing process; what Balkan termed "the barely legible hand that sprawls across the pages".

According to Catherine Bates, this was "yet another example of the author's inherited characteristics, passed down from his part fictionalised, part real-life father"; a reference to the "spindly, doctorly hand" described by the narrator in 1.1.

As outlined earlier, once Balkan completed the transcription in July 2003 and an extract was published by Otherworld that December, sections of the manuscript were, in Jacob Manson's words, "conveniently lost" following the death of David Balkan in March 2004. At the time this was of little consequence. After all, the book had been completed and, given its negligible sales and mixed reviews when published in full later that year, there was little call to preserve the manuscript. However, in light of the Bracewell case everything changed. Every page, every line, every word, mattered.

Crucially, several lost sections of the manuscript were those that contained, what Manson labelled, "the potentially incriminating passages". As a result, it was impossible to verify the text to ensure that the published version adhered to the original. Moreover, these sections were, by Balkan's own admission, "heavily edited due to their verbose nature". This opened up the possibility that they originally consisted of additional incriminating passages which were not included in Balkan's transcription. That is not to say that there were not already sufficient parallels between *Broadlake*'s published version and the events of August 2002 for the text to be considered as legitimate evidence. It simply meant that "further key passages relating to the events of August 2002 were conceivably edited out or manipulated, distorting the truth". This was the view of Damascus' barrister, Oliver Mandelson, on 17th January 2005. Conversely, some, such as Damien Grey, have suggested that these supposed key passages being lost provided Mandelson with a license to speculate, and hence exaggerate, what might have been written: "The defence surely distorted the truth by overstating the potential sinisterness within the lost extracts."

Despite Balkan's efforts to trim the text, he still came under criticism for including certain sections that some believed should have been cut from the final version. Manson panned their "highly tangential relevance to what remains of the chasm-infested plot", referencing in particular, "the fatuous drivel of *Jake, Klaus & Twain*". Yet, as Edith Ratchet has since retorted, "the fiercely intelligent, emotionally illiterate Manson wouldn't know a heart-warming yarn if it hit him in the face - repeatedly." Perhaps, on reflection, Balkan would wish he had omitted the tortoise and hare anecdote. For, despite the author's unlikely role in the murders, some have referred to the narrator's desire for Jake and Klaus to be "savaged" and "shredded" as indicative of the author's violent state of mind. Regardless, or perhaps, because of the conflicting viewpoints, *Broadlake*'s readership has continued to grow, precipitated by the book's role in the trial of Ivan Damascus; the findings of which we shall start to examine at the head of Part 4.

3.0

1:19 p.m.

Returning to the flat, I creep to our room,
Tiptoeing through so as not to wake Blair.
Yet, peeping inside, he's writing, I presume,
What looks like a letter as he leans on a chair.

Clocking me stood by the brimful drawers,
He stashes the pad under his pillow.
As he does so his pen drops to the floor
And rolls to a bag beside the window.

"You frightened me," he gasps, thumping his chest.
"What you up to?" I say, rubbing my heel.
"Nothing," he claims. "Nothing?" I contest.
"Why the inquisition? What's the big deal?"

"Well, what's all the pens and the paper for?
Are you composing some verse?" I say.
"Behold the new Whitman or Wordsworth, or,
Let me guess, you're writing a play!"

"Whatever," he says before changing tack.
"Enough of me. Where have you been?"
I am inclined to hold the truth back
Yet I cannot withhold who I have seen.

"Fucking hell!" whoops a gobsmacked Blair.
"You didn't say she was at the service."
"There's a reason for that. She wasn't there."
My explanation begins in earnest.

"You walked straight past her on the way
To Trish & Ian's the other day."
"Wait, so she's the one that you thought…"
My quick-fire nods stop him short.

"We're meeting tomorrow to have a chat."
"Really? You think that's a good idea?"
"Why not?" I say. "What's wrong with that?"
"Well, surely you need time to clear

Your head before you try to help her, too."
"We're both grieving, we can help each other."
I'm quite put out by his point of view.
"Why should she be the one to suffer?

She's just been told her sister's…" I pause.
"I'd say she needs support pretty badly."
"But you can't put her needs before yours.
You need some distance from her family."

"So that's how you treat those in need of help?
Her sister has died and now you infer
That she has less needs than myself."
"Why are you making excuses for her?"

"I'm not. Christ, you have a warped rationale."
"She betrayed her family." "She was young."
"But she didn't have to wed that traitor, Al.
Unless you haven't noticed, you're the one

Who stuck by her sister through thick and thin,
Who's come all this way to sort yourself out.
I'm just loathed to see you caught up in
Something that prevents this coming about."

"I'm only meeting her once, for Christ's sake.
Given everything, it's the least I can do."
"I know-I know, but I think a clean break
From their family would be best for you.

You never know what might happen."
I frown, bemused. "What do you mean,
'You never know what might happen'?"
"Listen, forget it, I'm just not keen."

"You think I like her, Blair. You think - "
"Are you mad?" "You heard me," I say,
"You think I'm vulnerable and would sink
So low that I would try to have it away

With her sister, of all people. Jesus, Blair,
Just because they are two of a kind
Doesn't mean I'm up for some tawdry affair.
And for you to think it has crossed my mind

After all that's happened. It's only, let's see,
Two months - two months - since she died."
"Never even thought it. You said it, not me."
"Yeah right, you didn't. You might take pride

In getting up to those things but I do not."
"What the hell?" says Blair. "That's really low.
I know you've been through an awful lot
But you twist things to make it sound as though

I was accusing you of trying it on.
And that I'd do the same. Well, you're wrong.
Sure, I sleep around, sure, I play about,
But your assumption is frankly way out

If you thought I implied you'd get her in bed,
Let alone that I'd do it in your position."
He puffs his cheeks. "But after what you've said
I now have a horrible, sneaking suspicion.

Should I be accusing you of such a thing?"
I gaze forlornly. "Of course not," I say.
"Of course not," I affirm, "there's no way in - "
"Alright, just leave it. Enough now, okay."

He flicks on the boombox under the chair.
"Look," he concludes, "if you have to go,
Promise you'll do it but then leave it there."
"I promise," I say. "I really do, you know."

As *Imagine* fades in, I take to my bed.
Blair plays his Game Boy as I browse a mag.
Restless, I scan round the room instead
Until my eyes settle on Blair's taupe bag.

"When are you giving me that thing?" I say.
"I thought you promised when we arrived
That you would hand it over today."
"I will when it's right. Just let me decide."

I'm sorely tempted to take a quick look
As he rises up and goes for a shower.
Deciding against it, I snatch at my book
And stare through the pages for a good hour.

3.1

In bed by half eight and waking at nine,
I doze till half ten then dress and slip out.
Keeping eyes open for the Europcar sign,
I trek up the drag and after about

Ten minutes' walk it looms in the distance,
Jutting like an elbow from the roadside.
Relieved though I am at its appearance,
My nerves, it seems, are along for the ride:

Is this really the right thing to do?
She needs my support, that's why I'm going.
Blair said I shouldn't yet do I not have to?
Such is my mind's toing and froing,

I soon find myself beside Europcar,
A touch surprised at having come thus far.
I look along the line of advertising boards,
Past the gleaming rows of Renaults and Fords,

And sandwiched between new-builds and Europcar
Is a model of the town's absurdity:
Viewing three villas, their traditional facades
Are wholly incongruous with the modernity

Rising up daily about their walls;
As if they are the ones now out of place.
As I move on, a canvas banner hauls
My gaze to the tower's sun-streaked face:

Streisand Developments glistens in the light.
Viewing activity on the structures lurking,
It strikes me how, passing building sites,
Workers never seem to be actually working.

Midst reflection, I've dropped my speed,
And, checking my watch, I'm running late.
I dart by a scaley flicking worry beads
And approach the first villa's wrought iron gate.

Hunting its name, I spot a wooden sign
Roped to a pole nearly halfway down.
Villa Daglas is sploshed on the pine,
The hotchpotch lettering a ruddy brown.

Paralytically shy, I tease open the gate
And take the stone path, wasps buzzing at my shin.
At the awning-covered door I knock and wait;
The whisper of water sounds from within.

A soft fizz gives way to footsteps, pacing.
The door creaks open and I feel myself blushing
At the towelled figure that I'm now facing.
I force out a "Hi". She turns and says nothing,

As if I'm not there, like her sister would do.
I enter and close the door on the town.
"Let me put something on." She leads me through
Into a small courtyard, where I sit down.

Walking off, she chirps, "Won't be long."
As she dips inside I shift my seat
Beneath a shade that shelters me from
The tarmac-melting late morning heat.

I look around the vined courtyard:
The whitewashed walls, Capri blue shutters,
Cobble fish mosaic, all picture postcard,
Above which a palm tree tamely flutters.

Then, staring ahead to the open window,
Her bare back hovers by the Roman blind.
I divert my eyes to the mosaic below,
Deleting the image from my mind.

As I rest there sweating and scarlet-faced,
She returns now clothed in a teal bikini
And plum sarong, floating down from her waist.
She pulls up a chair and sits beside me.

"Don't say it," she huffs through gritted teeth
As I survey the abutting block.
I switch gaze to three novels stacked beneath
A clothesline drying a mint green frock.

"So," I say warily, "are you okay?"
"Not bad, I guess, considering everything."
She takes my hand. "Thanks for today."
"It's fine, I didn't have plans or anything.

Nice place you have." "It was nice, you mean."
I'm unsure whether to pull my hand away.
"When we first came - I must have been fifteen -
It was open farmland right down to the bay."

"Crazy," she says and I grunt in agreement,
Before adding, with the moment convenient:
"I'm sorry for spilling the news on the beach."
She slides back her chair, emitting a screech.

"Can't be helped," she states matter-of-factly.
"It's lucky we met at the end of the day."
"But it wasn't ideal." "Yes, but how exactly
Would I have found out she had passed away?

Unless my folks, who I've not talked to in years,
Had written or phoned I might never have known.
It's a nightmare," she says, verging on tears,
"Losing all contact with family and home."

"I know just how you feel, I truly do."
"How do you know?" she says. "Don't try and be - "
"I have lost touch with my family, too."
She sheds her frostiness, brushing my knee.

"Are you serious? Sorry, I did not know.
Most people don't understand one bit."
She sniffs then wipes her bloodshot eyes. "So
You and your family, tell me about it."

"What, now?" "Why not? We've got all morning."
"It's a long story. Haven't spoken in years.
That's all." "That's all?" she questions, yawning.
"You speak like it's nothing. Come on, I'm all ears."

"I don't want to burden you. Honestly, it's fine.
The last thing you need is another sob story."
"Oh, please don't worry. Can't be as bad as mine.
Tell us what happened, I swear you won't bore me.

In any case, it might help me feel better
Hearing from someone in the same position."
"Some other time," I say, under pressure
And conscious of our role's transposition.

"Aren't I meant to be helping you,
Taming your grief, not the other way round?"
"Perhaps," she admits, "that may well be true,
But are we not covering similar ground?"

She takes off for drinks, alive to my thirst.
Returning, she mentions the service in the bay.
"Let me tell you," I glug, "about that first,
Then we'll move onto my family, okay."

She seems content to accept my proposal
And my description eats up the minutes,
Before we use time at our disposal
To discuss her family's summer visits.

Fresh tears in her eyes, I quickly digress.
"Where is work?" I ask, allaying distress.
"Oh, I'm with Libra, a Kos travel agent."
Her words are distant, her expression vacant.

"Look," she says, "I've nothing on tomorrow.
Fancy meeting up?" I ponder briefly.
"Don't see why not. Where do you want to go?"
"How about the beach? If you meet me

Here I'll show you this lovely cove.
Fifteen minutes walk, three if we drove.
Away from all the crowds." "Cool, around ten?"
"Great, sounds good. So where were we, then?"

She sips from her still untouched glass
And, before her words can outdo mine,
I shriek, no less, in something of a farce:
"God," watch-glimpsing, "is that the time?

Look, I'm so sorry but I've got to shoot.
Meeting a friend at a bar, Red Skies."
I bolt from my chair and she follows suit.
"Really?" she queries as we adjust our eyes

From glitterball sun to Stygian hall.
"I guess I will see you in the morning."
"The morning it is," I primly drawl.
I open the door and, beneath the awning,

Bid goodbye then march off manfully.
Nearing the gate, I hear her explode,
"You never told me about your family!"
"Tomorrow!" I cry as I streak up the road.

Although Ivan Damascus was viewed as the chief suspect - *Broadlake*'s author now seemingly discounted as the perpetrator - two other individuals were also questioned. The most lengthily detained was Lucy Freeman, a former heroin addict who had three previous convictions for robbery. Five years after the latest of these misdemeanours, she had been employed as a cleaner at Mills Apartments - a role that included working at number 60, Damascus and Bracewell's home - and accordingly she knew the layout of the building. Furthermore, having been spotted outside the property on Barrett Drive approximately one hour before the murders occurred, police raided her rented room on Gosse Street. Amongst a drawer of utility bills and receipts, they found a key to the Mills Apartments' entrance lobby. Freeman maintained that she had lost this key a week before she was dismissed from her cleaning role; a sacking brought about by persistent lateness and smoking marijuana in the staff toilets. Given these findings, Freeman was held for further questioning. However, crucially, no one had seen her entering or inside Mills Apartments, and there was no CCTV in place to verify her whereabouts. In addition, Freeman's fingerprints could not be found in Bracewell's apartment or on the Kookaburra cricket bat, hence she was released without charge along with another suspect, Oliver Myers. Myers had been questioned nine months before in relation to the recent spate of burglaries in Alice Springs, and was also seen on Barrett Drive on 10th August 2002. Yet, following further investigation, it was found that he had left the area at least ninety minutes before the murders took place to visit a family member on nearby Newland Street.

From *The Kookaburra Killer* by Arthur Hamlin

3.2

As it transpires, I try a taverna,
Choosing Fina off the main thoroughfare
In the middling unlikelihood of her
Passing and seeing me without old Blair.

As a checked paper cloth is pegged down
My disquiet gathers momentum once more.
A cupola-crowned church above the town
Reminds me that I have been here before.

Silent but for the cicadas' chirr,
I take her hand as we finish supper;
As always, though, I am holding onto her
Rather than us holding onto each other.

I lunch on calamari and Greek salad,
Bolted with a carafe of Retsina.
Bloated and little short of bladdered,
I pay then zigzag out of Fina.

Fabric gluing to sweat-drenched skin,
I pass the showpiece Streisand Tower.
Stumbling back, I find, sneaking in,
Blair, shorts down, asleep in the shower.

A right fine pair, intemperance is showing:
Who knows, asserts my irrational self,
I might have done it without him knowing.
"How zizzit it go?...Dizzit help?"

Dribbling, Blair lifts his zombie head.
"How do you know I even went?" I say.
"Do I look stupid?" "Well..." "You said
It was a pissabolity yesterday.

Why are you so reserved about it all?"
Blair slips, beer toppling, and faceplants the wall.
"I just knew you weren't keen on me going
So thought it was best without you knowing."

Even mid-sentence, I sense my blunder.
"It might be best without me knowing?
Whazzup with you? Sometimes I wonder.
I just want to...help," his wordage slowing.

He's set to resume but, flinching, refrains.
"You okay?" I ask, spinning from the wine.
"Oh, it's nothing, just a few aches and pains,
The odd giddy spell from time to time.

As you say, it's just a lack of sleep
And drinking like a Russian the last few nights."
"Are you sure, Blair? If these dodgy spells keep - "
"I'm fine." He scratches his swollen eyelid bites.

"Anyway, this meeting, you've done it, then.
You've played your part and talked things through.
There's no need to meet her ever again.
You haven't arranged to see her, have you?"

I mumble as Blair crawls to the bed.
"Please," he grimaces, rubbing his head,
"Just tell me the truth from now on, okay."
I look him in the eye. "Will do," I say.

Rushing next morning, approaching her gate,
She's checking her watch, waiting to go.
Speeding, I holler, "God, am I late?"
She shakes her head and assures me, "No."

I'm set to pause and take a breather
But, like a baton change in a relay,
She tears off, jet-heeled, before I reach her.
"Chop-chop," she cries, pulling away.

"You know this doesn't mean anything, right?"
"I'm sorry?" "You heard me." "I don't quite - "
"Nothing's gonna happen between us, okay."
I trip, confused. "Never in question," I say.

"It's just all my friends are guys out here.
We've more in common. Glad that's clear, then."
I hear Dad at some do, slurring in my ear,
"Beware the lass who gets on better with men."

Saddled by my parasol, she struts ahead,
Fawn espadrilles trailing wisps of dust.
"Lucky you've a shade," leaving me for dead,
"The one I brought over is now bust.

Got us some lunch from the deli store."
She pats the bag swinging at her side.
Onward, the land can breathe once more.
I picture it now as scorched hills ride

Off to our left whilst a glassy sea
Spills to the horizon, a distant right.
The road steers inland as a track, and we,
Cut through the scrub then, spared sunlight,

Hug the shadows of a slim rocky path,
A steep cousin of that to The Villa's shore.
Descending, I use my shade as a staff
Until parting beach grass, nature's secret door.

Fighting the glare, we are not let down:
The cove arcs round, a perfect crescent,
The grains a sweep of golden brown.
Crystal waves lap, in the sun vitrescent,

The hiss as it gushes then falls back
Only broken by a pair's dampened speech
From the corrugated grey iron shack
That borders the rocks behind the beach.

Stomping across, nearly two-thirds along
I stab my parasol into the sand.
We down our things, she removes her sarong,
And plants some sun cream in my hand.

Her dark olive skin is accentuated
By her bikini's snow-white straps.
"Hurry up, then," she clucks, agitated.
"We've not got all bloody day," she snaps.

Shades slipping off, I squirt cream in my hand
And coat her back. "Sorry," I grovel.
Meanwhile, she starts to cover her thighs and
Drops her sarong atop a novel.

She swings me round to return the favour
Before we settle, facing the sea.
"You have a nice back." "Really?" I quaver.
"Yes," she affirms, "you have, trust me."

Looking away to collect myself,
She adjusts a lens that has come loose.
"Hate these things," she mutters to herself.
With the lens aligned she puts it to use.

"What's that?" she asks of my curved chest scar.
She pre-empts my words. "No, let me see,
From when you pushed her away from the car?"
"Uh-huh. Got this one, too, on my knee."

Gathering herself, she picks up her book;
Still *Saving Agnes*, if I recall correctly.
She rolls onto her front and unhooks
Her top, then begins to read directly.

I blench at the brightness: "Jeez, where are my - "
"On your towel," she drones, her head still bowed,
My man-look drawing a despairing sigh.
Donning my shades, momentarily cowed,

I seize my bag, a small black affair,
One I'd grabbed in the dash of departing.
But, delving inside, I see that it's Blair's,
Finding *Loaded* and *The Little Book of Farting*.

Resigned to tanning and garishly white,
I snatch the cream, warming in the sunlight.
I plaster my torso then, in a dozed blur,
Sink into my towel, dreaming of her.

Two minutes in, I glance the heavens:
Far clouds, like a mountain range in the sky,
Fragment and reform in soundless procession,
Finally disbanding as they pass by.

Limbs out-turned and spread like a starfish,
I sit up abruptly, besieged by the heat.
My chest glistens as if glazed in varnish,
My skin pulsates with every heartbeat.

Her book bridges our towels, arched like a tent,
As, cross-legged, she observes a tanker.
"We would snorkel here," she nigh on laments.
"We'd sail from The Villa and drop anchor."

She's swift to discard talk of these shores.
"Ah, yes, families. Speaking of which,
You said that you'd tell me all about yours."
My heartbeat surges, like she's flicked a switch.

"Come on now, please. As I said, I'm all ears."
"And as *I've* said, we've not spoken in years.
It's a long story, not worth sifting through."
I try turning the tables. "What about you?

Why're you still fighting with your family?"
"Don't try and twist things back onto me!
It's you we're talking of, you sly so-and-so.
I've explained my position, now it's your go."

She takes my forearm: "Is it like with me?
My folks sent over letter after letter,
Begging me back, saying they forgave me,
But I'm not sure they had and if it was better - "

"Why would they say they wanted you back
Or that they forgave you if they had not?"
I press home my point as she looks to the shack.
"Could you not give things just one more shot?"

"I don't know," she replies, "it's such a mess."
"You really can't justify not trying," I say.
She withholds a response in her distress.
I relish the silence but she won't give way.

"Isn't it the same with your family?"
"No, not even close." "Are you quite sure?"
"God, what a question," I answer cattily.
"Why not?" she says. "What are *you* fighting for?

All you say is you haven't talked in years
And it's 'a long story'." She's growing impassioned.
"You can't give one reason that makes it clear
Why you've not spoken or how the split happened.

Or why the situation is beyond repair."
"We've tonnes of issues." "Like what?" she entreats,
Raising my hackles. "Let's not go there.
It's complicated." "Like *what*?" she repeats.

"Tell me, what the hell are *you* fighting for?"
Blind to hypocrisy, "Shush now!" I bawl,
Rousing the sleeping pair up the shore.
"I don't have to explain myself at all."

I leap to my feet and, without a plan,
Cross the burning sand into the sea;
Diving then swimming as fast as I can,
Trying to get away from, if anyone, me.

With thrashing strokes I make for the deep,
Ungainly writhing eschewing technique.
Lungs soon bursting and leaden arms spent,
I can go no more and, in the event,

My lactic limbs flop to a standstill,
Spreading like sails on a windmill.
Back-floating, paddling, I turn about.
Viewing the cove, I feel miles out

But, as ever, the distance from sea to shore
Seems to far exceed that from shore to sea.
Recovering my breath, I slowly withdraw;
My coasting, however, hardly calms me.

I'm striving to bury what she had said
Whilst also trying to argue against it.
I'm scouring the "reasons" I'd taken as read
As to why relations had become tainted.

So wrecked am I from my freestyle sprint,
I now boast the buoyancy of a large brick.
Bobbling and treading water for a stint,
I make for the shore with a butterfly kick.

Toeing the bottom, I take stilted steps
Then, soles fully planted, wade wearily in.
I offer apologies, which she accepts,
And we sunbathe without saying a thing.

B r o k e n

Splintered

                    Fractured

        Fragmented

                            Severed

Shattered

                        Destroyed

        Forever

            Lost.

                    Mother

            We

                    Are

        B r o k e n.

                            17th June 2000

A transcription of one of three poems discovered in the
author's black Nike rucksack on 28th August 2002.

3.3

*G*wen, *I appreciate the end is nigh*
But wailing and being quite so distraught
Is deterring the listeners and passers-by!
I'm sorry, my friend, you're such a good sport.

In fact, before things get out of hand
I ought to explain a little bit more
About the council and what they have planned,
Lest you'll get quite the shock at half four.

See, the reason behind our collective doom
Is bared on the bypass, heading southbound:
LUXURY APARTMENTS COMING SOON;
Half four being when they first break ground.

The details have been filtering through
From both our listeners and prospective buyers.
Architects lately have been heard, too,
Meeting at length with housing suppliers.

As for why the build is starting so late,
It seems road closures have delayed their arrival.
With such tight schedules they simply can't wait,
Hence out-of-hours work is now deemed vital.

The Church Conversion (or *Stage A*)
Will be completed with minimum of fuss.
Meanwhile, *Stage B* will get underway,
Blitzing the graveyard - in other words, us.

Backhanders afoot and PR fine-tuned,
Essential new housing is the council's line.
Yet where will we go when we are exhumed
And what of future "dead" when it's their time?

They have a solution, Reg has found:
Biodegrading coffins, which they say
Fulfils the required ten-year turnaround;
Large scale graveyards have had their day.

But picture the scene as family arrive
And find dear Ken is now Mrs Pickle,
Adored wife of Gerald and mother of five.
Ken's poor folks, expecting tears to trickle,

Will howl with grief at this loss upon loss.
On returning home and calling the council,
A PA will excuse her liquid-lunching boss,
And whose assistant's calls she's had to cancel:

"In a meeting with the marketing team."
On hold to panpipes - *Home to Donegal* -
Forty minutes later a message will beam,
"I'm afraid there is no one to take your call.

Leave a message, we'll be in touch shortly."
"Shortly" an eye-watering seventeen weeks,
Whereupon a standard letter will courtly
Explain the *transfer* and details one seeks.

Unfortunately, the site of your ~~daughter/son/mother/~~father's grave
Has to be reused due to lack of space.
Despite intentions for all sites to be saved
This has regretfully not been the case.

Owing to the coffin's decomposition,
Your ~~daughter/son/mother/~~father's details have been transferred
To a plaque <u>by the bogs</u>, a prime position,
On which we've engraved the relevant words.

For this honour, please send a cheque at once
For just £5000, made payable to:
Council Rip-Off Scheme, 4 The Cunts,
Fleece Lane, Scandalville. ~~Screw~~ Thank You!

3.4

Returning under cloud as evening beckons,
  She asks if I'd like to meet the next day.
  I think about it for at least two seconds.
  "Sure, sounds great. Where to?" I say.

  "How about the quiet little cove again?"
  I nod approval. "Great, meet me at mine
  At - let me think now - around half ten?"
  "You're on. And I'll bring lunch this time."

We reach her villa and say our goodbyes.
  But as she regards the patchwork cloud
  She turns and catches me by surprise,
Pecking my cheek as I stand open-mouthed;

  Flustered, guilty, but worse than anything
  - Christ, far worse - with joy unconfined.
"See you tomorrow," she says, back-peddling,
  Our hands as they brush briefly entwined.

  Dawdling back as dusk cloaks the bay,
    I am attempting to concoct an excuse
    As to why I can't see Blair the next day.
    I fear, from my absence, he will deduce

  That something's afoot; yet, fortunately,
  He has been priming his own get-out clause.
    "About tomorrow," he says cautiously,
  "Can't make it now." With a pregnant pause,

  He gauges my face as I swipe thick sweat.
    Clearly, I dare not appear too pleased.
    "It's just I really like this Kate I've met.
  And as we fly back soon I think that she'd - "

"I was quite looking forward to it," I say.
"But I guess we can do it another day."
"You're certain? I don't want you to think - "
"It's fine. Besides, I'm a little pink

So a full beach trip or island cruise
Wouldn't really work, to be honest, Blair."
"Sorted," he says. "So what's your news?"
Contented, he plucks his nasal hair.

"You were on the beach, I guess, from your colour."
I take from this he was not there himself.
"Yeah, with the tanners. Cancer central," I shudder.
"Where were you? I was down there myself."

I cup my chin in faux recollection:
"Having got burnt I stayed under cover.
In the middle somewhere, the busiest section.
With all the crowds we must've missed each other.

The sea was so warm it felt like a bath."
I attempt to dispel his scathing stare.
"From all the menopausal women," I laugh.
As, aptly flushed, I take a chair

He blurts, revived, "Read some *Catching the Rye*."
"Did it blow your tiny mind? Hooked, no doubt?"
"That J.D. Slazenger's one screwed-up guy."
"It's *Sa*linger, Blair. Must I spell it out?

And just 'cos it's all about a troubled fellow
Doesn't mean he *is* that person or thinks like him.
Narrator and author are distinguishable, you know."
"Yeah, but sometimes aren't they one and the same thing?"

"Now we're Shakespeare, are we?" "Oh, sod you."
With a balloonful of puff he expels a sigh.
Frustrated, he crunches a can of Special Brew
Then frisbees back my *Catcher in the Rye*.

"You know," says Blair, "I still don't understand
How we missed each other on the beach today."
   "Really?" I reply, as if my spiel beforehand
Had done quite enough to explain it away.

   "I was looking out for you a helluva lot."
"Given the hordes it was hard to see anyone."
"But you would think that one of us would spot - "
"And now we're Poirot. With luck we would've done.

In fact, I was lying there twiddling my thumbs
- I remember precisely it was two thirty-three - "
(Odd numbers more authentic than even ones)
"And was thinking to myself, Where could Blair be?"

     Though blunted at first, in his face I see
     The telltale signs of deepening suspicion.
     Before he even has time to accuse me
     I pounce upon his festering supposition.

   "For God's sake," I cry, pummelling the wall,
"You think I've seen her sister. Say it's not true.
I thought we'd cleared that up once and for all.
I can't believe you'd think that I'd lie to you."

   "Look, I'm sorry," he counters, taking a stand,
   "But from my position something's not right.
I know the beach was completely rammed
     But for you to be totally out of sight

Is more than a little improbable, no?"
   "It may well be but that's what occurred."
Blair retreats to the bed and lets it go.
"Alright," he says, "though it does seem absurd.

If I'm wrong I'm sorry for doubting you, okay."
   I look him in the eye but at once cut away.
   "It's alright," I reply, "let's leave it now,"
   Rubbing a bite on my sun-sore brow.

A silence follows my sign-off sentence,
Sustaining the tension of our bluing.
As when uncomfortable in someone's presence,
I start to commentate on what I'm doing

- "I'll put them there," I say, downing keys -
And whistling to infer casual contentment.
Nothing, however, can disguise my unease
Or old Blair's fast-growing resentment.

3.5

Boy, is Blair keen on his new flame, Kate,
For the next morning he's scarpered by nine.
Lazing a while but loathed to be late,
I gather my things and leave in good time.

Outside, I'm struck by the temperature,
Or more the lack of it, attuned as I am.
Being, like most, a sun-seeking adventurer,
I tut at the bulbous clouds that hang

Like a fleet of Zeppelins above the bay,
As if the roof on the world has been lowered.
I leave the shade and take the alleyway,
Past a night owl, barefoot and feather-boaed.

With lunch aboard, I'm there at half past,
And by quarter to we're at the cove once more.
Despite the cloud cover a disparate cast
Of wishful bathers border the shore,

Waiting more in hope than expectation
For skies to clear and service to resume.
Yet as we lie down, having set up station,
I am at one with the cooling gloom.

Turner-swirled clouds plug the sun's escapades
And the cove assumes a lethargic air.
Lazing on towels, the light lapping fades,
Faint voices dwindle, and the fitful glare

Passes unnoticed as heavy eyes close
And soon we are both sleeping soundly.
Stirring, I wonder how long we have dozed:
Her arm, I conceive, is locked around me,

Her head is nuzzled into my shoulder
Whilst curled feet press against my shin.
My body is stiff, the air around me colder,
As her sprawled hair tickles my chin.

I ease away but, as I do so,
She tightens her grip and takes my hand.
About us stiff winds have begun to blow
And, with a shiver, I glance up the sand:

Our fellow bathers have upped and gone.
Staring through fluttering strands of hair,
The granite cloud waits like a ticking bomb.
A glimpse down my chest, the beach we share

With encroaching surf, bubbling at our feet.
She wakes and charts our despoiled retreat:
Sitting up, she wriggles onto her knee
Then, steadied, fixes her gaze on me.

She contorts her hands behind her back;
Her bikini top falls, resisting lightly.
Sliding off straps until they are slack,
It drops to her thighs, now splayed slightly.

The rain fizzles down then freely flows
As wicked winds whip up the sand.
Waves are charging and, as bedlam grows,
She climbs to her feet and lowers her hands,

Pulling down briefs from her slender waist;
Slithered to the ground beside her top.
She moves to my towel and, in haste,
Tugs at my trunks. "No," I say, "stop."

She waves aside my lily-livered pleas.
"We can't," I urge, "we can't," I implore.
My trunks are slipping over my knees
As along my legs her slight hands claw.

I plead again as she casts them away.
"For God's sake," I cry, "we can't, I've - "
But then she kisses, she kisses me the way
Only She could and my heart is alive

Like I never thought possible again.
The forever feted, lost sensation
- Her breath, her taste from way back when -
Revived by our clinch's violation.

Insides melting and on the threshold,
Appeals from my conscience are in vain.
Our cold lips meet as the storm takes hold,
Our bodies knotted in the driving rain.

My hands slide over her dampened skin,
Her body pressing down on mine one moment,
Mine on hers the next as we spin;
Until then, with a sudden, urgent

Twist of her legs, I am pinned to my back,
And she's astride me, facing the shack.
Tensing, she guides me inside of her.
I look up, gasping, her face a blur

From the rain and sea darting at my eyes.
Her body begins to move with mine,
Quickening with cracks of bursting skies.
Leaning back, she arches her spine,

Spawning a moment not of this earth;
Guilt overrun by crazed carnality.
We are impervious to the grey surf
Spilling over us as, in our voracity,

She quickens our rhythm one last time;
Her fragile gasps supersede mine
As down she crumples into my neck,
And we lie midst waves, a human shipwreck.

The stately billows ignored in our lust
Grow taller with the ocean's every thrust.
Rising, I snare our costumes and trunks
And, turning, we stagger onward like drunks,

Fleeing from the front line, as it were,
Drained legs wrenched by the ruthless tide.
The deep, in its role as saboteur,
Has scattered our belongings far and wide:

Only our towels somehow remain
From where we had lain just moments before;
The rest we are now compelled to regain
As they're spat out along the shore.

My deck shoes, though, are lost, it appears.
We scour the sand and, after fruitless checking,
Hotfoot to the shack at the beach's rear,
Mounting three steps onto spindly decking.

Seeking protection from the elements,
I try the front door, wrestling its handle.
Despite my heaving's growing vehemence,
It will not budge so, like a vandal,

I punch the panels then take a step back
And try to shoulder-barge into the shack.
The door stands firm and, admitting defeat,
We hunker down on the frail porch seat.

The riotous deep drives up the sand
Then, in one fell swoop, floods our sanctuary.
Refuge short-lived, I take her hand
And, hunched, we venture into the savagery.

Surf tugs at our legs, almost taking us down,
As we wade through the frothed, roiling brown.
Slushed sand is sucked from beneath our feet
As the undertow strikes and waves retreat.

Then, just a dozen laboured strides later,
My foot snags on what feels like stone,
Cutting my sole like scissors through paper.
I look down, scowling, through the foam

As blood clouds the swell about which I stand.
The wave reveals, as its powers decrease,
A fragment of wood submerged in sand,
Its black border jagged like a puzzle piece.

Initially, I am far more concerned
With my slashed foot than what it might be.
But, as the incoming wave overturns,
Reality hits and I plunder the sea.

Water tears past, a rampant brown-green:
Discarding my things, I vainly endeavour
To grab the said piece before it has been
Devoured by the waves and is lost forever.

Gagging on water, I hear her calling,
Her strained voice smothered by the peaking squall.
To the sound of thunder she is bawling
Fevered objections as my hands trawl

The churning sand, hunting for the piece.
Swaying and set to be overrun,
I'm prey for the ocean's next release:
My kneeling's stability is undone

By the lunging bank of seawater.
Toppling back, too weak to compete,
Waves climb over me and, like torture,
Pin down my flapping arms and feet

To the sullied sand of minutes ago.
My attempts to escape are in vain,
The muted drone as I struggle below
Like the far rumble of an Underground train.

My strife, lasting mere seconds no doubt,
Appears eternal and ends with a hand
Seizing my arm and hoisting me out,
Supporting my weight until I can stand.

Yet beneath my foot something is wedged.
Wheezing, I search the withdrawing water:
Strangled in seaweed the deep has dredged,
I spy the fragment. As if relishing torture,

I pull free of her grip as again she pleads,
And quickly swoop to swipe the piece up.
I pick out the fragment from the seaweed,
My hands fanned round in the shape of a cup.

"What is it?" she shrills. "What have you got?"
I hold it out. "What *is* it?" she repeats.
For a brief moment I cannot say what,
I'm back at the service watching Rev Keats.

"It's the urn," I pant through a croaked cough.
"What urn?" she screams. "*Her* urn," I impress.
"What do you mean…" But she breaks off,
Grasping the reason behind my distress.

The Sydney Morning Herald

June 21ˢᵗ 2005

BRACEWELL LOVE AFFAIR CENTRAL TO MURDERS, CLAIM DEFENCE

"As the novel's protagonist declares in 3.7, 'nothing stirs the heart like forbidden love.' And so, bonded by their shared appreciation of literature, the two embarked upon a clandestine affair that would end in tragedy."

3.6

Fleeing the drowned cove in stumbled retreat,
We join the steep path as storm clouds pass.
I mince along on the balls of my feet,
As if beneath us lies broken glass.

Onto the rugged stone-strewn track,
Each step needles the cut at my sole.
On through the scrub, we join the road back,
The route's depressions and odd pothole

Kindly exchanged for tarmacked straights
That hail new-builds on the edge of town.
Barely a word uttered, we reach her gate.
Halting, she sets her drenched towel down,

Stoops to a squat and ransacks her bag.
Reaping a biro and damp scrap of paper,
She quietly curses as the split pen snags.
"Give me a call. We'll do something later."

She hands me the slip then turns for the gate.
"Later? Later when?" I ask, bemused.
"If you mean tonight how about if we ate - "
"Whenever," she says, somewhat amused.

I watch her strut up the path to her door.
"Oh well, bye, then," I mumble meekly.
Griping, I spasm onward as before,
My twisted foot weeping beneath me.

Sensing a spike rubbing at my thigh,
I probe my pocket, extracting the fragment,
Salvaged in raid from sea and sky.
It must end now, of that I'm adamant.

Back at the flat, I'm puzzled to see Blair
Lounged by the bed on his Game Boy.
As he observes me I pull up a chair,
Dabbing my foot, asking as a decoy,

"So where's Kate gone?" "Left an hour ago."
"Didn't work out? I thought you were keen."
"No-no, all good, we're meeting tomorrow.
Fuck, look at you. Where have you been?

Thought you said you were staying in today?"
"I know but I fancied a trip this morning
So tried a small cove just up from the bay.
Completely ignored the storm clouds' warning."

"Numpty. We lunched in The Vine on the strip
Once driven off the beach by the weather."
"And tomorrow?" I inquire, biting my lip.
"Well, providing that conditions get better

We're taking a boat to a beach somewhere."
He senses I wish to do something together.
"You don't mind, do you? It's just that there - "
"Don't worry," I insist, "you do whatever."

I was not consciously hatching a plan
To profit from Blair being away,
But perhaps it was brewing: on the slam
Of the door at ten the next day,

I'm snatching her slip from off the floor.
Raring to call yet checked by compunction,
I simply can't take it a moment more.
Conceiving that the slip's destruction

Will kill possibility once and for all,
I begin ripping the paper to shreds;
The debris soon so powdery, so small,
It lies like sawdust between our beds.

A sole reckless act and nothing more,
I scoop up flakes into the wastepaper basket,
Then check the urn fragment is safe in my drawer.
Needing supplies, I'm set for the market.

Yet still - still - all I see is her scrawl:
As I repeat, I have to forget her,
The digits appear in perfect recall,
And comes a louder, I must remember.

I see the number, *49532*,
Bittily scrawled in her pen's light blue.
My brick back in Blighty, I exit the flat.
Slipping the door key under the mat,

I hirple, footsore, to a payphone;
One of two past JUICE below our room.
Receiver in hand but no dialling tone,
I note the black cord has been given a prune.

Switching booths, I complete the sequence
And press the receiver hard to my ear.
Fourth ring she answers: defying prudence,
I ask her round, heart throbbing with fear,

With guilt, regret, hope - that old foe -
Hope she'll accept and hope that she won't.
"When?" she asks. "Half an hour or so?
I've got to nip to the shops. But don't

Fret if I'm not back when you reach our place,
I've left the door key under the mat."
I'm poised to ring off but, in my haste,
I've failed to say what address we're at.

"Where are you staying?" she sputters, panicked,
Rightly suspecting intent to hang up.
"How was I going to find you, by magic?"
I give her directions. "You got that?" "Yup."

Striding through pain, I spy on the drag
KONVENIENCE STORE. Swooping the aisles,
On paying I see they're out of plastic bags,
So are using brown paper things, Yank-style;

For a land that prides itself on invention
You'd think they'd have thought of handles by now.
Convenience, I note, is a pretension;
My server a sloth with advanced monobrow.

Slow-motion packing - near reversing time -
She flicks worry beads as she takes a breather,
Sending blood pressure of those waiting in line
Crashing through the roof and into the ether.

Impressively late, I approach the flat,
Forearms aching with fat-filled provisions.
Gulping for air as I trip past a cat,
The door is ajar and, making transitions

From doorway to hallway, I hear the sound
Of slow-spilling water from the bathroom.
Enticed, and with the shopping downed,
I pursue the trickle, the water's volume

Rising with my pulse as I near the door.
Water patters at the shower curtain
As shampoo slops to the tiled floor;
Desire, for now, has freed guilt's burden.

Forward though it is to take a shower
- It's the kind of thing her sister would do -
I guess I'd been gone for nearly an hour
And she, like me, sought to freshen up, too.

Hard-turning the handle, in I tread,
The plip-plopping shower masking my entrance.
I pull my damp T-shirt over my head
And draw back the curtain to reveal my presence.

Yet the flawless figure that I remember
Possessed slimmer limbs and longer hair.
A burnt shaggy creature tugs at his member;
The creature in question, of course, being Blair.

Horrified by each other's presence,
Blair, at full mast, cowers as I cry,
"What the fff…" But I don't finish my sentence
As I pirouette and cover my eyes.

Before Blair twigs and ire takes grip,
I leap at once on the offensive.
"Why you back? Flogging the log?" I quip.
Blair's retort is more comprehensive,

My intentions by now becoming clear.
"Why am *I* back?" he bawls, face on fire.
"Who exactly did you think would be here?
Actually, don't tell me. Jeez, you liar."

Blair berates me as I seek a truce.
"Who was it that told me they were afraid
The trip over here was not an excuse
To cavort round the island and get laid?"

He flicks off the shower and retrieves his towel,
Wiping soaped water but not his scowl.
He steps past the sink, clenching his jaw,
And barges out past me through the door.

Swallowing hard, I follow him out,
Staring at my feet as he drops to the bed.
Watching him dress, I await the fallout.
"The reason I'm back," he spits, purple red,

"Is 'cos a friend of Kate's - remember her, right? -
She came off her scooter and went to hospital.
Kate has gone with her but hopefully tonight
They'll be discharged and we'll meet, if possible."

Beating the mattress, he takes to his feet
And stomps, kicking *Catcher*, to the balcony.
Muttering to himself, he looks to the street,
Resting on the rail with his back to me.

Yet just as he's set to restate his case
There comes a loud knock at the front door;
Deep shame is splashed right across my face.
Blair groans loudly as I squirm, done for.

"Hadn't you better go and get that, then?"
Guilty as charged, I skulk from our room
And open the door, eyes down once again.
Before me, though, is the head of a broom

Parked next to a pair of stocky white pins.
"Maid service, sir. You like me clean now?
Is good time, yeah?" the dumpy lass grins.
Itching to decline, I agree anyhow.

"Y-e-s," I stutter as she duckwalks past,
Broom in one hand, mop and bucket in the other.
I slam the door against a freak wind-blast.
As she enters the bathroom we brush one another,

And I sit wearied by the false alarm.
Yet deferred fear is soon all too real,
For my return to comparative calm
Is dashed as I watch a piqued Blair kneel

To cram soiled clothes into a case.
"Where you off to? It's the cleaner," I plea.
Doubling his efforts, Blair crimples his face.
"You know that was not who you thought it would be."

Blair heaves a bag from under the bed,
Full to the gunwales with unused clobber.
As he hoovers up clothes, still widespread,
I try sweet-talking but I needn't bother.

On reaching the sagging bedroom door,
He suddenly stops and drops his luggage;
Precisely why, I am not yet sure.
He clasps the taupe bag and I watch him rummage

For a cardboard box bound by yellow string.
Sweating, he straightens. "Take it," says Blair,
Shovel-hands shaking. "Yes, but what's in - "
"Just take it." Shuffling across, grazing the chair,

I seize the box and his hands snap away
As he turns to shepherd his bags once more.
"Can't we resolve this? Where will you stay?"
Then in desperation: "Come on," I implore,

"Let's not fall out over something so trivial."
"Triv - " "I thought you came out here to help me."
"Oh, don't try that one. It's the principal.
I did come to help you, I totally agree,

Only for you to throw it back in my face,
By lying to me. I thought we were friends."
He motions to leave. "I'm at Kate's place."
"What? You only met her at the weekend."

"So? I stayed over a few nights ago
And she said I could do the same tonight.
We've got something pretty special, you know."
I can't help but laugh. "Oh, yeah, right.

Like with all the other tarts you screw.
It'll all be over in a couple of days.
When you fall out, then what will you do?
You're never going to change your ways."

"Who the hell says that we will fall out?
Besides, it's only until we fly back.
Jesus Christ," he snarls, turning about,
"You make these presumptions and attack

My feelings for a girl you've never met.
Yes, it's been quick but I really like her."
"So she's the one, is she?" "I'm not sure yet."
"Hang on, so the serial womaniser

Is now wooing the old-fashioned way,
Going about it in the 'proper' manner."
I don't think it would be unfair to say
That Blair was as tender as a sledgehammer.

"So," I sneer, "you're head over heels in love!"
I revolve to drop the box onto the bed
But, twisting back, I'm dealt a shove.
"Don't be stupid. You heard what I said,

I'm not sure *yet*. How can you be so flippant?"
"It can't happen so quickly. Just because - "
"What about you and - " "That was different."
"Why was it different?" "It just was."

"Typical," says Blair, "that's the thing with you,
You think you're special, not like everyone else,
That people don't feel the way you do.
All you think about is your bloody self."

He pauses for breath but then abruptly
Loses his balance and grapples the door.
"Are you alright?" "Don't even touch me.
Just leave me alone." "Blair, are you sure - "

"Look, I've been feeling giddy, okay.
But you'll dismiss it, like you do everything
That's not about you. In the same way
You always dismiss me feeling anything.

But I do feel, alright, I fucking well do.
I'm sorry she's gone, for what you've been through,
But that's no excuse to betray my trust."
"Blair, I really am sorry but I just

Didn't see the problem with meeting again."
"You didn't? So you've not had a fling, then,
Which you yourself condemned a few days ago
When you promised you'd never sink that low?

You don't think of her sister being laid to rest
Each time you meet? You don't feel guilty at all?
You don't think a clean break might be best?
That's the problem," he says, pounding the wall.

Humour the last hope of the vanquished,
"Careful," I grin, "it's not structurally sound."
"Go to hell," says Blair, stink-eyed and anguished;
Failed humour grating, not winning him round.

Steadying himself, there's nothing I can do
But sit and watch him as he struggles out.
I cannot pursue him, much as I want to;
It's a lost cause, of that there's no doubt.

A wall-trembling *whoomph* spells his departure
As knocking vibrates the bathroom door.
Stiff as a knight in full armour,
The maid toddles in. "Me clean your floor?"

"Sure," I sigh as I briskly sit up.
I watch her broom clack about the bed.
"Your friend now go?" "Afraid so, yup."
"You have big fight?" "A few things were said."

"Is no problem, soon again make friend."
Sweeping resumed, and exchanging smiles,
She sings until, with chores at an end,
She waddles out over the grout-chipped tiles.

It's strange but I wish she had stayed to chat.
You meet someone once and that seems that,
But you can always respect them from afar;
You're never let down by who they really are.

Looking to the footboard, I view the box,
And toe-poke the edge, as if it might bite.
A further bold kick and it rattles like rocks.
Lassoed with my feet and gripping it tight,

I slip off the string then pick at the tape
That runs, double-layered, along the seal.
Commandeering keys, I carefully scrape
Up the thick joins until the slits reveal

A contents that has me scratching my head.
"Tapes," I say. "That was worth the wait."
Gripping the box, I tip them on the bed.
"And some old papers. Thanks a bunch, mate."

I take a random tape box in my hands.
Like so many, it is scratched and broken,
The two halves conjoined by elastic bands.
I pick up another that has flopped open

And place it onto the dishevelled bed,
Spilling out a tape and inlay card.
I note the writing, a crabbed dark red:
March '81 - Tin Pan Alley/Scarred.

Then another: *June '80 - The Escape/
Wasted Dream/Out of Sorts/Castaway.*
I work through the pile until on one tape
I spot dashed initials, *HDA.*

Citing "coincidence", I look once again:
Why would *he* have a set of demos?
It can't be, I think, it can't be; but then,
Spying crinkled papers beneath my elbows,

I see the same hand, the same *HDA*
That is emblazoned on the tape cases.
This time my mind is in disarray:
I recall as across the paper it races,

The hand outstripped by our writer's thoughts.
A batch of tapes cascade with a clatter
As I pluck the sheet for *Out of Sorts.*
I note drinks rings as they bespatter

The fading lyrics to the said song;
The demo of which I'd just picked out.
Placing it down, I scan *So Long,*
Then *There Was A Time When I Did Not Doubt.*

"Make God laugh," I read, *"tell him your plans,"*
A Mexican lady once told a young man.
Dropping browned papers, I slot a marked tape
Into the boombox and await *The Escape.*

With cellar-like echo comes a clearing throat,
Then glassware clunking onto a table.
A tinny guitar rings, he sings the first note:
Taking to the bed, I am barely able

To contain myself, eyes hazing with tears;
It could well be me as the verse trips by.
My God, I never dreamt in a million years
That we were so alike - Dad and I.

3.7

What with the recordings and Blair having fled,
I'd almost forgotten she was coming round.
She was late as she'd lost her purse, she said,
And so couldn't leave until it was found.

She stayed the night, slipping off at one.
With things as they were, I skipped the flight home.
I called up Drew, saying I'd met someone,
And gave him my new Kos landline to phone.

For, yes, on her return I went too.
I sub-let the flat but, parked at Heathrow,
Was forced to ask a favour of Drew:
"If I sent you the key - " "You owe me." "I know.

The passenger and the rear doors are broken,
So I fear you will have to climb in the back.
The hinges have gone so prop the boot open
With one of the golf clubs under my mac.

The wedge works fine but, if still a bit low,
The three or four iron work an absolute treat."
"Are you taking the piss?" "Afraid not, no.
You can park it for free on Blondel Street."

"So who is the mystery bird?" he asks.
I refuse to say but, badgered, cave in.
"Jeez, straight out of Jerry Springer," he laughs.
I play along at first but the joke wears thin.

"When are you coming home, then?" "Not really sure.
Maybe Christmas." "Ah, in time for the birth."
"Birth?" "We're having twins." "Shut the front door!
Double trouble. You got your sperm's worth."

One problem solved, another was at hand:
Namely my guilt's ever lengthening shadow.
Make God laugh, I'd say, tell him your plans,
And, for a while, this guilt would plateau.

Our honeymoon phase seemed here to stay;
Desire undimmed, a "blessing from above".
How the first cut is the deepest, they say,
But nothing stirs the heart like forbidden love.

Yet beyond twisted thrills and warped reminiscing
Lay a joy equally wonderful and strange.
I sensed a peace I never knew was missing,
Until one morning when everything changed.

Waking, **5:10** beamed the bedside clock.
I see myself drowsing but, turning over,
Catch the click of the bathroom lock.
Nothing unusual but, listening closer,

I sense this is no call of nature.
She starts to cough which, double-quick,
Leads to retching moments later,
Until, quite violently, she is sick.

Feeling just a tad queasy myself,
I assume it's the fish from the night before.
Poised to crassly ask if I can help,
I throw off the sheet as she opens the door.

"I'm late," she gripes, somewhat surly.
"Late? No you're not," I say, eyeing the time,
"You've got hours till work, just how early…"
Her sober expression mimics mine.

I disguise inner panic with The Speech.
"Wow, that's amazing. We could be a…family.
What we've both dreamed of." She looks to the beach.
"That's what you want, yes?" "Course," she says angrily,

"But with all that's happened isn't it...wrong?"
"Nothing's certain yet." I feign composure.
"But what if I test and I'm a week gone?"
And, just like that, the honeymoon was over.

Part 4 Introduction

Broadlake's role in the murder trial

One of the most notable things regarding *Broadlake*'s involvement in the Bracewell case was that Oliver Mandelson, acting for the defence, only cited the novel's pertinence two weeks into proceedings. This was due to him initially believing that the evidence arising from the text bred an argument that was unlikely to stand up in court; hence submitting it as a means to exonerate Damascus was effectively a last resort.

Mandelson had first claimed that the Bracewell deaths were the result of a failed burglary, one of an increasing number of thefts and attempted thefts during the second half of 2002 in Alice Springs. He alleged that the perpetrator had entered the apartment on Barrett Drive and, in attempting to steal a wallet and some bank notes, had been confronted by Rose Bracewell, who was cradling her child, Mary. Following a scuffle, Bracewell had supposedly been struck on the temple by Damascus' Kookaburra cricket bat, an object stored beside the unstable bookcase that contained Bracewell's collection of novels. The alleged blow sent Bracewell and her daughter over the balcony to their death, following which the attacker fled the apartment. Inevitably traumatised by what had happened, it appeared that the culprit abandoned Bracewell's wallet and bank notes, which were later discovered by police beside the balcony door. Although this sequence of events was plausible, most glaringly Mandelson could not identify the offender.

Alongside Ivan Damascus, Lucy Freeman and Oliver Myers, *Broadlake*'s author was at first under suspicion, but any case against him had been dismissed following the pathologist's ruling that the author had died between three and four days prior to the murders. The narrator's erratic behaviour and references to such things as a Kookaburra cricket bat - combined with his questioning of whether he would "kill one day" - were thus deemed mere coincidences in relation to how Rose Bracewell, her unborn child and Mary Bracewell had died.

To further weaken Mandelson's claims, there were no signs of forced entry to the apartment (Damascus had the only key besides Bracewell), no possessions had been taken, and no one could vouch for Damascus' whereabouts at the time of the murders, thereby providing him with an alibi. Consequently, Damascus seemed certain to be found guilty, and so Mandelson was left with little alternative but to turn to *Broadlake*. Yet even delivering this account, let alone convincing the jury of its relevance, was problematic enough. Seemingly so farfetched was Mandelson's argument that the presiding judge, Mr Justice Ronald Stewart, was reluctant to let him proceed with the alleged evidence. Eventually, Mr Justice Stewart agreed to listen to Mandelson's proposal so that he could decide whether the barrister could make his case to the court.

The defence now planned to focus on events surrounding the death of *Broadlake*'s author, in addition to "suggestive" extracts from the book itself. As the former concerned the study of authoritative medical documents, Mandelson did not require permission from the judge for them to be presented as evidence. Nevertheless, in order that *Broadlake*'s text could be referenced, Mr Justice Stewart had to decide whether this supposedly fictional account was a reliable source. The submission of diaries in the Richard Overton, Marcus Wesson and Madeleine Smith trials was one thing, but submitting a novel was an altogether more venturesome, if not unprecedented, proposition. To recap, Mr Justice Stewart had to consider whether events in the book that mirrored those of the Bracewell case were clear references to what happened or merely unintentional echoes of the incident. He also had to decide whether Balkan's editing could have altered the writer's intended version, and, in doing so, perverted the meaning of certain passages. Before the book could be submitted, therefore, the manuscript would have to be examined to confirm that the published work was in keeping with the author's original text. This was by no means a flawless solution as some of the manuscript's "incriminating sections" were now missing, but the defence claimed that there were "a sufficient number of implicative passages within the available papers to justify such an exercise".

After lengthy deliberation, Mr Justice Stewart delivered his decision: he agreed, in principle, to *Broadlake* being referred to in court. Nevertheless, to ensure that the "incriminating sections" within the available manuscript could be thoroughly analysed and compared with the published version, the trial was adjourned for six days. On 31st January 2005 the inquiry's findings were revealed, the conclusion of which stated:

"Although a small number of substantive edits have been made to the text and accidental variants are common, in no way do they cloud or alter the events and opinions being recounted. If anything, they serve to clarify what is being said."

Mr Justice Stewart was now satisfied as to the published text's authenticity and Mandelson was free at last to proceed with his new line of defence. This by no means guaranteed Damascus' reprisal but it at least gave fresh impetus to a dying cause.

Setting aside *Broadlake*'s textual evidence for the culmination of his argument, Mandelson queried Damascus over his living arrangements prior to Rose and Mary Bracewell's deaths. After several objections from the prosecution over the relevance of this line of questioning, Mandelson made his first breakthrough. For his client now belatedly admitted that he and his partner housed a male lodger in the spare room of their apartment from August 2000 until June 2002. Throughout previous questioning Damascus neglected to mention the man's existence. This was originally due to him long discounting the individual, who he now named as Lawrence White, from having any part in the murders. Nearly two months before the deaths, the lodger had been asked to move out and had informed Damascus that he was heading to Thailand. Furthermore, when Damascus had been probed over his living arrangements by the defence team prior to the trial, he had guarded against disclosing such an illegality. For not only would he have been party to the murder of his partner and child (and Rose's unborn baby), he would also have been in contravention of The Residential Tenancies Act of 1997 by not declaring that he was housing a tenant, and not lodging the tenant's bond with the Residential Tenancies Bond Authority. Hence, it would have provided an inauspicious precedent in relation to this present and gravest of charges.

When, on 1st February 2005, it was revealed that Damascus and Bracewell had taken in White to supplement their income, the accused was thereby confessing to the above crime. However, Mandelson reasoned that, to preserve his client's otherwise innocence, it was a small price to pay: "Although he may be guilty of this infringement, for which he will be punished, to assume he is also a murderer is both unreasonable and, quite simply, incorrect."

Damascus described White to the court as a man "who kept himself to himself", but, bucking this trend, he purportedly became "increasingly friendly" with the now pregnant Rose Bracewell. Damascus stated that the pair would often be in discussion when he returned home from work. As a result, Damascus became suspicious of Rose's relationship with the lodger, resulting in an argument between the three on 12th June 2002. It was this argument that prompted Damascus to evict White from the apartment, upon which the lodger declared that he was heading overseas. Yet, on tracing White's movements following his departure, Mandelson found this to be untrue, and thus the complexion of the case altered dramatically. It transpired that White had not travelled to Thailand, or indeed anywhere else, but had remained in Alice Springs up until the time of his death.

Moreover, having investigated White's passing further (details of which we shall examine in Part 5's Introduction), Mandelson had reason to dispute the reliability of the information provided by the authorities. This gave rise to White's innocence being scrutinised once again. Except, of course, the man whose innocence was being questioned was neither Lawrence White nor any of the other names displayed on the counterfeit passport and identity cards that he carried.

This was the unidentified author of *Broadlake* who, it would seem, had set about writing the very book you are now reading within the apartment that Damascus and Bracewell shared.

4.0

2:02 p.m.

The best advice I received on parenthood
Was not to take too much advice from others.
Just as well as, back in England for good,
We hid ourselves away like runaway lovers;

Ashamed, perhaps, into self-isolation
Yet blessed by the everyday miracle of life.
Mary we named her in our elation
Before sleepless reality rallied the strife.

Still, to hold Mary was to hold our world
As the dream I never knew I had came true.
I pictured my olds as I cradled our girl,
For now we felt the love - and sacrifice - too.

Oh, yes, the love, how it spilled over,
Drowning, at times, that which we shared.
You'd hope the experience would bring you closer,
Not stir the feeling that war was declared.

Reviewer roles in short supply,
I settled for temping outside King's Cross,
"Admin" for PR firm, X & Y;
Or runner/tea boy for my desk-chained boss.

Boosting modest pay with her dwindling savings,
We battled through the tongue-tie, colic et al.
Propped at my desk, nursing caffeine cravings,
I was textbook new dad who had fallen foul

Of thinking The Slog sole domain of his friends;
Who thought, with routine, that things would settle,
That soon I would write and rest at weekends,
That Mondays would find me in fine fettle.

Nothing irked like another parent's success:
"She sleeps through," pouted too-posh-to-push mother
- Straight from spin class in her size 8 dress -
Whilst award-winning couples regaled each other

With tales of toddlers chatting at a year,
And phonic-savvy by two, for that matter.
No doubt by three they'd be quoting Shakespeare
And fielding offers from Oxbridge and NASA.

We endured NCT, at least for a time,
Before the forced friendships took their toll.
Play dates, birthdays - human zoos - we'd decline,
Being, for the most part, crowd control.

Shying away from those in our position
Wound us only tighter into our bubble.
Needing an outlet from the attrition,
Anything, in fact, to stay out of trouble

- And douse skipping marriage with thoughts of divorce -
I mooted weekly "jamming" with a local band.
That went down like a shit sandwich, of course,
As did mere mention of the book I had planned.

I see myself now as that Autumn fell,
Scanning the uncommitted October sky.
Mary down at last, I contemplate hell;
Or, put another way, some DIY.

Contemplating being the operative word,
I drag a creased *Times* from off the floor:
Diana's still dead, Saints remain bottom third,
I browse until I can defer no more.

I set about opening my fern green tool box,
Which is going really well until, touching the side,
I cut my finger on one of the locks.
Grabbing a tissue, and with pressure applied,

I eye the flat-pack - tower shelving, no less -
Then glance the destructions with fatal disdain
Whilst trying to fend off the Ikea Stress™.
As founding boards sway like a proto-biplane,

I re-skim the guide's microscopic Chinese,
Then wrestle with fixings, rage on full power.
My legs soon shot, requiring a new set of knees,
Plus the shelves aping a certain Pisan Tower,

The doorbell rings like manna from heaven.
Like a lame dog, I crawl on all fours
Past *Private Eye*, my limbs still leaden,
And twizzle the latch to open the door.

I stand, finger bleeding, as it slowly dawns.
"Drew. Bloody hell. Long time, no see.
How are you?" I say, smothering yawns.
"Yeah, I'm fine thanks but it's not me - "

"Oh, did you get my postcard from way back?
For collecting the car from Heathrow."
"The card…ah, yes." A train brakes on the track.
"Sorry I've not called. Been lying low.

How did you figure we lived up here?"
"We just moved in to the road next door.
I saw your car when I went for a beer.
I guessed you'd be number two or four.

Are those *padlocks* I see on the boot?"
"Ah, yes, top of range security measure."
"Priceless," he snorts, brushing fluff from his suit.
"I'll come back if another time's better,

But could we just talk? I've got some…news."
"Sounds ominous," I say, lightly chuckling.
My mood, though, is not matched by Drew's.
As he steps in, we hear the shelves buckling,

Shooting our heads round the sitting room door.
"God, I'm in trouble." "Worse than useless."
They fold like a wounded beast to the floor.
With my efforts to tidy up fruitless,

We retreat to the kitchen's damp-infused air.
Scraping by the pram, Drew promptly admires
The photo of Mary above the stairs.
"So you have a girl?" he gaily inquires.

I dab my cut finger. "Three months old."
"Is she napping? Haven't heard a peep."
"Just two hours to get her down, all told."
"Fuck, I do love it when they're asleep.

You can clear all the plastic crap you collect.
Need a Jumperoo?" "Jumperwhat?" "Bouncer thing.
Or as the boss calls it, The Circle of Neglect."
"I think we're alright." "Just you wait," he grins.

"The voice of experience. How are yours?" I say.
"Urgh," he groans. "They're fine, Jane and Molly.
But," he sighs deeply, "we've a third on the way."
"Oh goodness, Drew, I'm…" Set to say "sorry"

- Hell, that's what I mean - I do not dare
And I tamely trot out the accustomed line.
"Congratulations, mate." "Don't, it's a mare.
Still," he says, "there's a good chance it's mine."

We snigger like schoolboys. "Your other half in?"
"Out shopping," I stammer, eyes evading his.
Drew appears lost. "Not sure where to begin.
Guess the best way is if you just read this."

Rooting his pocket, he submerges a hand
And plucks out a folded newspaper cutting,
Sending my mind into No Man's Land.
He opens it out, as yet saying nothing.

As across the page my fraught gaze flashes,
Drew motions me to read the sectioned print.
A sea of hatches, matches and dispatches,
He taps the paper but, insensible, I sprint

Through forthcoming *Marriages*, blind to my goal.
Then, as along the two *Births* columns I scroll,
I'm drawn to the namesake of an old friend.
Stymied, Drew taps beyond the *Births*' end:

Blinking, I see one name I recognise
Under the bold font of the next heading.
This time I don't want to believe my eyes
For this is no birth or future wedding,

But a brief tribute above *Chris Dent*.
I murmur the words: "*CARVER. - Edward Blair,*
Passed away peacefully at home in Kent,
Dear son, husband and father to Claire.

Fought an all too short cancer battle,
Courageously and most bravely borne."
I stare at Drew as the train tracks rattle
And drizzle pre-empts the pending storm.

Pushing back tears, the least I can do
Is attend the funeral on 10th at two.
Glimpsing the date inscribed on my watch,
Stifled tears I can no longer scotch:

Its number succeeds that on the page.
I curse myself, my last words with him,
A pain no memory can ever assuage.
"I can't believe it," I say on a whim.

He folds the sheet. "I thought you should know.
When you weren't at the service yesterday
I presumed the only reason you wouldn't go
Was as you weren't aware he'd passed away.

I realise last year that you'd fallen out,
But when he was ill and nearing the end
We all tried to trace your whereabouts.
He hoped to meet up and make amends."

"You're serious, Drew? Blair wished to 'make peace'?
So what happened to him? To his health?"
"When he returned from your trip to Greece
He said he was not quite feeling himself.

It was diagnosed as a concussion
- He'd fallen, apparently - but some weeks on
Blair and his doctor had further discussions.
They started to sense that something was wrong.

Fighting headaches, dizziness, and being sick,
He went for some tests which revealed his fate:
It was glioblastoma, it was all so quick.
He hadn't much time but he and his Kate,

The kindred spirit he'd met out in Greece,
They got married and she gave birth to Claire.
Dying days later, though, was a release.
The pain, apparently, was too much to bear."

In the silence I hear keys in the lock
And, rain thrashing down, I try to take stock.
She enters, downing bags, shaking her head,
Tripping on a kite we had found in the shed.

"Is Mary alright?" "Still sleeping," I say.
She slings her coat on the washing-draped rail.
"That fucking kite. Are you okay?"
At last looking up, she cannot fail

To notice I'm shaking and red-eyed.
"What's up? What's happened?" she pleas.
"It's...it's Blair. Last week...he died."
"Blair? As in..." Dropping her keys,

She throws her wind-chilled arms around me,
Gripping my body, hollow and lifeless.
"Best be off now," and, turning, we
Address the figure standing behind us.

.

Burying grief, I make introductions.
"Won't you stay?" she asks. "No, it's alright,
I don't want to cause any disruption.
Besides, as it happens, we're out tonight.

A novelty these days so better hurry.
Going to that great English institution,
The Indian restaurant, for a curry.
Speak soon," he mutters in conclusion.

Schlepping to the door, I show Drew out.
As he darts off she's stroking my head
Then whispers something as I turn about.
All I can hear, though, is: Blair's dead.

Bewildered, I tramp upstairs to our room,
Where she brings me a cup of Earl Grey.
I thumb through my vinyl, prising *Pink Moon*,
But she clicks it off then twists my way.

"You'll hardly feel better listening to that.
Put down your cup and give me a hug."
Eyeing the drawers, she finds a drinks mat
And we cuddle bedside on the sisal rug.

Stretching, I nudge her willowy easel,
One bought to revive a childhood passion.
A small sketch aside of St Martin's steeple,
Her time, so far, was severely rationed.

Slowly uncoupling, she abruptly looks hurt.
"Can you not do that? Stop it," she blurts.
"Stop what?" "What you are doing with your hand."
"I'm wiping my tears, I don't understand."

"It's not just your tears. Must I explain?"
Rising, she snaffles the keys to her car.
I grasp as she runs out into the rain
That I'm rubbing my cheek - or more my scar.

Melbourne Times

June 23rd 2005

TURBULENT RELATIONSHIP SENT WRITER OVER THE EDGE

4.1

She later apologised for losing her head
Whilst I was deep in the throes of grieving,
And then for how she had thoughtlessly fled.
From the charged vibes, though, I was receiving

She did so more to clear her conscience
Than out of remorse for her fiery display.
As if her actions were of no consequence,
It appeared a task to get out of the way.

"Sorry!" she screamed, stamping off in a state.
I responded she may well be irate
But being indignant *whilst saying sorry*
Rather put paid to her apology.

When she returned with more Earl Grey
She apologised for *how* she'd apologised.
"I'm very sorry you took it the wrong way."
Which, of course, meant, if it were summarised,

"It is your fault that you were offended
By my vile behaviour and then losing the plot."
She even squawked back when I protested,
"Do you want my apology or what?"

"Only if it is a genuine concession."
"It is genuine, it really is," she cried,
"I'm sorry you got the wrong impression."
"Well, I'm sorry you gave it," I replied.

"Okay, I'm **SORRY**. Does that make you happy?"
I looked up at the ceiling. "Not as such."
"It's just bloody words, don't get all sappy."
"If they're just words how come they hurt so much?"

She burst into tears and, with fevered brow,
I embraced her until she was calm again.
Oh, the joys of your partner starting a row
And then you ending up consoling them.

Plus this, clearly, was no typical spat
Over money, sex, daily chores, the usual.
I was battling bereavement, and not only that,
The hurt of how I had missed Blair's funeral.

I recall my mumblings, slipping off to the can:
"Christ, she doesn't have a short fuse," I scoff,
"She doesn't *have* a fuse, it's simply ****!BANG!****"
She was like a bomb constantly going off.

Maybe old Bertie - you know, from the Such's -
Maybe he was right and no one's *truly* happy.
Why, some stop trying once you're in their clutches.
Come "anger holidays", when less snappy

And kindness flowed, I feared I'd break her heart;
Yet mostly I'd wonder if there was one to break.
In the fallout, upstairs, I'd make a fresh start
On my solo LP, my poor man's Nick Drake;

Short-lived for, like clockwork, Mary would stir
And, burying the hatchet, we'd attend to her.
I'd offer my apologies to keep the peace
And long for the office, that newfound release.

Why, after work, as the nights closed in,
I'd visit Blair's grave and, there, reminisce,
Reliving his antics and Colgate grin;
His vexing habits the ones I'd miss.

I'd ask his forgiveness, often staying till dark,
Then wander home to Mary's bath and bed.
Come the weekend, we'd take walks in the park
Where I'd fly the kite we had found in the shed.

"Childish", she called it - perhaps she was right -
But I liked to imagine that up there, somewhere,
Were their souls drifting just out of sight,
The spirits of Dad, her sister and Blair.

In some ways, I think, we were a "normal couple":
We'd get on one day, have a good row the next,
Make up, row again. But, beyond the struggle,
She kept her cards ever closer to her chest.

She became guarded over calls she received
And then, without reason, she would badger me
- Often mid row, taunting the aggrieved -
To make contact again with my family.

It was the strangest thing, it truly was.
I guess she had been in touch with her olds
For the first time since she fled to Oz,
So felt for Mother being out in the cold.

She would make beelines for the morning post,
The act that, I think, disturbed me most.
It's dreadful, I even went through her mail
But all my efforts were to no avail.

I didn't wish to come over all dramatic
And ask her straight out, sparking a blue,
So I resorted to my favoured tactic
Whenever broaching a delicate issue:

I professed I had a dream about it.
"It was awful," I blubbered one winter's morning,
"I dreamt you were out - in town, I think - and hit
It off with some Spaniard, some Don Juan, spawning

Weeks of meetings and a full-blown affair."
"Oh, honey," she said sympathetically,
"Don't be silly, I'm not going anywhere."
Her reply seemed authentic but, essentially,

It neither solved things nor stopped me musing.
Still, I felt better for asking the question
Without really asking or sounding accusing.
Yes, say that you dreamt it - just a suggestion.

4.2

The shit you pull to stay in the game,
To not lose the war, to win the battle.
Smouldering doubts had grown to flames,
And, as with Her, we were scraping the barrel.

As a last resort we considered marriage,
Like a concept could save the ruin we'd built.
Our love for Mary glossed over the damage,
But always there lurked that scoundrel, guilt.

How I tried to cast our origins aside,
Yet daily reminders exposed my shame:
The scar on my face, the urn fragment I'd hide,
The way I'd clam up at the sound of her name.

How I lied to myself, to her and the rest,
That I'd moved on and we'd find our way.
Lying comes easily when taught by the best;
Her sister once more rejoining the fray.

Dancing with the truth as means to an end,
Her greatest lie of all, her tour de force
- I should've told you, I'm sorry, my friend -
Was that which defined my later life's course:

Her vow that her beau was her half-brother,
The one I'd "mistaken" for her new lover.
My mistake, though, was to believe I was wrong;
He was, dare I say it, her date all along.

Boy, how she laughed when I revealed my fright
At spotting them there in the box that night.
How she smiled when asked why a half-brother
Would implore us to be with one another.

So coolly did she dismiss my case,
I fell for it all - and I mean Everything.
I guess say something with a smile on your face,
And you can get away with almost anything.

And the reason she called that night on the train?
Well, her date, one Piers - her partner-to-be -
He'd returned to his pad on Merton Lane,
So when she couldn't find her front door key

She had phoned to pick up the spare,
Forgetting that I should have been on tour
And not, as I was, staying with Blair;
When the key came to light she rang no more.

Oh, and do you recall when she asked why
Piers hadn't stayed if she was having a fling?
He had left that night as he was set to fly
On business that morning out to Beijing.

I see her Piers on the boat in his Sunday best,
Eyes fixed on The Villa, suppressing his pain.
Opposite, nursing a tightness in my chest,
I'm drawn to his wrist and his silver chain,

One identical, it appeared, to my own.
See, mine was for Piers but, savvy as ever,
She had given me his - unbeknown
To us both - to ensure her alibi hung together;

She'd bought him another, always the schemer.
The thing is, my friend, she didn't want me
Or me to be with anyone else either.
She was a terrific liar, to quote HC.

Gwen always says that she saw it coming;
And, deep deep down, maybe I did, too.
In love, the whole world sees you succumbing
Yet the one who cannot admit it is you.

Yes, how I blanked the Red Flag before me
When, island-hopping, we docked in Greece.
"How I so wish we could choose who we…"
I begged her at once to say her piece

Even though I knew full well her thinking.
I still feel the sun beating down from above,
I swear my heart has never stopped sinking:
"How I so wish we could choose who we love."

See, she'd already picked this Piers above me.
Yet what irked, what really made me choke,
Was the way that folks would rave about "Piersy"
Or "good old Piers", or "Piers, top bloke";

Or if asked about him, "Legend!" they'd reply.
In fact, do you know what bothered me most?
It turns out he *was* one truly special guy.
Following the service off the island's coast,

He ambled over at the gathering,
Doing his damnedest to make conversation.
And he wasn't just inanely blathering:
He was offering *his* commiserations

For *my* huge loss, pitying how *I* felt,
Saying how highly she thought of *me*.
There's no way on earth that I could have dealt
With such a scenario if I were he.

And, despite events, he still found a way
To be ever so winningly - irritatingly - droll;
Like he'd been given the best lines from a play.
I felt as thrilling as a lump of coal;

Like I was reading a dazzling tale's first page,
Its Wildean wit and breathless élan
Drawing nothing but jealously then writerly rage.
Not that it mattered, he was the better man.

In other circumstances - had we not met her -
I would've been honoured to call him my friend.
I've tried to hate him but the more hate I stir
The more the voices of reason descend.

Hell, when I am done putting him down,
I catch a glimpse of his buffed black Church's,
Of them lodged by my head at the crash in town,
Him tending to me as the rushed crowd searches

For an escape from the inconvenience.
I see his bloodied shoes, steadfast at my side,
A faceless saviour in unerring allegiance,
Straining to staunch the seeping red tide.

Later, I heard that he dropped by the ward.
I was in theatre, broken-boned and bleeding,
But his gallantry deserved a reward,
Which would come in the form of them meeting.

I guess they crossed paths whilst she awaited
Treatment for her fractured arm and wrist.
That evening we met and months later dated,
Both of us ignorant of the other's tryst.

Even when "exclusive" the games persisted;
On her tour to Belfast they had been in touch.
I had my suspicions her feelings had shifted;
A stashed invite from Piers hinted as much.

She played us for fools, yet I still hoped
That, despite the pains, one day we'd be happy.
We were "destined", I'd say - that way I coped -
Telling myself we'd eventually marry

When she'd grown tired of this Piers Delatte
Who, I would reason, was a short-term thing.
I fear, however, he was far more than that:
They married in the March of the following spring.

I still see them emerging from the hotel doors,
Slouched in my banger on Liverpool Street.
Sheltered from the deluge, at first they pause,
Then flee the reception for their honeymoon suite.

Scurrying to the Jag through biblical rain,
They wave to the guests and tumble in.
Flashbulbs ignite, fleeting white flames,
Capturing the bride's invincible grin.

They're drawing away, coming right at me,
Deep puddles fountaining as they pass,
Splashing the car, dripping down the chassis,
Falling like my tears behind the glass.

Lonesome as hell, as Holden would say,
I would seek a place a whole world away,
Somewhere we had never ventured together,
That bore no reminders whatsoever.

Starting the engine, my tears having dried,
I see myself heading out of The Smoke
To the hill I'd frequent after she died.
As rainfall relents I push in the choke;

Clouds roll back and the moon is exposed.
Threading on through suburban overkill,
I join the motorway then the B-roads,
And, slowed by the incline, puff up the hill.

Parked on the verge, with stiffened calves
I jink through elms to the mud-churned path
That leads to the bench above the valley.
I behold the moonlit, rain-glistened alley,

It's moss-mottled sign; and, leaning, I strain
Tear-filled eyes to make out the name
Etched in faint letters across the pointer.
I reach the bench but, still sodden, I loiter,

Shaking, drawing tight my moth-holed scarf.
Viewing the landscape, the illumined forest,
My sobbing's so frenzied it sounds like a laugh.
    I feel like ending it all, to be honest.

The Northern Territory News

July 1st 2005

BLOOD ON THE PAGES

"Following on from the protagonist's acknowledgment of his unreliable narration and subsequent stalking of the elder sister, the culmination of 4.3 can only be viewed as a veiled - and quite repugnant - admission of guilt."

4.3

Perhaps all those years on I was still bitter,
Resentful of how she had indeed won.
Perhaps if we'd met without ties to her sister
We'd not have been over before we'd begun.

Hindsight, perfecter of the imperfect past!
As for her temper, that gravest of signs:
If she allowed it to show from the start
It was hardly going to improve with time.

A year on and, hope renewed with spring,
We'd stumble upon a lease of happiness
Before hostilities once more crept in.
We sought to blame parental crabbiness,

As if that excused the toxic divide.
One day above all, though, replays in my head
As we wake to the radiant world outside.
Squinching, I try to slip out of bed

But, despite our rift, she'd had no qualms
About spooning so tightly I could not breathe
And had lost feeling in both of my arms.
Reclaiming my limbs, I straighten a sleeve.

Ensuring days had the worst possible start,
By my lamp she'd hung a piece of her "art",
A modernist splat that resembled diarrhoea.
Keen that my scorn was made perfectly clear,

I asked if it was the work of a child.
"Was it Mary?" I added. "What?" she replied.
"Seriously, was it her?" Suitably riled,
We had since put the episode to one side.

Yet that week at an art show, *The Silent Skit*
- Stuffed pigeons, gold cocks - a thought crossed my mind:
When does a piece of art become a piece of shit?
More often than not, you invariably find.

"Fancy," I say, "a chilled trip to the coast?
We'll take your car...did you hear what I said?
The sun is shining so we ought make the most - "
"I heard you," she chides as I worm out of bed.

Mary fed, I peek through the sitting room door
And check that the shelving is still standing
From when I'd rebuilt it the night before.
A drunken curvature notwithstanding,

I punch the air. We slip out for a paper,
Returning at the call of a leaking nappy.
A housework dispute and shelf row later,
Mary wades in with a car seat paddy.

After much dallying we'd opted for Dover.
Granted, The Arsehole of England, no less,
But we had ultimately been won over
By cliff-walk ads doing rounds in the press.

I see us driving under a brooding sky,
Bullied by a breeze that's begun to blow.
"As the wind's up let's give the kite a fly.
It's still in the boot from a while ago."

"Huh?" she responds, head buried in a book.
"I thought you said this was a chilled-out day."
"Kiting is chilled and since I last took - "
"Alright," she says, "whatever you say."

As to her preference I am still unsure.
"So, hang on, you'd like to fly it?" I press.
She withholds a reply so I ask once more.
"Sorry, but do you want to - " "I said *yes*!"

I flick the radio to avoid conversation
And catch sports chat on a local station.
"Saints won," I say, enticing a smirk.
"Oh, great, well done for all your hard work."

I shake my head. "They're on TV next week.
Let's hit the shops early to make sure we're home."
"Can't you record it?" "*Record* it?" I shriek.
"They'll lose anyhow." "Not the point," I foam.

Thumping the dial, in searing silence
I contrive to miss the turn for Dover.
"Who did you bribe for your driver's licence?"
"I'm sorry?" I say, hands poised to pull over.

"Can't you read signs?" "Wait, just 'cos I miss - "
"Hopeless," she says through a marital hiss.
Her shift from unpleasant to deeply unlikeable
Makes a riposte, to say the least, inadvisable.

She continues to read as I find a route back
And, bristling from the morning's mandatory tiffs,
We bump down a road, one like the Greek tracks,
That leads to a glimpse of The White Cliffs.

Parked, donning hats and yawning together,
We clamber out into the ghostly light.
"Brilliant," I say, "classic suicide weather.
If you'd not dissed the shelving then we might - "

"Oh, don't you go there, that is absolute - "
"You're only pissed off because I'm right."
Checking on Mary, she tramps to the boot
And there withdraws the contentious kite;

A sludge green diamond, red stripe up the spine.
"You're keen," I say as she untangles the line.
"You must be joking. I'd so love to throw it - "
"We just got here," I rave, "and before you know it

You're ogling the blackened skies with glee.
It's hilarious how you've swiftly backtracked.
Earlier you sneered and looked over at me
Like I'd suggested the most heinous act.

The turnaround has been fairly immense."
"I've changed my mind." I sarcastically smile:
"You snap at me and that's your defence?"
"Defence? It's a kite, not a murder trial."

A gust exceeding the sustained keen breeze
Whips the kite from her grasp and it flips away.
As I snag it in the grass I sink to my knees.
"Why do you always look for arguments?" I say.

"Me? You're the one always spoiling for fights.
I swear you've been cooped up far too long.
You take it out on me then slink off at night,
Writing your damn novel or some new song.

When did you last go out or see anyone?
You really need to find more of a balance."
"A balance?" I say. "Oh, isn't this fun!
Since when was this all about bloody 'balance'?"

I mean that is the world's favourite soundbite.
Ask anyone anything and, somewhere down the line,
They brandish the b-word. Of course, they're right,
I just wish that folks wouldn't *say* it all the time.

"Now you *want* me to go out? Is that your thinking?
When I mentioned the band thing you went berserk.
I thought you'd be pleased that I'm not out drinking.
And I'm now earning so you don't have to work - "

"You're only temping, it's not serious money.
When will you start living in the real world?"
"Oh, now the 'real world'. Are you trying to be funny?
Please don't get started on the 'real world'.

That's where I'm trying to escape from," I yell.
"Everyone always tells me, 'You know what, sonny,
You've gotta do this, you gotta do that.' Hell,
Don't you think that by having no money

Or luxuries, or prospects, almost nothing,
Makes me realise what the 'real world' means?"
"If you realise that then why not *do* something?
Get out of your ivory tower," she screams.

"I *am* doing something, I work hard each day."
"But it's not proper work or one that gives - "
"Art's only work in retrospect, okay."
"What mansplaining tripe." "But it so is.

Failure and you have been 'piddling about',
Success and you've 'worked yourself to the bone'.
My book needs trimming before sending it out."
She responds as I trap the kite with a stone.

"But sitting on your arse writing all night - "
"Wait up," I say as I kick broken glass,
"How precisely do you think I should write
Apart from doing it sat on my arse?

Is writing whilst sitting not the done thing?
Should I now do it whilst cleaning the house?"
"Don't be pedantic." "Well, don't slip it in
If you don't actually mean it," I grouse.

"Look, it's lovely for you to have these hobbies - "
"They are not hobbies." "Does it earn you money?"
"Not yet but it - " "Then they are hobbies.
And without, in your words, 'trying to be funny',

Given all these projects have taken so long
How are they still not good enough for me - "
"How do you know they're not?" "I've heard your songs."
"They're not even finished." "They never will be."

Approaching fury, I yank at my hat.
Fair do's, my works did recall The Great War;
It will be over by Christmas and that.
Cruelly exposed, I protest all the more.

"I *will* finish soon and they *will* sell one day.
I do understand what 'real life' is about.
I haven't just got off the ark," I say.
Grappling the kite, I turn to shout,

"Why can't you support me?" "What? I do.
The sad truth is, all you have is a dream
That, more than likely, won't come true,
And I've still got your back. But you don't seem

To grasp that all my savings are for - "
"Here we go again, back to bloody money.
I had the same problem with your…"
She's not heard, thank God, above the flurry.

"When are you going to grow up?" she utters.
Consumed by grievance, I vent my wrath:
I throw the kite down and, as it flutters,
Stamp my chilled feet and, cursing, storm off.

"That's it, walk away, like you do from the truth!"
Increasingly narked at my puerile strop,
She calls out at the top of her lungs: "Strewth,
I don't see why I should take the cop

For just stating facts." I turn towards her
As she grapples with the backflipping kite
Whilst skewing an eye to our daughter,
Still sleeping as we duel in the half-light.

"God, you're infuriating, you realise that?
And, for Pete's sake, take off that stupid hat."
I glower, affronted. "It's not stupid," I claim.
"Oh, puh-lease, you only wear it as what's-his-name

From that teen book wears one. That not so?"
"No," I object. "It is, it's ridiculous.
You're too old for aping your schoolboy hero."
I rant as if her words are blasphemous

But, dropping her attack, she cuts me short:
"We've fought long enough. It's a lovely day - "
"Oh, positively tropical," my retort
Coalescing with the heavens which, by way

Of accord, pat rain on my shoulder.
"It's only water," she dismissively snaps.
Choking on laughter, before I've told her
That most "lovely days" constitute, perhaps,

Cerulean skies and a glistering sun,
Not iron-grey clouds the size of small states,
She's back peacemaking, saying she's done.
"Can we just leave it. For now at any rate."

"Agreed," I concede, "I'd like nothing better."
I glimpse above: "Shall we stay to fly the kite?
I mean in view of the worsening weather."
She scans the angry mass, closing in, stage right.

"We've come this far." "Let's do it," I say.
She hands me the sails. "Where are you going?"
"Where do you think? To check she's okay."
Turned on her heels, the fresh squall is blowing

Her loosened locks into a storm of their own.
She hotfoots across to the solitary car,
Pulls on a coat then returns to intone,
"You don't think, do you, that we're too far - "

"She's totally fine." Wiping dirt from my knee,
I placate her fears. "She's perfectly alright.
What could possibly happen? We can see
Her quite clearly and she's strapped in tight."

I let out the lines and watch the kite climb;
Harried sails flapping like butterfly wings.
The diamond grows distant till, after a time,
The handle is shot of the spooling strings.

Glancing towards her, I'm set to enthuse
Over the kite's arcing and the wintry views,
But her focus is still on our daughter.
"You don't think, do you, that I now oughta - "

"No, I do not!" I cry, yanking a handle.
"We're in more danger than her, for God's sake."
I seek to adopt a more "comic" angle.
"Why, if I move just about..." And I make

My way towards the edge. "...Just about here,
Then, by my calculations, one strong gust
Should whisk me away..." I persevere
And, sure enough, it wins her disgust.

"Get back from there. Get back!" she shouts.
"Don't be so silly. Why won't you listen?"
My vertigo is now giving me doubts
As to the prudence of my position,

But I cannot resist one final gag.
"Alright," I exclaim, "I am just coming."
Yet, instead of retreating, I drag
Myself to a ledge, a slim shelf running

Below the grass; a good yard, though, from the drop.
As I await her I sprightly crouch down.
Oh, to go back and tell myself, *!STOP!*,
To unlive the fate of this miserable clown.

Though my spot's clear from the kite overhead,
She is still fretting as to where I might be.
"Where are you?" she calls, her cheeks glowing red.
"Stand the hell up, please, so I can see.

I'm begging you now, stop fooling around!"
Her tone grows desperate as she draws near
And, like a salmon, I leap from the ground:
   "Got you!" I holler. "Got you!" I jeer.

"Oh, fuck you!" she fumes. "Fuck. You.
You're sick, you know that, you're fucking sick.
I thought..." Turning, she curses anew,
   Slating my royally insensitive trick.

Accepting my actions, and also banter,
Are about as funny as stage four cancer,
I roar my apologies and steady myself,
Then creep off the cliff's white powdery shelf.

Yet, jolted by a sudden tug from the kite,
   It's suddenly my turn to feel the fright.
I redouble my care, parting the ledge;
But one false move and I'm back at the edge.

Pain at my hands, palms as they're skinned,
I shriek like a madman, a banshee-like plea.
Perhaps she can't hear for the screaming wind
That's whisked the green kite and my hat out to sea.

I can only guess she's continued apace,
   Perhaps to the car, to Mary, who knows.
All I can see is crumbling rock at my face,
My wired hands scraping as I glance below.

The dissolving surface may as well be sand
   The way it is slipping through my hand.
    My God, I think, my God, this is IT.
   Yet my fall is broken as my feet hit

A ledge and my hands snatch a hold;
Wind beats at my back, now bracingly cold.
Clawing at the rock, I hear her yelling
Above the furore of the ocean's swelling.

I bark repeatedly, sensing she's near.
"Go back, for God's sake, it's too late to help."
"No, I can reach you, there's a route from here."
"It's way too steep, I'll have to do it myself."

She flatly defies me or can't understand,
For muddy soles appear above my head.
As I pule she begs that I place a hand
On a nose-shaped rock. "Do as I've said.

Do it," she demands. "But I'll slip on the moss!"
"Just bloody trust me for once," she bawls.
"I won't make it," I say, but scrambling across,
Somehow I do and, as sluicing rain falls,

She's urging me to chance a second lunge,
And again I protest but again I make it.
Dislodging stones, I hear them plunge,
Then spy a nook and, fumbling, take it.

"I'll have to pull you up." "But there is no way - "
"I have to, I have to," she says on repeat.
"You can't, it's just not possible," I say.
Peering up, our eyes finally meet:

Her slender jaw trembles as she cries,
Mascara running with rain and tears.
"You ready?" I ask. She tardily replies,
Sniffling assent as the moment nears.

She leans down, quivering, and, this time,
I shoot out my arm: in a heartbeat,
Her right hand dives to gather up mine;
Groping thin air, with a clap we meet.

She's wrenching me up, her taut arm jerking,
My free hand scrabbling for extra purchase.
Inching up, it seems to be working
Until one misjudgement has turned this

Strained manoeuvre, literally, on its head.
I pull too hard and she cedes too much:
My weight is dragging her down instead.
As she tumbles, I desperately clutch

A nook with one hand, her hand with the other,
And, with a jolt, she comes to a stop.
One descent must be followed by another.
As both she and I are set to drop

I bellow her name: with no strength as such,
She has enough to glance up, reveal her shock,
Shock that we're done for but, just as much,
That her sister's name rings off the rock.

As it echoes she seems to give in.
Her firm grip loosens, I try to cling on,
But lashing rain has moistened her skin,
And, fingertips brushing, she is gone.

Part 5 Introduction

The case against *Broadlake*'s author

In turning to the text as a means to exonerate Damascus, Mandelson claimed that *Broadlake*'s author was a lonely yet harmless drifter who had been driven to kill by an intense relationship that had turned sour; the result of which was a book that intermittently pointed towards an elaborate confession. Mandelson argued that these "confessional passages", combined with numerous references to objects and scenes that echoed the events of June-August 2002, indicated part of the author's motivation for writing the story. Thus the case for the defence was potentially strengthened, particularly when in conjunction with fresh evidence concerning the author's death.

The success of Mandelson's argument depended on two things: whether the body found at 38 Larapinta Drive was that of the couple's lodger and *Broadlake*'s author; and whether the pathologist's report could be proven to be inaccurate with regard to the man's time of death. For if he had died four days earlier than the report stated, it opened up the possibility that he had murdered Rose and Mary Bracewell. Problematically, the man's only means of identification were the photographs within his counterfeit passports and identity cards, and the pictures taken by the pathologist, Dr James Radcliffe. Therefore the only individuals who could identify the man as the lodger were either deceased (Rose Bracewell) or were an unreliable and hence discountable witness, namely Damascus himself. What is more, although Sarah Ainsworth, amongst other neighbours, had seen the man in the photographs outside Mills Apartments, she had never spoken to him or entered Damascus' and Bracewell's home since December 2000 following the string of arguments over loud music. For this reason, neither Ainsworth nor the other residents could say for certain that the deceased lived at the property.

Compelled to find alternative means of proving the man's identity, Mandelson requested that Mr Justice Stewart grant permission for the corpse to be exhumed from Alice Springs Garden Cemetery in order for DNA samples to be taken. These would be compared with samples from the room allegedly used by the lodger in 60 Mills Apartments. The risk of contamination was relatively minimal as the property had been left vacant since August 2002 due to the tragic events and the considerable publicity surrounding the case. Mr Justice Stewart had no option but to adjourn the trial and, since the present jury members would be prejudiced having heard previous evidence, they were dismissed. A new jury was sworn in for the retrial which would begin on 9th June 2005.

Mandelson took further steps to ascertain the man's identity. He believed that the narrator's father's initials, HDA, and the character's death in 'Broadlake', could be a direct reference to the author's own such relation. Since the period in which the narrator's father's death was announced in 'The Times' corresponded with that of the newspaper found beneath the manuscript ("that clement May day" and 6th May respectively), Mandelson investigated the names listed in the edition's Deaths column. The only possibility was one Henry Dominic Angus of Battle, East Sussex. However, with the assistance of the METMPB and the NMPH, Angus was found to have fathered only a daughter, Jennifer.

Following the trial's adjournment, crime scene investigators examined 60 Mills Apartments on 4th February 2005. They initially concentrated their search on the box bedroom next to the kitchen, where the lodger had supposedly stayed. Although this appeared the most likely area for DNA samples to be found, it was ultimately in the kitchen that they discovered the most significant evidence. On taking up the floorboards, the investigators uncovered a number of letters and notes addressed to Bracewell, signed simply "L". Mandelson would later produce this correspondence to help explain what happened on the night Rose and Mary Bracewell died. Beneath the sink, they also found a bundle of polythene bags, one of which contained several rags which were used, according to Damascus, "for jobs around the apartment". Some of the rags, Damascus claimed, were ripped-up pieces of the lodger's discarded clothes, and, if so, they would potentially contain traces of his DNA. Consequently, they were taken away for examination.

These rags were purportedly used by Damascus and their cleaner, Lucy Freeman, before she was dismissed for persistent lateness and smoking marijuana on the premises. Given Freeman's links to Damascus and Bracewell, coupled with her possession of the entrance lobby key and her presence outside the apartments on the night of the murders, Freeman was questioned by police for a second time on 6th February 2005. She confirmed that she had occasionally used the rags for cleaning but, ultimately, she was again released without charge.

The letters and rags were not the only items of interest found in the kitchen. In his eagerness to prove the identity of the lodger, Damascus had seemingly overlooked another key object that lay under the sink. Behind a broken Zippo lighter, once owned by Freeman, and a large tub of multipurpose grease - used, according to Damascus, to alleviate the "squeaky" bathroom taps - the investigators uncovered a tin of arsenic; an exact match of the one found beside the deceased's body. Damascus maintained that the poison was used to control the rodent problem in the apartment, a situation that had got progressively worse since the death of the couple's cat in February 2002. Although this occurrence seemed incidental, the cat's name was then revealed to the court; Damascus disclosing that the feline in question was called Blair. If true, this evidently linked the author to the apartment. Moreover, the lodger apparently become extremely attached to the cat and was "deeply upset" when Blair was put down following persistent seizures brought on by meningioma, a form of brain cancer.

Following Blair's death, and with rodent infestation evident, it seemed plausible that arsenic trioxide could have been used by Damascus for legitimate purposes. Yet, given the arsenic detected in the author's blood, it was also possible that Damascus had played a role in his death - unless the deceased was the lodger and he had stolen and ingested the arsenic himself. Hence, it was all the more paramount to prove the dead man's identity.

It took nine days for the rag samples to be analysed, after

which it was announced that they did indeed contain traces of DNA matching those extracted from the corpse. This was not in itself incriminating evidence, since it only proved beyond all reasonable doubt that the lodger was the man discovered at 38 Larapinta Drive, and thus *Broadlake*'s author. Nonetheless, it meant that the author could have stolen and consumed the arsenic, and allowed his part in the murders to become feasible if his recorded time of death was inaccurate.

When the retrial began on 9th June 2005, Mandelson set about questioning the pathologist's findings. Dr Radcliffe confirmed that the author had been discovered on 28th August 2002 and that, according to his report, he had been dead for "between 21 and 22 days". Yet Mandelson then disclosed that at the time of the investigation Dr Radcliffe was still a junior pathologist and was under the supervision of Dr Martin Brooks. From this, one might have assumed that Mandelson wished to cite Dr Radcliffe's inexperience as the reason behind any inaccuracy in the timescale. However, this was not to be the case. Mandelson recognised that the slightest misjudgement would most likely have been corrected by his supervisor - the exception being if the supervisor himself was at fault. Substantiating the possibility that blame lay at the feet of Dr Brooks, Mandelson revealed that on 21st December 2002, less than four months after the Bracewell report was written, Dr Brooks had been struck off on grounds of negligence and malpractice. This raised considerable doubts over the senior pathologist's competence. On further questioning, Dr Radcliffe declared that he had examined the lodger's body on 28th August but, having completed his investigation, Dr Brooks had overruled his assessment that the man had been dead for "between 17 and 18 days". Both men testified this to be true. Instead, Dr Brooks affirmed the time span to be "between 21 and 22 days". It was the latter figure that was stated on the report and which had, until now, prevented the author from becoming a feasible suspect.

Once the unreliable nature of the pathologist's report and the identity of the deceased male were confirmed (if not in name but his role in relation to Damascus and Bracewell), it was put to the court that Ivan Damascus did not commit the murders. Mandelson asserted that the perpetrator was, without question, *Broadlake*'s author. Accordingly, Mandelson reverted to Damascus' statement that he had become suspicious of Bracewell's relationship with the writer. His concern was heightened since their budding rapport coincided with Damascus and Bracewell having "significant difficulties", which resulted in the couple sleeping in separate rooms for several months. Damascus said that he grew increasingly paranoid whilst he worked during the day as an electrician on the state-funded housing development on Anzac Hill Road (the site of the recently deconsecrated St. Peter's Church and former graveyard). Not only would the pair often be in conversation when Damascus arrived home - invariably, he alleged, discussing literature - Bracewell also began to empathise with the author over the frequent late payment of rent; even asking Damascus to reduce the amount by 10% in order to ease their lodger's financial burden. In clarifying the reason for these late payments, Damascus revealed that the author had lived off savings for much of his stay in order to devote time to writing his "experimental novel". When these savings ran out in early 2002, he had taken to the relatively new innovation of betting online (mostly "exchange betting" whereby customers place bets between themselves). This inevitably produced an infrequent source of income, causing additional friction between the lodger and Damascus over internet usage and costs.

On 12th June 2002 Damascus reportedly returned home early from work to find his partner in what he termed a "flustered state". The author's door was apparently slammed shut as he entered the hallway and, according to Damascus, it was clear "that something had been going on between them". Bracewell and Damascus became embroiled in a fierce argument which spilled over into the box bedroom beside the kitchen, where Damascus admitted to striking the author across the face. Damascus proceeded to ask the man to leave immediately, and this he did, falsely declaring that he was travelling overseas to Thailand.

Damascus admitted that thereafter the relationship between himself and Bracewell became "extremely tense".

This culminated in their separation on 9th August 2002 at the The Golden Inn on Undoolya Road. Then at 8:15 p.m. the next day, Damascus was seen entering Mills Apartments. Mandelson claimed that he was visiting purely to pick up some belongings and that he departed, unseen, at 8:25 p.m. This left his former lodger free to enter the apartment any time within the next hour. In order to explain why *Broadlake*'s author returned to number 60, Mandelson read out one of the letters discovered beneath the kitchen floorboards. A transcription of it is shown below.

9/8/2002

Dearest Rose,

I have written and rewritten this letter so many times. In the end, all I want to say is that I love you and want nothing more than to be together.

So please, I'm begging for the last time, let us start a new life: you, me, Mary and our daughter-to-be.

I hope you can find it in your heart to forgive my behaviour of late. I never meant to say all those hurtful things. Can we just put it behind us now?

I will call tomorrow when Ivan is out to hear your decision.

L x

For the record, the handwriting and Qwerty ink matched that of *Broadlake*'s manuscript. Mandelson deduced that when Bracewell did not answer the telephone the following day the author panicked: he entered Mills Apartments at approximately 9:20 p.m., not caring whether Damascus was at home and unaware that he and Bracewell had separated. It was proposed that he entered using the key that Damascus had neglected to take back in the heat of the eviction, removing any need for forced entry. The Yale (the same make as that used by the narrator in 1.6), was later found in the author's black Nike rucksack, but it was not until examination of apartment 60 that its corresponding lock was known. When Bracewell refused to elope, *Broadlake*'s author supposedly lost self-control and struck her with Damascus' Kookaburra cricket bat, knocking Rose Bracewell and her child, Mary, over the balcony railings to their deaths. Although Damascus' fingerprints and those of several others were found on the bat, the author's were also present, ensuring that this version of events was entirely plausible.

Finally, Mandelson asserted that, having killed Bracewell and her daughter, the author took one of the two tins of arsenic from the kitchen cupboard and fled the apartment. As previously stated, a man with an English, Home Counties accent then made an anonymous telephone call to police at 9:38 p.m., notifying them of the bodies' whereabouts. It seems likely that this was *Broadlake*'s author acknowledging the crime, alluding to it but not fully confessing, as he appears to do within the novel's pages.

5.0

2:51 p.m.

Set to follow her onto rocks below,
A last-ditch lurch pulls me back from the edge.
How I have the energy I do not know
But I manage to crab across to a ledge.

Above me, I anchor blood-smeared hands
Whilst wild winds snap at my coat's scythed sleeve;
Quaking feet crumble the lip where I stand
As aloft gulls wheel to mark my reprieve.

Iced rain arrowing from grey globes above,
I plan my next lunge, near double in length.
Only thoughts of Mary, of a depthless love,
Imbue my limbs with a vestige of strength.

Clamped to the cliff, I dare a peek down
Through the tunnel of my trembling frame;
Past cramped feet, my shoes' scuffed brown,
To the hulking waves sent to reclaim

The land: they explode on rebuttal,
Erupt with shards of luminous white,
A perpetual ferment as they shuttle
Into shore. Growing faint at the sight,

I stare straight ahead, arms rigid as cement,
Then view the peak, the scene of my slip.
Tears clouding vision, I'm braced for ascent:
Fighting for air and toiling to grip

Against cloudburst rain and hostile gusts,
I launch my hand at a jutting rock
Which, of course, I can only trust
Won't tip me into the chasmic drop.

Bullseye, it loosens, gives way then plunges,
Bouncing as it goes, and I'm hung by a hand,
One slipping - like hers - as the other lunges
For a secondary hold. Grabbling, it lands

On the moistened stone, scratching its surface,
Scraping like a cat sharpening its claws,
Until, when struggle seems almost worthless,
It jams in a crevice whose merciful jaws

Hold firm at the pull of my grateful hand.
Yet grip is perilous, there's no ledge to stand,
And, although I am essentially blind,
I chance an overhang, a treasured find,

As fissured rock grants firmer holds.
Creeping, eyes forward, I've soon assailed
The first protrusion, and growing bold
- My lottery of lunges at last curtailed -

I'm heading upwards, climbing steadily,
Face at the rock, till with some surprise
I slump on the grass, breathing heavily.
Defying exhaustion, woozy, I rise,

Teeter to the car and, my phone now dead,
Spot the profiles of three distant houses;
I will have to call from there instead.
Tumbling inside, the clanking rouses

Gurgling Mary from the calm of sleep;
Grazing the horn brings a comical *BEEP!*
I drag out my keys and turn the ignition,
Once, and then again, until repetition

Produces the same strangled squeal.
I scoop up Mary then arthritically peel
Away from the car and lumber on.
Searching the houses, they've almost gone,

Mantled by a pixelated curtain of mist.
It's all too late but I must keep going.
Crossing ploughed fields, deep furrows twist
My aching ankles, cruel gusts throwing

Me as I strive to hold course.
A snag too many, I hit slurried mud,
Running like custard, the wind hoarse
In my ears; my slashed hands' blood

Tinting the pool of cloudy brown water.
In my stupor I wriggle up - just -
Cradling, kissing my whimpering daughter.
I press on till suddenly, like thick dust

Parting to bare that hidden beneath,
The blanket of rain thins to a spit,
Unveiling, as if three giant stained teeth,
The dishevelled white houses that wearily sit

At the dank base of a sheep-sprinkled hill.
Mary's dress stained by my bleeding hands,
I blunder onward as the air grows still.
We drop over fencing as, twisting, it fans

Out from the houses and zips away,
Yielding to contours of passing fields.
Along a flint path I make my way,
Panting as the sky belatedly wields

A rod of light through the parting cloud,
Relieving the land of its former shroud;
The gravel's dull browns turned sparkling beads
Of yellows and oranges as their glint leads

To a tired abode's mint green back door.
Clunking the knocker, I gaze inside.
It seems no one's home but it's not long before
From an upstairs window a voice has replied

And I'm relating the horror of it all.
A stubbled soul swiftly reveals himself.
Noting Mary, he unearths a red shawl
Then shows me the phone where I ring for help,

Relaying events and where she might be.
Towels slung on seats, we take his Chevrolet
And negotiate side roads down to the sea,
Now lustrous in the sun like The Villa's bay.

We enter a car park above a grass bank
That bears stone steps down to the shore.
"I'll take her," says the man, whom I've yet to thank,
So frantic has it been since I rapped at his door.

"You'll take her?" I respond as Mary cries,
More stalling tactic than bona fide question.
"If you want to move quickly," he replies,
"Then go by yourself." I gauge his expression.

"It's unsafe to take her, she will only slow - "
"But she's - " "You run ahead, I'll wait with her."
I'm loathed to simply leave her and go
And, in two minds, I continue to dither.

Deducing that he has got me this far,
I resolve to leave her in his care.
I hand over Mary then step from the car.
Flouting damp steps, I veritably hare,

Skidding carelessly on slippery stone,
Body running on adrenaline alone.
Clattering onto the plump-pebbled beach,
I forge on, reeling, till at last I reach

The epicentre, it seems, of our mission;
A factless punt on her current position
Given the turned tide, the ocean's power,
And the passing of time, perhaps an hour.

Though a fall precious few would survive
How hope toys with me, vowing she's alive.
I comb the area where I believe she fell,
Hopping over rocks and the odd shallow well

Of cloudless water abandoned by the tide.
Promptly, though, I'm distracted from my quest:
Head turned, I watch the coastguard ride
Across stilled waters and, at my behest,

They approach my spot, slowing as they near.
Ashore, a bobby is pacing my way,
Escorting paramedics, saddled with gear.
Rehearsing my account amidst replays,

I'm drawn to the lifeboat as it pulls up.
Someone calls out: "You alright?" they're saying.
"I'm ok," I shout. "Round here?" "Yup."
The engine rallies and, silver surf spraying,

They speed away, skimming up the shore,
Allowing, I presume, for the turning tide.
I watch bobbing heads, now three or four,
Navigating rocks with impaired strides

As they rise and fall on the undulations.
A thickset bobby is first on the scene.
He's scarcely arrived but, fearing accusations,
I rush to explain and thus come clean.

"It was an accident, nothing I could do.
I couldn't hold on. You must understand - "
"Alright, sir, I know it's hard for you
But take it easy, yeah." He spies my hand,

Imbruing my coat sleeve a ruby red.
"Before we talk, let's get that dressed first,
And that nasty gash you have on your head."
"Jesus Christ, we've gotta find her!" I burst.

"We're doing all we can," he dryly replies.
"The local coastguard are out on a search
And my colleagues and I are doing likewise.
For now, though, sir, just take a perch

And we'll have someone down to get you cleaned up."
I grudgingly obey and they tend to my head
Whilst I sip water from a white paper cup.
I trace our last steps in foggy retread,

My restless feet crackling on the blue-grey shale.
"We'll have two more of us down here shortly
But would you be able to give us more detail?"
I stare at the cliffs. "Could you do that for me?"

Nodding, I clear my throat to explain.
He slips out a notebook and takes my name,
Then inquires how the whole thing came about;
Like my body, though, my mind is worn out.

I'm relaying events but partway through
I start losing track, wittering to myself.
It's like I'm a madman: "I so wanted to…
But she couldn't…she fell…I tried to help…"

He concedes defeat, pocketing his paper.
"Let's leave it, sir, and get you out of here.
We'll try again at the station later."
Though my parlous state of mind is clear,

I plead to remain down on the rocks,
Where I see out the rest of the hunt.
The wait is not long, for at five o'clock
She is found in a cove along the front.

Mandelson revealed to the court that traces of whisky were found on several pages of Parts 4 and 5, suggesting that the author may have read - and occasionally extended - this section of the manuscript whilst drinking on the night of 10th August. One page in particular validated this assertion, the author having updated a verse in 5.0 (dated "10/8") which detailed the protagonist's opening remarks to the police officer: "It was an accident, nothing I could do./ I couldn't hold on." Given these lines appear to have been inserted on the night of the murders, Mandelson argued that "I couldn't hold on" was a direct response to the tussle with Bracewell on the apartment balcony. Having struck Bracewell with the cricket bat, the author supposedly tried to prevent her from falling over the railings as she was still cradling her child, Mary. Indeed, according to the autopsy report, the abrasions found on Bracewell's left wrist could well have been sustained when the perpetrator attempted to pull her back onto the balcony.

From *The Kookaburra Killer* by Arthur Hamlin

5.1

Is that the clock chiming three, my friend?
I must push on if we're to reach the end.
What with the diggers chugging at the gates,
We've barely an hour to explain our fates.

Why, what has become of my fellow stiffs?
Gwen, Zac and Reg - are you still there?
Gwen likes to mull over events on the cliffs
But I guess she's now too depressed to care.

Zac's a quiet one but old Reg Kent,
He's hardly backward in coming forward;
Even he has taken to silent lament.
If we had time and things were more ordered

I'd give you the lowdown back at the station,
The nightmares I suffered reliving her fall,
The quandary of burial versus cremation.
Fast-forward we must, though, through it all,

And hit *play* on the eve of the funeral.
Mary down at last, I collapse on the sofa.
Closing my eyes, more tired than usual,
I long for tomorrow to finally be over.

Yet what happens next truly confounds me.
I'm lying there listening to *Burn* by The Cure
When the phone seems to ring particularly loudly,
Like they do in movies to put shits up the viewer.

As opposed to many who had been in touch,
This was no token, "If there's anything I can do".
They had not rung to give sympathy as such
- They didn't know she'd died - and, in lieu,

Asked to put her on, saying they were "old friends".
  Then - and this is what I found most intriguing -
    As I faltered through how she'd met her end
      They repeated my account, as if reeling

Off the tale to someone stood nearby.
  I'm dreaming it or she's in shock, I thought,
    But it continued till we said goodbye,
      Her recaps, it seemed, increasingly fraught.

That night was the first that Mary slept through,
  Yet could I sleep? Nudging quarter to two,
    I knelt by her cot, half hoping she'd stir,
      So I could hold and take comfort in her.

She woke at five as I flicked through my vinyl.
  I fed her and then, with the wake here later,
    Began to prepare for the caterers' arrival.
Though for "caterers" read "retired waitress and waiter",

Pat and Jim Steyn; both so frail I'd surmised
  They'd begun life when God was still a boy.
    Hiring heaven-ready help was clearly ill-advised
      But, with my budget search bringing no joy,

I'd settled for the couple's *Entry-Level Buffet*.
  I did have more luck, though, with Mary's minder,
    Booking Drew's suggestion, one Dee Moray.
      As Pat staggered in - Jim rattling behind her -

I reviewed my eulogy, battling self-doubt,
  Removing a comma then putting it back,
    Amending a clause then scrubbing it out.
      One setting down from a panic attack,

I busied myself: like an OCD cleaner,
  Re-dusting the house, battling sleep deprivation,
    Hiding a remote later found in the freezer,
      Plumping up cushions with a stylist's dedication.

On Dee's arrival I explained the routine,
Then the cortège appeared at ten fifteen.
There I am kissing Mary countless goodbyes
Then scuffling out the door under mackerel skies.

Inside, I sit alone on pristine grey seats,
Staring, inconsolable, at the hearse up ahead.
We glide like stingrays up stock-still streets
Until blocked by two workers unloading a bed.

One bellows orders but, noting the hearse,
Tips his skewed cap in bashful reverence.
A six-minute drive, rarely out of first,
I alight, stomach knotting, by St Martin's entrance.

I spot the mourners in the window's reflection,
Beneath the bower of a drooped silver birch.
Beyond the bonnet, in the opposite direction,
A couple roam the square fronting the church.

A chief mourner in the company of strangers,
I scutter on through the graffitied lych-gate,
Grazing the path's mauve purple hydrangeas.
At the narthex her parents solemnly wait,

Then, entering, I pass the empty pews.
I sit by the lectern, tribute on repeat,
Organ humming gently as soles of shoes
Swish on the flags, guests finding their seat.

Church full to bursting, the organ dies,
Whispers diminish, and austere calm
Is dashed by the rustle of feet as we rise.
Sweat is fast-forming in my tensed palms

As pall-bearers slow-march, funnelling past.
Onto pine trestles her coffin is placed
And I watch, horrified, numb, aghast.
Attempts at composure are laid to waste

As I fight tears throughout the first hymn,
In the knowledge I must make an address;
In time I desist but more croak than sing.
The last chord fades and, reining in distress,

I edge to the front, shoulders stooped, head down,
Flattening the folds of my rumpled sheets.
Silence sucks in the tumult of town;
Pews creak as mourners shift in their seats.

I stumble, frog-throated, through the opening line,
Hundred times rehearsed, read and reread,
But now the words alien, the voice not mine.
I sense my audience are losing the thread;

I consider stopping but, just as I do,
I spot two faces way down the back,
Past the grand piano: Sam and Drew.
Checked yet heartened, I briefly backtrack

Then resume, back straightened, loud and clear.
I say how immensely proud she would be
To see all her friends and family here;
How, on returning to England with me,

She had found happiness in family life;
In motherhood, of course, first and foremost,
But also as my partner and future wife.
I refer to the accident down on the coast,

The shock for all those that she leaves behind;
Our one comfort being - my breaths growing shorter -
That the final thought passing through her mind
Would have been of her love for our daughter.

Rising, the pastor resumes the service.
Yet where is the relief? Beyond wishful truths,
I sense I've been merely scraping the surface;
That my account is one elaborate ruse,

An excuse for a past I do not understand.
Why, it's only then, as I relive her fall,
And a stranger plays Chopin on the grand,
That I realise I barely knew her at all.

I sit, whey-faced, as my case gathers clout,
Peaking as the service comes to a close.
Yet even as the coffin is borne out
Down the aisle beyond the last rows,

The agony's not done, the burial's to come.
Trailing pall-bearers, we file outside,
And beneath a broad oak and a saffron sun,
Gather for interment at the graveside;

A plot by her sister's porcelain plaque.
As a dog walker strolls casually past
The pastor completes the ring of black;
And so the interment begins at last.

Breaching stony earth, her coffin disappears.
We observe the prayer then, breaking the chain,
A quartet depart, dabbing at their tears;
The rest follow suit until just I remain.

5.2

Ensuring I'm home when the mourners arrive,
I jink past minglers in talks with the pastor.
Ferried back, I check Pat and Jim are alive,
Then dart up to Mary, catching faint laughter,

The rising murmur of babbling downstairs;
The clink of glasses as more join the fold,
Floorboards groaning under dragged chairs,
Bringing to mind do's held by my olds.

In fact, I muse, as my left temple aches,
It's almost funny, their do's sounding like wakes.
I wander downstairs, taking in the sounds,
Acknowledging Piers before doing the rounds.

Yet it seems I've become the ultimate bore,
Hasty exits greeting my verbal nadir.
My lowlights on par with, "How is your lawn?" or,
"What are you doing for Christmas this year?"

Five empty chats later, possibly more,
I'm reduced to browsing condolence cards
Displayed on the dresser, read three times before.
Flagging, I'm caught slightly off guard

As a stern girl, circa eight, saunters up.
"How are you?" I ask as she draws near.
"Existing," she says as I sip my tea cup.
"That's a smart dress." "It's a skirt," she sneers

Then stares at the shelves parked in the bay.
"They're wonky," she states, shaking her head.
Must be family, I think. "Some Pepsi?" I say.
"Yuk, no thanks. Is there Coke instead?"

Unsure, I scour the milling guests for Jim,
Currently drooling into the mayonnaise.
"Can't get the staff." As he spills the Pimm's
The girl eyes me: "Who are you anyways?"

I stare at my tea as she looks askew.
"You shouldn't have drinks parties here, you know."
"Oh, really, why's that?" "There's only one loo."
She observes the queue that's begun to grow.

"My first funeral," she beams. "Oh," I say, "right.
How're you finding it?" "Yeah, pretty cool.
Dead bodies and that. It was an early flight
But the best thing is, it gets me off school."

"Ah, fantastic." "Did you see it?" "See what?"
"The coffin." "Er…yes," I drawl remotely.
"I couldn't because we had such a bad spot.
Mum said the guy doing the speech was phony."

"Oh, did she now," and, with that, we're done.
"Forget the Coke, I think we are going."
She skips to the hallway. "See ya, have fun!"
As loose-lipped guests keep cheap wine flowing,

The jollity has me somewhat vexed.
I guess it's relief that the worst is over.
"I'm sorry," says one, "*So* sorry," says the next,
Hollow consolation as I claim the sofa.

Drifting into replays of her cliff fall,
A stout guest joins me, jolting me awake;
His head, bald and shiny as a cue ball,
Bobbles as he bolts his weight in cake.

He looks up, chomping: "Hi. I'm Neil."
"I'm sorry," he says and I try not to brood.
"Thank you," I reply, "that means a great deal."
"Oh, no, I just mean for eating all the food."

As he staggers off in search of thirds
I spot her pensive mother stood nearby.
I seize the chance for a brief word.
"I thought...I thought I should come and say hi."

"Ah, yes," she says, "was going do the same.
I saw you chatting with her friend, Neil Vine."
Her pleasantness dampens my fears of blame.
There's nothing for it but to utter The Line.

"Look, I can't tell you how sorry I am - "
"So am I," she utters, "so am I."
Her warmth dissolves as she clocks our pram;
A film of moisture envelops her eye.

"Nothing I say can bring back your daughter,
But just know I did all I could to...save her."
"It wasn't your fault. Could I have some water?"
I start to well up. "Let me - " "Speak later."

She stumbles off in growing abjection,
Heading to the stairs where she slows to a halt.
I stand there shaking in snivelled reflection.
"Yes," like she's there, "it was no one's fault."

Semi-composed, repressing thoughts of Dover,
I'm approached by Flick, wife of Sam.
"How is little Mary? You must pop over
For lunch or supper whenever you can.

Do be quick, though, off to Kent next year.
Our flat's too small and dark as a dungeon."
"But I thought you guys - " "We're done living here.
Most come to London to get *out* of London."

Flick's the kind of woman other women abhor:
Beautiful, successful, content and, what's more,
To complete the whole unrelenting misery,
With a 1st from Cambridge in Biochemistry.

She jokes of how Sam - who, unlike me,
Had stayed on to scrape a Desmond from Bath -
Had then bagged a diamond such as she.
"Opposites attract," she says and we laugh.

She mutters, pointing, as I drain my cup:
"That old girl's looked unwell for a while.
She'll need a doctor if she doesn't perk up."
"Oh, don't worry, Flick, she's the help," I smile.

Pat's not alone in her lethargy, though:
The sisters' grandfather - who, at the memorial,
Had aired his memories of The Lady Mo -
Can barely hold still his glass of cordial.

"Have they found her?" he asks a kindly acquaintance.
"Sarah, darling, do you think she'll pull through?"
Sarah strokes his wrist with nurse-like patience:
"This is her wake, dear. She died last week, Hugh."

I talk to friends from London and Greece,
Doing their damnedest to dispel my gloom;
Taking their turns to say their piece,
Gushing with how "she lit up the room"

And "displayed kindness so rarely found".
Her qualities, it seems, are irrefutable:
"So thoughtful and loving, a joy to be around."
I ask myself if they're at the wrong funeral.

Or maybe it's simply the standard spiel,
The ever obligatory five-star review,
Before, months later, comes the big reveal
As mourners recall the The Real You;

Sensitivity gradually drifts away,
And the halo hovering above your name
Fades as they feel at liberty to say
That X was a grump and a bit of a pain.

I hail a lulled duo. "Thanks for coming guys,"
And, joining Sam and Drew, we play at best friends.
It's just like old times but, saying their goodbyes,
I can but wonder when I'll see them again.

Rechecking on Mary, I ascend the stairs,
The queue for the loo now having dispersed.
Yet on reaching her door I am aware
Of noise from my room, so look in there first.

I notice, winding my head round the door,
A gaunt, thinning soul, sunken head in hands.
Sensing me, he looks up from the floor,
Wipes his flushed cheeks and abruptly stands.

I stare at her father, crumbling inside.
Awkwardness building, the train line clatters.
In my disquiet I cough, tongue-tied;
My vacuous question hardly helps matters.

"Are you alright?" "Yes, perfectly okay."
"Are you quite sure?" "Absolutely," he snaps.
He tweaks his cufflinks then smooths the duvet.
"Looking for the bathroom. Could you perhaps

Show me the way," clearly keen to save face.
"Sure," I respond, "down there on your right."
Fuelled by a panicked injection of pace,
He totters inside, fumbling the light.

Viewing a snap of us up on the wall,
I linger a moment, rocked back on my heels.
I look in on Mary then make for the hall
Where I am met by pocket-bulged Neil,

Doing, it would appear, his weekly shop.
Lining his coat with fruit, cake and beers,
He conjures a bag of bags from his top
Then slings in two apples: "Nice spread, cheers."

I take a livid swig of a cast-off gin:
"Need a hand there?" "No thanks, I'm done."
Nearly taking the doorframe with him,
He squeezes through the porch and into the sun.

I watch as, laggardly, Neil makes for home,
A common conviction, guests drifting away.
By twenty to three I am slumped there alone,
Slipping down Bell's, chewing over the day.

Though the service was only hours before,
I wish to return to reflect in peace.
Asking minder Dee if she'll stay until four,
I wander, half-cut, back through the streets.

The church's grounds now lie deserted;
In sunlit silence grief's been averted.
I reach the spot to the chime of the bell;
My throat, as I kneel, begins to swell.

I glimpse her sister's final resting place,
The soil piled high by the digger's spade.
Tears first seep then course down my face
As I stare at the plaque that had been made.

The Australian

June 16th 2005

SECRET LETTERS TO BRACEWELL MIRRORED IN 'BROADLAKE'

5.3

Closing the lych-gate and securing the bolt,
A black-skirted figure looms into view.
As the blur sharpens I'm forced to a halt.
"Lara?" I say, eyes strained, head askew;

Her features matured yet somehow the same
As when I last saw them from the London train.
"This cannot be real." "You're telling me."
"How long's it been?" "Too long." "I agree."

From awkward embrace she edges away:
"I just can't tell you how sorry I am,
Firstly for what happened and then today.
The front of the car got hit by a van."

"God, are you alright?" "Yeah, I'm fine.
Car not so much, so missed the whole thing.
I hailed a cab but it took so much time,
And then didn't have your number to ring.

How come you're here and not back home?"
"I wanted to have some time on my own."
"But you're free to talk?" "Of course," I say.
"Another cab, I hear, is on its way

But with the traffic they're running late.
Picking up the kids from a place in Dorking."
We take a weathered bench beside the lych-gate.
"So how did you know all about this morning?"

"Well," she says, "that's why I hoped to chat.
I'm here, for the most part, because of Mum."
"Mum? What on earth do you mean by that?"
"If it wasn't for her I wouldn't have come.

For years now she's been relaying your news.
She had been finding out how you were
Through your friend, Blair, until he would lose - "
"What the hell's he got to do with her?"

"You haven't changed, have you?" she responds.
"Blair and Mum were pretty close at the end.
Him coming to Dad's funeral was down to their bond."
She takes my hand. "He was such a good friend.

Every few months he would try to call,
Or send some photos and a short letter.
He was so kind to Mum through it all,
When we knew Dad would not get better."

"Hang on, wait, there must be a mistake.
Blair used to call and *write* to Mother?
He'd misspell 'typo', for goodness' sake."
But then I recall that fateful summer

When we flew to Greece. She cracks a smile.
"His letters weren't easy to understand,
But they kept Mum going for a good while.
Blair had to keep it all underhand.

He knew you'd go crazy if you found out.
Since you left, he'd been in touch throughout,
Knowing how much Mum relied on his news.
He couldn't, out of nowhere, suddenly refuse."

"So that's how Blair got hold of Dad's songs?"
She nods. "Everyone knows you and Dad fought
But Mum hoped you would see that, all along,
You had more in common than first thought.

She dreamed it might - despite what happened -
Spur you to change your mind one day."
"But why didn't Dad share his passion?"
"I guess he was just too embarrassed in a way

To admit he'd not had the perfect career.
Music was one thing at which he'd failed.
He was simply too proud to discuss it, I fear.
Never dwelling on failure, what could've prevailed,

Dad lived as if it had never occurred.
That talk of 'successful men with talent',
It was to *him* that the comment referred.
You striving for your dreams was not gallant.

It was foolish to Dad, a waste of education
When there was so little chance of success."
I sit, arms folded, in hushed resignation.
"He knew what it was to be thwarted, I guess."

"But all this," I say, "still doesn't explain
How Mother kept tabs on me once Blair died."
"Well, when Blair's health was on the wane
Mum did her best to heal the divide.

One weekend she drove up to yours
But when she arrived you had gone walking.
Or was it shopping at the local stores?
Your partner answered and they got talking.

Mum wanted to wait but it was made clear
That staying was not such a good idea.
Any word of us, she said, and you tried
To dismiss the subject, brush it aside,

Shunning any wish to see your family
Or the chance to revive what we once had.
Like you had done with Blair, apparently."
She sighs. "You might resent Mum sticking with Dad,

For subjecting us to their constant rows,
But you can't blame her for Dad's mistakes,
For being so loyal - we're beyond that now.
She was doing it for all our sakes.

She stayed with him over the years for us,
Solely to keep the family together.
Maybe once you'd reason to kick up a fuss
But you can't bear a teenage grudge forever.

Anyway, your partner said she would try
To talk you round and, with luck, bring about - "
"So Mother visiting was the reason why
She kept on saying I should reach out?"

"Yes, in essence she took over from Blair.
She'd write to Mum or occasionally ring.
You never found out, they took such care."
"No wonder she got so stressed about things."

"She kept Mum updated about Mary at times...
Gosh, I've not mentioned her in all the strife.
It might appear a strange request of mine
But I would so love to be part of her life."

"Me too," I say, "same with Saul and Mia."
She blinks, confused. "How did you know?
Their names I mean. I had no idea - "
"Through a friend of a friend a while ago.

How are they?" I ask as thick cloud descends.
"They're good but, with work, Todd's rarely about,
So it's often just me and the kids at weekends.
With little ones, as I'm sure you've found out,

It's never easy managing by yourself.
You must let us know if you need any help.
And if anything should ever happen to you,
I am here for Mary. I really mean that, too."

"You don't have to say that. We've been apart - "
"Mum would say the same, if you asked her.
She only has your best interests at heart.
That's why she kept speaking with your partner.

And when, last week, she heard nothing back
She truly freaked out. You know how she is.
We spoke every day, so I took the flak.
She longed to phone and got in such a tizz,

She had to know why she'd not been in touch.
Mum was too flustered to call herself
So she asked a friend - remember Ros Such?
And the phone was answered by yourself."

As she takes my hand her mobile rings.
"Mum believed that by showing we care,
By coming today, it might kick-start things."
Muting her phone, a cab enters the square.

From a bag she plucks two straggly receipts
And a ballpoint pen: "Give me your number."
We scribble in turn as the taxi bleats
And, papers exchanged, we're cast asunder.

As the cab leaves I look into my palm
And carefully flatten the ragged receipt.
The slapdash digits fill me with alarm,
Forcing me once again to my seat.

I scan the first line, its workplace extension,
Before the second row demands my attention.
For written before me is none other
Than details for - you guessed it - Mother.

I dawdle to the car, reciting her number,
Then labour back home, processing events.
A heavy shower hits and, with it, thunder,
Before, parking up, it quickly relents.

With Dee and the caterers finally gone,
I trade prickly suit for jumper and jeans.
I play dolls with Mary like nothing is wrong,
Then, alone downstairs, fall apart at the seams.

I down double Bell's like it is water,
Crying hysterically in the gloam.
As my head spins I rise from the corner,
Then take the receipt and sway to the phone,

Thrusting the receiver up to my ear.
Set to dial, fingers hovered, I freeze;
Maybe it's resentment or guilt or fear,
Maybe it's all three to varying degrees.

I slam the receiver back on the hook
And toss the receipt on the dresser shelf.
Seeking a distraction, I seize my book
- *Franny and Zooey* - and lose myself.

During questioning, Damascus stated that the lodger, "often liked to play with our cat, Blair, encouraging him to chase a golf ball that he would roll down the corridor outside his room". The lodger would also allow the cat to sleep beside him on his desk as he worked. Blair had apparently become homeless five years previously following the death of his owner, Daisy Lyle, a Scottish immigrant who had run Kirk's Tea Rooms and lived at 10b Mills Apartments. Although, according to Damascus, Blair was "incredibly lazy", the author would increasingly have to dispose of mice "that the cat brought him as gifts". Furthermore, Blair was rumoured to have fathered several of the litters in and around the apartment block. Such was the lodger's affection for the pet, he even contributed a small sum towards initial investigations into Blair's persistent seizures; symptoms caused by the onset of meningioma. Some observers have proposed that these experiences are reflected in the intermittent references to cats and cancer throughout the book.

From *The Kookaburra Killer* by Arthur Hamlin

5.4

With my X & Y contract nearing its end
I began teaching guitar; evenings by and large
Or, during Mary's naps, at weekends.
An ad in the rag and my moderate charge

Enticed two victims to take up lessons.
Classic non-teacher, how hard could it be?
The answer emerged a minute into the sessions
When I learned my pupil was better than me.

Needing "help with his pieces", said mum, Ms Tate,
She failed to say Dom had breezed Grade 8
And was, to my horror, clawing the sofa,
Now in fact studying for a diploma.

As he handled Tárrega with consummate ease
He posed the one question I had been fearing.
"Could you just play me the first page, please?"
"What, me?" I asked mid panicked throat-clearing.

"No problem, Dom, I'll do that next lesson.
Run the other piece so I know the arrangement."
Naturally, there was to be no "next lesson".
As Dom finished playing and I broached payment

I sensed him wonder who should be paying whom.
I told his mother he should practise more,
Then phoned to say I no longer had room
As my new band were now going on tour.

The relief ringing off switched to sadness
As Lara and Mother hijacked my thoughts;
Briefly, though, as reviving the madness,
There came a challenge of the opposite sort.

For next was beginner, one Joe Buxham,
A novice at guitar but also sitting down,
Keeping still and following instruction.
Surmising a circus was missing its clown,

I asked what genre he would like to learn.
"Dunno. Don't listen to music," he yawned.
"Could be an issue," I dryly discerned.
By the fourth lesson reality dawned.

"Can I ask," he said, flicking snot to the ground
Whilst holding The Axe the wrong way round,
"Am I the best pupil you've ever taught?"
Jingle Bells proving harder than I thought,

I wondered what precisely I had taught him.
"So have you practised at all this week, Joe?"
"Ummm...a bit." Viewing the chances slim,
"From experience 'a bit' means 'no'."

"Been very busy." "Oh, really, doing what?"
"This and that." "Have you watched TV?"
"Yeah, I saw *Star Wars* then afterwards got - "
"So you have had time, it would seem to me.

Don't worry," I said. Joe took a breather:
"Phew. Good to get that one off my chest.
You know you are my favourite teacher."
"That's kind of you." "Wait, no, third best."

"That's still...quite kind of you," I replied.
"Just be upfront if you haven't practiced."
Hence next lesson the door flew open wide
And Joe foghorned, "**I HAVEN'T PRACTISED**!"

"Truly appreciate the honesty, Joe.
How was half-term?" "Had a funeral in Stowe."
"Gosh. I know how you feel so we really won't - "
"Both grandparents." Okay, maybe I don't.

"Natural causes, just three days apart."
"Christ, that really is awful," I shuddered.
"Mum said Gran died of a broken heart.
That's bullshit, though, they hated each other.

Apparently Gran tried to poison him once
But I think she was just a terrible cook.
Dad said they were both miserable cun - "
"Ok-a-a-ay, shall we play? Did you buy the book?"

"Uh?" "Just do the last riff that we discussed.
What were we playing?" Joe pulled out a sheet.
"Ah, here it is: *Another One Bites the Dust.*"
A week later, as Joe tapped out a beat

With less rhythm than a hiccupping drunk,
In walked his mother. "Is he getting better?
When's Grade 1? Can we do it next month?"
Of course, doing any practice whatsoever

Would have rather heightened his chances;
As would playing something resembling a tune.
Keeping cool under the circumstances,
I thought of his strengths but realised soon

That picking one's nose was not on the syllabus.
"Before starting Grades we'll need some more sessions."
"Sitting scholarships should provide the impetus.
We're investing lots of cash in these lessons.

He gets it from his father." What, being inept?
(I didn't say that.) "He would've made it except - "
"He still plays?" I asked. "Did you hear me, Joe?"
"He's nearly fifty-five now so, well, no."

"How's aural?" Mother probed. "The singing back?
He has a great sound, way over and above - "
"Really?" I said. "Shall we give it a crack?"
With a voice only a mother could love,

The more he strained the more cross-eyed he grew
Until his eyeballs had switched sockets, it seemed.
Citing throat pain and a touch of flu,
Joe's blush deepened as I intervened.

I proposed a diary in which he could write
Precisely how long he'd practised each day.
So he appeared the next Thursday night
And thrust the dog-eared book my way:

Monday - 88 Tuesday - 91
Wednesday - 45 Thursday - 84
Blow me down, I mused, doing the sums,
That's five hours' playing, possibly more.

Admiration, though, was somewhat lessened
When I perceived that what Joe had practised
Was gauged, not in minutes, but in seconds.
He balked when I quizzed his shady tactics.

"You said little and often would provide - "
"Yes, but there's little and there's…nanoscopic."
"Nanoscottish?" "Extremely small," I sighed.
He ignored my efforts to change the topic:

"Wow, learning guitar and new words each day."
He tugged at his music, a chewed ball of paper:
"Your lessons are pretty good value, I'd say."
"Are they," I said as he murdered C major.

From shaky beginnings persistence bore fruit:
A trickle of pupils became a steady stream,
So much so I'd ditch the city commute
And the odd hours became weekly routine.

The more I charged the more they came,
Covering Mary's nursery three days a week.
Cocooned at home, as means to entertain
I sought out the Web and, on a hot streak,

Gave in to the rush of betting online.
Dabbling on horses, on a hiding to nothing,
I of course blew all I made over time;
Why, I've no doubt that some are still running.

Then one fine Tuesday, Mary at nursery,
My lesson postponed, I am at a loss.
I heat up some soup and turn on the TV,
Expecting the customary daytime dross.

Yet the strict diet of property programmes,
Quizzes, 40's flicks and chat shows
Has been banished - the schedules are jammed
With ad-libbing journos as they disclose

The "facts" behind the footage on screen:
Camcorder film of a passenger jet
Striking a high-rise, an act they deem
- But which they cannot confirm as yet -

Is terrorist-lead, an attack on the West.
They switch to footage of The South Tower
As it stands crippled, a black hole in its chest,
Smoke spilling forth in its final hour

As smog defiles the azure on high.
A deck of cards, the walls then crumble,
"Like a freight train coming out of the sky".
An ash cloud follows the guttural rumble,

Chasing fleers down adjoining streets.
On a loop, they show the camcorder clip,
That of two officers out on the beat;
The camera quivers and giddily flips

Up to the aircraft droning overhead.
They keep playing the clips again and again,
Keep saying the same things, but instead
Of tiring I just want more, replay ten

As horrific, as engrossing, as the first.
Groping, transfixed, for my soup bowl,
They talk four to five thousand dead at worst,
Leading to stories of the poor souls

On the hundredth plus floor, if I recall,
Jumping from windows like skydivers,
But with no chute to break their fall.
The ground reached up - there could be no survivors -

As, doomed, they bombed to the ravaged ground.
Soon there are reports filtering through
Of the plane passengers, Twin Towers bound,
Making last calls home, a final "I love you",

Words they may've voiced last night in bed,
Or perhaps this morning, or at the weekend;
Habit or heartfelt, now being said
With peerless meaning as this is The End,

And what else exactly is there to say?
Except that they wished they'd said it more,
Every minute, every hour of every day,
For however many times it was said before

There would always - always - be more to tell.
We hear of those who'd not had the chance
To make that last call, that final farewell.
Agog, I watch appalled, entranced,

As the low plane glides through cloudless sky
And strikes The North Tower, sealing its fate.
They never had the chance to say goodbye,
To make their peace, it was just too late.

Never had the chance, I keep saying to myself,
Over and over; I'm not sure why
- Mind racing ahead - till on the dresser shelf
The crinkled receipt catches my eye.

Rising, I snare it, then bound to the phone,
Tracking the recurring footage en route.
I stiffen as I hear the dialling tone,
And switch the burbled reports to mute.

Eager, petrified and all in between,
I plug in the number as my heart rate builds,
The wait producing an endless stream
Of trilling couplets that have me drilled,

Marching double time up and down the room,
The cord stretching as it yanks at the wall.
I stride back and forth until I assume
That she is not there to take my call.

"Hello?" comes a voice. "Hello?" she appeals.
A "Hi" emerges from my ums and ahs,
Fighting street noise, rain hissing under wheels.
"Oh, my golly," she says above passing cars.

"You alright?" "Er, think so, more or less."
"I wasn't sure I should come to the service…
You got this number off Lara, I guess?"
Swift to reply, she seems not to notice.

"I'm just so pleased that you finally met
And were able to talk. It's been so long.
I don't know if she has had the time yet
To fully explain what's been going on?"

My words are swamped by throttling traffic.
"I can't tell you how great it is to speak."
The rising road noise sounds like static.
"I was about to call you the other week

But I thought you'd hate me butting in."
Her slammed-shut door kills the mulch of noise.
"You don't need me to complicate things."
"Complicate?" I say, regaining my poise.

"It would mean the world to have you around."
"Really?" she whispers. "Really," I say.
"I'm done with fighting over old ground.
I want us to all move forward, okay.

I'm just so sorry - " "Listen, you don't - "
"No, please," I cut in. "Let me say," I implore.
"I won't let you down, I swear I won't.
And I know that I've said all this stuff before

Then gone back on my word. It won't happen again.
I should have reached out when encouraged by Blair.
And I'm sorry I bailed on you way back when,
Never meeting in London or calling you there.

But everything I say right now is true.
Say you believe me, say that you do."
"For sure," she answers. "Positive?" I press.
"Oh my goodness me, absolutely yes."

I'm set to respond but, stalling my reply,
The maimed North Tower is reduced to dust.
"Have you seen the news?" "I know," she sighs.
"Unbelievable." "Isn't it just."

We arrange to meet in two days' time.
"I'll come to London." "You will?" "It's fine."
We settle on a spot at Euston station.
"How does three sound?" Without hesitation,

"Can't wait," she says as her dashboard dings.
"Ditto," I reply. "Ditto," I repeat.
Hanging up, and with a hint of a grin,
I take to my chair and put up my feet.

I pick up *Review* from *The Sunday Times*
And slip on *Cahoots* by The Band.
In critique mode, I read the first lines
Of the featured articles until I land

On a small piece by one Erin Feliz.
Five hundred words tops, at its core
It highlights the eight hundred thousand Tutsis
Slain in Rwanda in '94.

History is written by the victors, we're told;
Now it's rewritten by the losers, she claims.
I read of the butchery that took hold
Before she raises the question of blame:

Why did the West, with Clinton as head,
Never heed the UN's cautionary words?
Why did it turn its back on the bloodshed?
Why only now is the truth being heard?

5.5

The following night, my pupils long gone,
I sort through her clothes, untouched all the while;
A small step, you'd hope, in moving on,
Yet which I'd resisted in my denial.

A few favoured items stored safely away,
I divvy the rest into black bin bags
And drop them next morning at Age UK.
Waiting for our meeting, how time drags:

I clock-watch through lessons until, at last,
I'm free to head into town at two.
Arriving early, the crowds thrum past.
I do not see them - all I construe

Is they are not her and the search goes on.
Glimpsing my watch, it's a minute past three.
She's always punctual, something is wrong,
Then rationale strikes and reminds me

There are umpteen reasons she could be late;
If you can call one minute late at all.
I'm feeling a touch unwell as I wait.
In fact, I half wish that she would call

To say she's delayed and we'll postpone today.
In truth, though, all I want to see is her
Strolling up the station's thronged walkway.
A jackhammer fights a siren's whirr:

My ears full, still the decibels soar
As a car alarm joins the chorus,
Which, as ever, we wholly ignore.
I glug at my water as, before us,

A hooded Asian struts to and fro,
Tightening the straps of his tan rucksack.
I tell myself he's just an Average Joe
"Going about his life", but with the attack

On the Twin Towers and all the talk
Of suicide bombers on the Underground,
I can but mistrust his frenzied walk.
Paranoia, I fear, soon abounds:

What if meeting gets us blown sky-high?
What if it's us who, when the moment comes,
When all hell breaks loose, are stood by,
Dreaming of the future? As my heart drums

I twist to view a second rucksacked Asian.
He approaches the other and they yabber away
By the newsstand at the front of the station.
A feverish exchange and they turn my way,

Like I am the one acting suspiciously.
Downing his rucksack and foraging inside,
The former stomps towards me officiously,
My unease heightening with every stride.

Three steps away, he pulls something out:
A bundle of leaflets entitled *Unity*.
He divulges what the bumph is about,
A call for calm within the community

Following the recent New York attacks;
A plea that Muslims are not victimised.
I take a sheet, thank him, then stand back
As my two neighbours are politicised.

Their appeal - though one I'm pleased to scotch -
Has momentarily outstripped my dread.
But how it floods back as I check my watch:
Nine past, it reads. "Three o'clock, we said."

Nudging despair, I find myself praying.
A fusty tree-hugger, puffed up with piety,
Is shooting the bull, some hogwash saying
That I should join his green society.

"No thanks," I snarl, waving him away.
I wonder if I said *precisely* where I'd be.
The greenie's still going. "Not now," I say.
I recheck my watch. "Fuck, where is she?"

To think I'm so close to finding an end
To our decade's divide, our phony war.
So how it pains me to tell you, my friend,
The wait never ended; I left alone at four.

There was no kind face easing into focus,
No stammered first words to slowly digest,
No feeling of renewed sense of purpose
As ten years of feuding was laid to rest.

I still can't believe that she never came,
And the worst thing is she never said why;
No calls, no letters, nothing would explain
Why she left me there as the world sped by.

5.6

"All will be fine," olds are programmed to say.
Yet sometimes it won't be and, despite forbearance,
Shit truly happens and you must face the day;
Even if that shit *is* your parents.

How exactly, though, do you recover
From such rejection by your own mother?
Even accepting I'd drawn out the feud,
It was the not-knowing that I now rued:

Why had she behaved - like me - so callously?
Why, after wishing for nothing more,
Had she blown the chance to unite the family?
And why thereafter would she ignore

My constant pleas for explanation?
To cap it - and capping I could ill afford -
She had cemented our alienation
By leaving Blighty and moving abroad

For a new life in Gore, New Zealand.
Lara broke the news, calling that October,
Returning from a Seychelles trip to England.
Mother, it transpired, had sold up in Cromer

- Where she had moved soon after Dad died -
And flown out the week we'd planned to meet.
"What on earth made her do that?" I replied.
"On holiday last year she met this chap Pete - "

"Pete? I thought - " "Please, just let me speak.
A friendship blossomed and it grew from there.
At Easter he flew to England for a week,
So clearly it was not some short-lived affair.

Then when she went back Down Under in May
He asked her to join him, an offer she'd accept."
"Mother did that? She wouldn't, no way.
She wouldn't run off with a guy she's just met."

I mean "love is a leap", she'd often proclaim,
But some leaps were surely further than others.
"So she risked everything for some new flame?
No chance," I pressed, "there's no way that Mother's...

She wouldn't..." But she had, she damn well had.
At first, I was pleased, almost overjoyed,
That she'd found love after years with Dad.
Yet this ripple of happiness would be destroyed

By the hurt of her never saying goodbye,
By the pain that gripped me now she was gone.
"Why didn't she warn me? Please tell me why.
Why vow to meet when she had plans all along?

You can't promise such things then take a flight - "
"Perhaps she hoped to meet but then opted out.
Maybe she sought proof that you were alright
And were coping okay, but then she had doubts

Over whether you'd snub her, like before."
"I wouldn't have, though." "How could she ignore - "
"Because this time round it's totally different.
This time it's for real." "Not to her it isn't.

She could never quite trust you, don't you see?
She could not face it if it didn't work out."
"She's chosen some guy she hardly knows above me.
Christ, she was the one always preaching about

Not deserting your kids, whatever they do.
'Never give up on them,' that's what she'd say.
And now she discards me by shooting through - "
"Heavens, it's not always about you, okay.

It's about her for once, *her* wants and needs."
"But she can't just leave. I can't believe what she's done.
She's our mother, for God's sake, and look how she leads - "
"Yes, she's your mother but you were her son."

The Sydney Morning Herald

June 28th 2005

MOTHER'S REJECTION LAST STRAW FOR FAILED AUTHOR

"Poems such as *B r o k e n* were found amongst the author's belongings, suggesting that he left England for Australasia when attempts to reconcile with his mother proved unsuccessful."

5.7

Three weeks later, I get a call from Sam.
"Flick's away, let's get cunted in town.
How about Saturday at The Ewe & Lamb?
Or we could try out The Triple Crown."

So that weekend, Mary at the minder,
I leave for the station at one fifteen.
Passing her car - a constant reminder
But one that had dulled with daily routine -

I glance inside and, by *Private Eye*,
Spot the red shawl swathing Mary's seat.
Accustomed to letting the triggers pass by,
This time I'm thrown from the purr of our street

Back to the fracas atop The White Cliffs,
To how one thing had led to another,
To the whys, wherefores and endless what-ifs.
Bumbling on with a fearful shudder,

I try walking it off but, as I pace,
The pictures, the sounds, they just follow me,
Chasing, threatening, like thugs at my face.
In no mood for false bonhomie,

I call up Sam to cancel our drinks,
Excused with some riff on a sickness bug.
Too flustered to care what he might think,
I hide the red shawl under a rug

Then climb in the car, thoughts miles from here,
At the hill I'd frequent after she died.
I drift through The Smoke then, as the roads clear,
Meander into open countryside.

Windows wound down, along B-roads I wend
Till, at the hill's base, I seek one last surge.
Approaching the peak, I stop on the bend,
Rolling back onto the long-grassed verge.

I rise from the car and turn to lock it
- Least I think I do, I cannot be sure -
Then post my keys into my pocket.
Hunting the bench, I briskly make for

The cluster of elms beside the road
That swarm, unbroken, up the hillside.
My undisturbed walk is at once slowed
As the tree labyrinth stunts each stride,

Renders them shimmies, until I am met
By the sharp camber of the mud-dried path.
I pause to mop up thick beads of sweat;
My collar stifling, as if it a scarf.

Gathering breath, I stare straight ahead,
The uncharted alley demanding my gaze.
On past the bench I gingerly tread.
The pointer before me has seen better days;

Strangled by ivy and, nearing, I see
The faint black letters have begun to flake.
Yet focussing in, I make out a *B*,
An *r*, an *o*, an *a*...*Broadlake*.

I say it aloud, averting my eyes
From the pearly sun above the valley.
Then - God knows why, please don't ask why -
I lower my stare and head for the alley.

What begins as a sluggish amble
Breeds a light jog, a canter then sprint.
Approaching the sign, I evade the brambles,
A boxer weaving, the late sun's glint

Snuffed as I enter the shaded alley.
Spider's webs snag at my flinching face;
A trip on a stick derails my sally
But, balance regained, I quicken my pace.

I feel my heart thrashing at my chest,
A stitch invading my dough-filled stomach.
Heaving, my body cries out for a rest
But I push on, up over a hillock,

Before the release of the brackened slope.
Hurdling the branch of a fallen tree,
Sprinted strides are reduced to a lope.
The declivity steepens and I can see

The waiting sun, a ball of amber light,
Converging at the tree-tunnel's end.
My listless legs are stirred by the sight
And, hastening briefly, I eagerly descend

Into a clearing, over shards of glass.
I wind to a stop as senses engage:
A *Broadlake* sign is rotting in the grass.
A burnt-out car commands centre stage,

All fire-warped doors and mangled bonnet;
Shunted off the hilltop road, I presume.
By the wreckage lies a pool of vomit,
A snapped syringe and a rusting spoon.

There is not even a goddamn lake,
Or if there was, it dried up years ago.
"Is this it? Is this *it*, for Christ's sake?"
Strewn shards crunching at my toe,

My ears are ringing like at Our Beginning,
Lying in the road in the wake of the crash.
The ground, the car, the forest is spinning
As I step over grey mounds of ash.

Rocking, I summon my stiffened legs:
Like rusty pistons, they grind me forward
Back up the alley, past spiders' webs
And dangling creepers till, senses disordered,

I take what must be several wrong turns
As the pathway forks and progress is slowed.
Only by fortune do I tramp through ferns
And find myself back on the hilltop road.

My car not far from where I emerge,
I fall inside and, hard-turning the key,
Wheel-spin away, churning the verge.
Time running short, I call minder, Dee:

No answer forthcoming, foot to the floor,
I miss the first turn - switching on the fan -
Landing me on the coast road once more,
The one where, perhaps, my End began.

I start to think as my world implodes:
If life is a journey then why am I always
Travelling the same familiar roads?
I cast my mind back and, at every phase,

All I see is the mess, the madness, the panic.
Why do I feel the whole time I have been
Rearranging deckchairs on the Titanic?
Unravelling again, I picture the scene,

Her cartwheeling off the Dover cliff edge,
The search, the grieving, her burial, the wake;
Scanning each detail my mind can dredge.
I screech to a stop, stamping the brake,

Fronting the junction at a crossroads.
Left and it is The Road to The City,
Right, it's my parents' former abode.
Maybe it's guilt or maybe self-pity,

Or I'm not the man I thought I'd be,
But Mary can't see this, of that I am sure,
Not if the last soul she can trust is me.
Left, no, right, no, and what's more

I can't go on for it's the road to Dover.
Picking my poison, hysteria swells;
Worse, there's nowhere to even pull over.
"What now?" I say. "What now?" I yell.

I scream so hard I break into a cough
And then without looking - I don't even *look* -
I step on the gas and just drive off.
Somehow, somehow, by hook or by crook,

I make it across; suffice to say,
A medley of horns ring in my ear,
Detuning, like cat wails, veering away.
I should pull over but, into fourth gear,

I make for Dover, fan frantically blowing.
Perhaps this is "destiny", perhaps it is key
To exorcising the brutal not-knowing,
The doubt over whether it was down to me.

Yes, maybe, I think, this is all for good,
Maybe returning will put me in the clear
And confirm that I did do all that I could.
Streetlights rousing, I slip down a gear

As a triad of cyclists savour their ride,
Fanning, freewheeling, across my lane.
At first I presume they will move aside,
But the sole movement I can ascertain

Is that of two riders turning around,
Staring, cackling, then, just as before,
A gleeful refusal to cede their ground.
Revving, I catch first sight of the shore:

Jinking by like a sidestepping winger,
I move past the cyclists, the outer of whom
- As a parting gift - gives me the finger.
Pushing on as rain augments the gloom,

I judder up the road we took that day:
Drawing up into the sparse car park,
I flop from my seat and make my way
Through the grim dusk's encroaching dark.

I reach where, jesting, I spread out,
Vertigo-dazed, just shy of the ledge.
If I hadn't insisted on fooling about
She would have never come to the edge.

I dare a peep down, I see us clung on,
Her scrabbling to grip my shaking hand.
If I'd not slipped she'd never have gone
Beyond the wild grass on which I stand.

I sense grip failing, see tears in her eye,
Her shock as she hears her sister's name;
It shreds my heart and I start to cry,
Wilting under the weight of blame.

How could I even debate the cause?
How, my friend, was there any not-knowing?
I shuffle forward and, set to pause,
Something stops me and I keep going,

I can take no more, it's too much to bear,
I'm at the edge, this is IT, my friend.
With one last step comes the rush of air,
As I hope and pray this is

THE END.

Part 6 Introduction

The fallout for *Broadlake*'s author

Having committed the murders and fled the apartment with the tin of arsenic, Mandelson stated that the author purchased two bottles of whisky (one Bell's, one Teacher's) from Lambert's off-licence on Mueller Street. The owner of the store, Luke Harper, confirmed that this had taken place at approximately 9:35 p.m. It was alleged that the author then made an anonymous telephone call to police before returning to 38 Larapinta Drive. During his final hours in the basement, he supposedly revised at least one passage from *Broadlake* and added several others that seemed to allude to the Bracewell murders. Furthermore, since the whisky-spattered and defaced dedication page was discovered beneath the author's left hand, Mandelson reasoned that he had carried out this defacement just before his death. This argument was reinforced by the disclosure of what the author had originally written. David Balkan had attempted to decipher the words but had only managed to transcribe "To" and "family". Yet upon analysis by forensic document examiner, Martin Scuthers, it was revealed to the court that the author had initially dedicated the book: "To Rose/And the family we shall have together". It seemed likely that when the author realised he had killed his unborn child and his hopes of a life with Bracewell were over, he defaced the dedication. Having reworked the manuscript and deleted his original inscription, it was claimed that the author was so overwhelmed by grief and guilt that he took his own life. This he did, Mandelson asserted, by consuming a dangerous quantity of whisky and ingesting at least 0.25g of arsenic.

Such an explanation seemed plausible, but particularly so in conjunction with further evidence arising from *Broadlake*'s manuscript. It transpired that one of the passages revised on the night of the murders was the climax of 4.3, which recounted the younger sister's death (the section was dated "10/8"). In the reworked version - the one that appears in

Balkan's transcription - her fall is portrayed as an accident; the result of an insensitive prank backfiring tragically. However, in March 2005, following the transfer of the late David Balkan's library to his widow's new home in Adelaide, a number of *Broadlake*'s previously lost drafts were found amongst a collection of unpublished essays. Crucially, one of the mislaid papers attained by Mandelson showed that the argument on the cliff top had formerly ended with the narrator becoming so enraged with his partner that he pushed her, quite deliberately, over the edge. The author defaced these parts of the manuscript but, again, thanks to Martin Scuthers, the defence were able to partially decipher the text. The following lines leave one in no doubt as to how the younger sister originally died: "Clasping her throat, I force her to the edge/And, screaming, she falls, temple clipping the ledge." This evidently raises the question of why the author condemned the woman to such a death and then chose to rewrite the passage on 10th August 2002.

At first sight, obvious parallels can be drawn between the deaths of Rose and Mary Bracewell and the younger sister in *Broadlake*; the original storyline appeared to be a fictionalised admission of guilt. Yet the passage had first been written on 27th June 2002, many weeks before their deaths, so it was plainly not an oblique confession. It was instead, Mandelson claimed, a statement of intent. For, as the papers found beneath the kitchen floorboards will soon prove, the relationship between Bracewell and the now homeless author had become so strained that the latter's love had turned to something bordering on hatred. He had repeatedly begged Bracewell to leave Damascus but on each occasion she had declined to do so.

Bracewell's procrastination generated a stream of pleading letters, which evidently increased the risk of Damascus discovering their affair. By now, though, the author did not appear to care. "For Christ's sake," he wrote despairingly on 21st June 2002, "come away with me like you promised last week, like you promised months ago. You promised." His increasingly distraught state of mind is clear from another letter he wrote four days later:

25/6/02

Rose,

Where the hell have you been? I tried to call yesterday but there was no reply, and when I came by the apartment at lunchtime you were out. How you can lead me on and say that you love me more than anything, but then tell me, "It's the wrong time"? You vowed we'd be together. And you say you're worried about where we'll go and how we'll live, but we'll <u>find</u> a way. In any case, when *Broadlake* gets published things will be alright. I know you think it's too niche and that I've spent far too much time on it, but I swear the book will eventually earn some money and I'll take care of us all.

You've no idea how hard this is. I pray this letter makes a difference because if I can't have you I really don't think I can go on. I won't lie, Rose, some days I wish I'd never met you. But it's because I love you so much that I can't bear what you're doing to me now. Please don't desert me, like my family has.

Remember my green T-shirt with the red stripe down the middle? Remember that blustery day when it flew off the balcony and we couldn't find it, however hard we tried? That's us - taking off, never to be seen again.

You and me, Rose, we share the same shadow.

L x

The author's belief that he and Rose Bracewell "share the same shadow" (alluded to in 2.4) has since been cited by Jacob Manson as a prime example of the author's plagiarism; this time borrowing from 'Boomerang Girl' by little-known and underrated English acoustic rock act The Good Ship Band. He also quotes directly from the song during the same passage in 2.4: "How do you let go when it's all you've got?"

Mandelson claimed that the author harboured such resentment towards Bracewell for not leaving Damascus that three days later he killed off a fictionalised version of her in *Broadlake* - namely the younger sister - in a perverse rendering of wish fulfilment. Indeed, given Bracewell's clear concerns over the author's career, apparent from the above letter's opening paragraph, it seems likely that her rebuff had centred around this issue; and, as a result, it was depicted in the row on the cliff top. Thus, according to Mandelson, when the author and Bracewell argued again and the author subsequently committed murder for real on 10th August 2002, he tried to right the wrong by reworking the end of 4.3. In doing so, he supposedly wished to convince himself and any future readers who might the see the connection, that it was a dreadful accident. He was ostensibly in denial and using his writing as a form of sanctuary from the truth; an impression corresponding with the narrator's statement in 1.8: "You see, until now I'd felt protected by 'art',/A shield from my troubles or chastened heart." The author, Mandelson said, was wracked with shock and guilt from not only committing the crime but also from witnessing his fiction becoming a sickening reality.

Mandelson then turned his attention to the end of Part 5. Although *Broadlake*'s ending had been written with the completion of Part 6 (dated 7th and 8th August 2002), and with it the fate of the narrator confirmed - or so it seemed - the author had yet to conclude 5.7 and thereby make known exactly how his fall came about. The only draft of the passage in question was dated 10th August 2002. From bullet points jotted at the end of 5.6, it appeared that the author had intended the protagonist to finally visit Broadlake and discover that the light at the end of the tunnel signalled an ethereal and unspoilt hideaway. He would then to return to the cliff top and, on placing carnations above where the younger sister fell, slip accidentally to his death. Yet Mandelson claimed that, as the author revised Part 5, he could no longer deny his guilt to himself or to those who might read his work; although he could insert lines claiming that her fall was an accident, the text's underlying tone told a different story. Consequently, at the end of 5.7 the author set about recounting the realisation of his culpability and his suicidal leap. It seems that he also added the fifth verse of 6.0 which makes reference to this act; the passage was crammed into the page's bottom left corner and was also marked "10/8".

It appears likely that some of the material dated 10th August may in fact have been composed in the early hours of 11th. If the author left Mills Apartments at approximately 9:30 p.m., it would have taken him at least ten minutes to return to Larapinta Drive by foot - perhaps more in order to purchase the whisky and telephone emergency services - ensuring that he could have only commenced writing at 9:40 p.m. at the very earliest. Given the amount of work completed that night, it is highly unlikely that he would have finished by midnight. Some, such as Edith Ratchet, have also since questioned the assumption that all the revisions were carried out after dark rather than earlier in the day. However, given all the rewritten passages appear to allude to the murders and bore traces of Bell's or Teacher's whisky, it seems most probable that they were completed during the author's final hours in the basement.

On confronting the horrific nature of his actions, Broadlake was no longer a haven but a wasteland, and the author's wish to die meant that stepping off the cliff replaced accidental death. The consumption of alcohol combined with a probable panic attack - denoted by the empty pack of Librium, an anxiety suppressor, found by the body - almost certainly caused the handwriting's deterioration in this section of the manuscript. Moreover, traces of arsenic were discovered on the first page of 6.0 and the defaced dedication page, indicating that the substance was ingested at this late stage, thereby hastening the author's death.

Despite this explanation, some have since questioned whether the author's likely rereading of Part 5 was central to his suicide. Edith Ratchet has asked whether his desire to die needed reinforcing if he had already planned to kill himself by consuming a lethal cocktail of alcohol and arsenic. "What else", she appeals, "was the poison for?" Ratchet has a further bone of contention: "It does seem justifiable that *Broadlake*'s author would have felt suicidal after events that night, just as the novel's narrator had done following the sisters' deaths. But one still has to be deeply sceptical that the narrator's demise is an elaborate suicide note." Even Jacob Manson sides with her on this matter. "Who, on the point of killing themselves, has the presence of mind to prefigure their own death? If the author wished to express his wish to die there are far simpler ways of doing so than confessing at the end of an almost illegible manuscript that may never be found and ascribed to him, let alone read. It is quite categorically not, as biographers have tediously become accustomed to saying, as though the author knew his own fate, since the events surrounding the Damascus case were totally unforeseeable." Unforeseeable they may have been but, as Mandelson argued, not out of the question. Hence the author's motives for writing certain sections of *Broadlake* cannot be discounted.

Mandelson gave further illustration of *Broadlake*'s text mirroring reality, overriding claims that the similarities were purely coincidental. He contended that the narrator's arguably unethical relationship with the younger sister, resulting in her pregnancy, echoed the affair between the author and Rose. He also argued that the letters and telephone calls between the narrator's mother and Blair, and, later, the mother and his partner, invited comparison with the secret correspondence between the author and Bracewell. Finally, Mandelson alleged that the elder sister's reasoning for splitting with the narrator in 1.3 - "wrong time, wrong place" - was merely an extended version of that given by Bracewell for not eloping with her former lodger (see the letter dated 25th June 2002). It is easy to dismiss this last parallel as coincidental, but it is surely more likely that Bracewell's response was inserted into the story on the back of her views on their relationship.

Aside from Mandelson's interpretations, other observers have proposed that the narrator happening upon his father "embracing" Sue and, years later, spotting Piers Strauss kissing the elder sister in the theatre, are both embellishments of Damascus entering the apartment and sensing something untoward going on between the author and Bracewell. What is more, these sections were re-edited on 14th June 2002, just two days after Damascus had uncovered their relationship. In 4.3, the kite's design ("A sludge green diamond, red stripe up the spine") is undoubtedly inspired by the T-shirt of the same colour and pattern that flies off the balcony and which the author describes in the aforementioned letter to Bracewell. Edith Ratchet has also suggested that the author's move to Australia in the hope of finding a better life, only to end up sleeping rough in a litter-filled basement, is the inspiration for the wasteland that is Broadlake. Indeed, was the road where this took place, Larapinta Drive, behind the naming of the protagonist's sister, Lara? Alternatively, perhaps we are trying to extract meaning from mere coincidence.

Despite the difficulties of separating fact from fiction, the trial of Ivan Damascus would reach a decisive conclusion on 30th June 2005. At 3:20 p.m. Damascus was cleared of both charges of murder and the killing of an unborn child. He faced only an $800 fine for contravention of The Residential Tenancies Act, a $146 penalty for speeding, and received 90 hours community service for resisting arrest. Mr Justice Stewart concluded that there was reasonable doubt that he did not cause the deaths: "There is insufficient evidence to convict the defendant but his cause has been aided greatly by the case against *Broadlake*'s author. The writer's guilt may not have been comprehensively proven, but the weight of evidence against him is such that it seems most likely that he committed the murders."

In the wake of the outcome, the majority of the Australian press demonised *Broadlake*'s author. The *Melbourne Times* ran the headline, "MOTHER AND CHILD CLUBBED BY KOOKABURRA KILLER"; typical of the reaction nationwide. In *The Australian* Geoff Kipling spoke of "the Englishman's psychotic attack", whilst in *The Northern Territory News* Camilla Watson lamented "the pseudo-poet's malevolent mind". It was widely assumed that the author was the perpetrator and, in a statement issued following the verdict, Rose Bracewell's family supported this notion: "*Broadlake*'s author should have received a life sentence for what he did, yet it is only us who have to suffer that fate." Their anger was by no means isolated and was no better demonstrated than by the unknown individual(s) who knocked down and desecrated the author's headstone; a rudimentary concrete marker that had been left standing in The Alice Springs Garden Cemetery following the body's exhumation. This act was seen by many as a deliberate attempt to turn the tables on the author by imitating events in the narrative; in this case, the impending demolition of the graveyard by the local council.

Despite the trial's outcome, some are still sceptical of Damascus' innocence. Questions remain over why he fled Alice Springs following the Bracewell deaths if he did not carry out the crimes. In an interview with *The Sydney Morning Herald*, Damascus protested that he simply panicked on hearing the news: "Without Rose I couldn't bear the place [Alice Springs], so I left and never wanted to return." Yet why did he try to evade capture for over two years? Perhaps he was on the run for something else; the murder of *Broadlake*'s author, some have proposed. It is also still unclear as to why Damascus stored arsenic under the kitchen sink. Although the substance is used for pest control, this appears more of a convenient explanation than a convincing counterclaim. In addition, the forensic pharmacologist, Dr Jeremy Back, may have confirmed that *Broadlake*'s author died partly from choking on vomit, but the ingestion of arsenic means that, even now, we are uncertain as to whether his death was the result of suicide, an accident or if it involved a third party.

Given the absence of bruising, abrasions or cuts to the corpse, it has since been argued that murder is out of the question. Such a death would have almost certainly necessitated some form of struggle, evidence of which would have been found on the body.

Several investigative journalists, including Arthur Hamlin, have also questioned why the cases against the other previous suspects have not been not re-examined; particularly that of Lucy Freeman who had access to Mills Apartments and whose whereabouts at the time of the murders could not be verified. Yet, given the sizeable evidence against *Broadlake*'s author, the Northern Territory Police have decided to take no further action.

Just as *Broadlake* received mixed reviews upon its publication, the Damascus case verdict has divided the critics. Damien Grey, who praised the story in 2004, has since apologised for writing the review owing to his disgust at the author's likely inspiration. Others, such as Edith Ratchet, have urged the public "to not take the author's guilt for granted or allow the trial's outcome to completely override the book's qualities". Jacob Manson, however, in a typically contrarian rejoinder, believes "the author should be declared guilty until proven innocent" and hopes that the verdict "does not negate the book's colossal failings". He goes on: "Despite the narrator's frustration at many pigeon-holing *The Catcher in the Rye*'s readership as potential killers or suicidal loners, the writer has ironically become this stereotype, this cliché he so feared, having committed both homicide and suicide." The warped beauty with which *Broadlake*'s "fictitious" narrative assumed a reality has drawn a largely condemnatory reaction. In a recent article in *The Australian*, Toby Brown has vociferously criticised Ratchet's "insensitive and debased attitude" whilst affirming that the author "went to the most hideous depths in insinuating the ordeals that he wished to inflict upon others". In *Blood on the Pages,* Catherine Bates states that the author "craved an attention in death that he never managed in life. His dream of notoriety has been realised through the most sinister of means." Echoing this sentiment, James Chilcott concludes in *Writing for Freedom*: "By producing a book that he hoped would bring fame and free him from his impoverished existence, the author has condemned himself to eternal vilification."

For every explanation or viewpoint offered an alternative can invariably be found, and it is this sway of opinion that ensures *Broadlake* will be debated long into the future. Indeed, whatever is said about a seemingly fictional story playing a part in matters of fact, it has undoubtedly struck a unique chord within both the literary and legal communities.

6.0

3:59 p.m.

*T*hat's where my End began! Forget the past strife!
Note to self: jumping off The White Cliffs…
Not recommended…for improving one's life.
A favourite jibe of my fellow stiffs.

The mystery goes on and we're foiled anyhow,
For is that the bell that I can hear now
Announcing my stay is nearing the end?
Is it chiming four? Why, it is, my friend.

An hour or so and I'll be gone from here;
As to where I'm going I've no idea.
To make best use of my every last breath
Let me tell you what happened after my death.

I use "death", of course, in the loosest sense,
As, despite it all, it seemed I'd survived.
You see, my "condition" would confuse events,
For, though I was paralysed, I felt alive.

God, I'm a failure, I pondered solemnly,
I can't even commit suicide properly.
I mean I doubt even those Quebrada divers
Would emerge unscathed or as mere survivors,

But, despite my efforts, I'd managed to catch
The crest of a wave to cushion my plummet.
I hardly got away without a scratch
- I'd clipped my head on leaving the summit –

But I'd not, as yet, passed into this world.
Naturally, I had been knocked unconscious
And, coming to, like a doll I was hurled
Through frenzied surf; walled waves, now monstrous,

Thumping at the cliff's boulder-strewn base.
I prayed one swell would slam me down,
Cull me with a final rap to the face.
Yet each time I sensed I was set to drown,

The frothing white deep, in fleeting fondness,
Spewed me up or didn't slam hard enough;
Saviour then tormentor, I lost conscious
Then regained it, lost it again, the rough

Seas rescuing then fetching me for more.
I must've passed out as I lay at death's door,
For next thing I recall is coming round,
Sun in my eyes, storm switched off, the sound

Of gulls mewing as they swoop overhead,
The plash of lulled waves lipping on rocks.
By miracle, it seems, I am not dead.
As I hear the clank of nearby docks,

Thoughts rush to Mary: what have I done?
What was I thinking? I wasn't, that's the thing;
She's left without family, without anyone.
I summon a scream but it echoes within,

A burning, furious desire to live;
Any life, *anything*, what I would give...
The sound of kicked pebbles pervades my thoughts:
Stones underfoot meet tones overwrought,

Slurred words of a soul in outraged muttering.
"Moody bloody woman," I catch him saying.
"And she believes that *she's* long-suffering.
And what is the reward for me staying - "

His venting ceases, his footsteps, too.
He's seen me, I think, he's seen me for sure,
Or maybe he's paused to admire the view.
But, no, he has clocked me as once more

Steps grow louder till, upon me, they stop.
"Good Lord," he warbles, dabbing his sweat.
He stands at my feet, eyeing the drop,
Bowling ball pate a haloed silhouette;

The reviving sun now briefly hidden.
He bends his knees, lips clenched tightly,
And eases into my line of vision.
He feels for a pulse, wheezing slightly.

His presence had come as mighty relief
- If it weren't for him I'd be left to die -
Yet in moments this turns to disbelief
As I fathom he's no plain passer-by.

My body craves to burst from its skin:
As he twiddles his tie and looks up the shore,
All I can think is, Chrrrist, it's him.
He's shaking his head and, what's more,

Is showing no signs of recognition.
It's me, it's me, I'm inwardly roaring.
I'm alive, don't you see, it's a condition!
As I protest his hand is withdrawing

As, joints now clicking, he stands, back turned.
Bertie, it's *me*. Bertie! I writhe.
You'd think that I would be far more concerned
With how he'd not grasped that I'd survived;

Not one sane thought flows through my head.
Jeez, even if he *did* recognise my face
How would that prove that I was not dead?
For God's sake, we met at the Such's place!

You worked with Dad before moving to Dover!
    Perhaps his memory is a tad shoddy
    Or perhaps my mug is so done over
    I'm a John Doe to, frankly, anybody.

He tugs at an object, what looks like a phone,
Then stabs at a button. "Technology," he sniffs.
He locates the *ON* key and, huffing, he drones,
"White male, thirty-odd, beneath The White Cliffs."

    He holds his gaze until the call has ceased.
    I reason that Bertie's no medical mind
    And that some quack or, at the very least,
    Pathologists will make the unlikely find.

6.1

A medic's cursory inspection later
And inky darkness has dashed my hope.
Stretchered up shore and beyond the breakers,
I'm borne up the steps cut into the slope.

Checking the bearers' keen weather discussion,
Doors click open and they slide me in,
Like chefs slamming trays of food in the oven.
The engine splutters and, turning up *Spring*,

We ride to the strains of Radio Three.
Above Vivaldi, the medics babble
Of the coming weekend and views of the sea.
Slowing for speed humps, metalware rattles

Until, at a standstill, the rear doors open.
Rolled out and inside, the trolley stalls:
"10b," comes a voice and, in one swift motion,
I sense the closeness of my new walls,

A deepening darkness taking hold,
A jarring grind as the door squeaks shut.
The air around me is bitingly cold.
I'm fighting the feeling in my gut:

Where are the shivers? Where is the pain?
How are my lungs and heart not failing?
How has the trauma not gone to my brain?
For a man on his deathbed I'm hardly ailing.

And yet, to this day, these feelings abide;
It was no anomaly or passing fad.
There is a reason they thought I'd died,
The reason being because I had.

6.2

It's no gentle passing, joining the dead.
Imagine conceiving your time is done
Just as you thought life stretched ahead.
You'd have a stroke - if you could have one.

All of us here have felt the same thing;
You'll see what I mean when you are no more.
Ask neighbour Reg: he swears it took him
A night in the morgue till he knew for sure.

That flick, *The Sixth Sense*, isn't far wrong,
What with old Bruce thinking all the way through
He's being ignored when he's dead all along.
That twisted the truth, though, like flicks do;

I mean The Departed don't stroll around.
Let's get real, they are either cremated
Or are left to rot in once hallowed ground;
Their oblivion, I fear, only abated

By regaling their tales to folk like you.
Yes, are you still there? Hello? Hair-lo-owe?
I seem to be sensing some déjà vu.
Is that you rising and preparing to go?

Have the gates opened? What's that you say,
The workmen are here? Is that them shouting,
Demanding that you now be on your way?
I can hear the snarl of engines mounting.

Oh, Mary, I'm sorry, you made me so proud;
Why-oh-why is love *never* enough?
I pray Lara cared for you, like she vowed;
Nothing hurts like missing your child grow up.

Boy, I can feel the whole ground shaking,
Above and beyond the bypass quaking.
What with the build seizing my attention
I've yet to answer the one key question:

Where - where exactly - did my End commence?
For all my efforts I *still* do not know.
If ever I pin it on single events
The more I doubt they're The Killer Blow.

A closureless tale, I have spun, I believe;
If truth sets you free then my shackles grow tighter.
I imagine the comments as listeners leave:
"I see why he never became a writer!"

Conclude we must with no conclusion, my friend;
My quest is destined for an endless end.
Watch them exhume me and concrete my space
As luxury apartments take my place.

That digger's so loud I can't hear myself think.
There goes the bucket gouging the ground,
Chewing up earth; we are on the brink.
It knocks at my lid - can you hear the sound? -

A donk then a crack as rotten wood splits,
The light's rushing in as workers cheer.
One's leaping down and upon me he sits,
Posing for pictures: "Say cheese!" they jeer.

Oh my, what class, what a glorious end!
Tell me you don't feel betrayed, my friend!
If there is one thing that gets my goat
It is to leave things on a bad note.

Farewell, Reg, it's been good knowing you;
I sympathise now regarding your wife.
And, Gwen, it is hard to believe it's true
But how I will miss you airing our strife

Every five minutes, come night or day.
Like Holden once said, in a strange way
I'll miss all of those I've spoken about;
Even Reg and Gwen, as it turns out.

Epilogue

"Hypocrisy is as much at the heart of human nature
as contradiction is at the core of the truth."

Daniel Foster, *Abandoned Logic*.

The revelations discussed throughout the second edition of *Broadlake* have merely fed journalists' and critics' pens, leaving its author cast as a much-maligned figure. Yet, over 17 years after Ivan Damascus was cleared of the murders, it is only recently that the case has been conclusively resolved. For on 26th November 2022, Lucy Freeman, who had been questioned and released on two previous occasions, walked into Alice Springs Police Station and confessed to the killings of Rose and Mary Bracewell.

It would appear that the version of events outlined by Oliver Mandelson in the first three weeks of the Damascus trial were ultimately accurate (the unspecified culprit aside), since the murders had indeed resulted from a failed robbery. In recounting events to police, Freeman explained that she had originally intended to burgle apartment 61 which belonged to Bracewell's neighbour, Sarah Ainsworth. Having observed the property for several days, Freeman noticed that Ainsworth would leave at approximately 6:15 p.m. each evening for her shift as a waitress at Matilda's restaurant on Todd Street. After this, Freeman said, the apartment was in darkness which suggested that Ainsworth lived alone.

With this in mind, Freeman entered Mills Apartments at approximately 9:30 p.m. on 10th August 2002, using the key that she had used when working there as a cleaner. She passed through the main entrance and climbed the stairs to the third floor. Having progressed along the corridor to number 61, Freeman noticed that the door to number 60 was ajar; it is thought that it had been left open to create a draft following temperatures of almost 35°C that day. Freeman's findings indicated that the occupant was at home and so any robbery was initially ruled out. She changed her mind for two reasons. Firstly, she realised that in forcing her way into number 61 she would potentially alert the neighbouring inhabitants to her presence. Secondly, on looking through the door to number 60, she spotted a brown leather wallet and several bank notes on the living room coffee table. Meanwhile, one of the inhabitants, Rose Bracewell, had her back turned and was humming to her child, Mary, on the balcony. Damascus later disclosed that the song in question was most likely to be Don McLean's *Vincent*, which had often been heard coming from the lodger's room and which Rose Bracewell subsequently liked to sing to her daughter. Although a robbery was still extremely risky, the above factors would be enough to convince Freeman that it was possible, and, as a result, she stole in.

However, on entering the hallway she tripped on a slipper that was lying upended on the Moroccan runner, and thereby alerted Bracewell to her intruder. Freeman stated that the untidiness had surprised her as, during her time as their cleaner, Bracewell had always "ordered the shoes - like her books - with military precision"; an uncanny echo of how the "rigid line of shoes parade to one side" in 1.6. Recognising her former cleaner, Bracewell rushed in from the balcony and confronted Freeman, who had taken hold of the wallet and loose bank notes from off the coffee table. Whilst cradling Mary in one arm, Bracewell seized the Kookaburra cricket bat from behind the living room door and threatened to strike Freeman unless she left immediately. A tussle ensued and this spilled out onto the balcony: Freeman snatched the cricket bat and, in what she termed as "a moment of madness", struck Bracewell on the temple, sending her and Mary over the railings to their deaths. Severely traumatised by what had happened, Freeman fled the apartment. She discarded the wallet and bank notes, later found by the balcony door, but removed the cricket bat for fear of leaving behind incriminating evidence.

Freeman went on to disclose that she had worn a pair of black leather gloves on the night of the murders, preventing her fingerprints from being detected. Under cover of darkness, she made her way to the Frances Smith Memorial Park and set fire to the bat and gloves in the scrubland behind the children's play area, utilising a Zippo lighter to ignite the flames. Yet, on seeing a police patrol vehicle pull up in the adjacent car park - and fearing that she had been followed - Freeman extinguished the fire and attempted to bury the charred items beneath stones from the surrounding scrubland. Unbeknown to her as she absconded, the police were investigating allegations of a sexual assault within the park's grounds. Freeman returned to the scene the following day to remove the bat and gloves, but they had already been recovered by police following a tip-off from a dog-walker who had noticed the smouldering objects earlier that morning.

Freeman confessed to nine further burglaries from July to December 2002, which had contributed to the record number of reported thefts during that period. She informed police that, having been dismissed from her cleaning role, she had taken to stealing to fund her heroin addiction, and impressed that she had absolutely no intention of committing murder. Living with what she called "paralysing shame", on 24th November 2022 Freeman left her home in the community housing on Renner Street and visited the author's overgrown and desecrated grave in the Alice Springs Garden Cemetery. No longer able to bear the guilt of seeing another man demonised for what she had done, Freeman confessed to the murders two days later. On 19th January 2023 she was sentenced to life imprisonment without the possibility of parole.

It appears that Edith Ratchet's request that the author's guilt should not be taken for granted has been vindicated. Yet these latest discoveries have left us less certain as to why *Broadlake*'s author committed suicide, if that is how he died. It was clearly not out of guilt for killing the Bracewells, as Mandelson alleged at the Damascus trial. One can only assume that, if he did take his own life, he did so out of despair at Bracewell rejecting his plan to elope; a hammer blow to his already fragile mental health. Alternatively, some have proposed that he heard news of the deaths and, as stated in his letter to Bracewell on 25th June 2002, could not "go on" without her.

Whatever the merits of the individual theories, it reinforces why the author defaced the dedication page and never inserted another name: without Rose his life seemed meaningless. He had no one else. The same explanation can account for why the author depicted *Broadlake*'s narrator committing suicide. Yet we cannot be sure how he came to possess the arsenic without entering the apartment that night. Again, we can only speculate that he took it without Damascus's knowledge before being evicted, or that he stole a tin on an undetected visit thereafter. Either way, it appears that he intended to commit suicide before 10th August or had in mind another use for the arsenic. Perhaps, as Catherine Bates has advocated, he planned to poison Damascus so that he and Bracewell could be together. Ratchet, though, has since poured scorn on such a theory: "However much Bracewell wished to leave Damascus and loved *Broadlake*'s author, it is nigh on inconceivable that she would wish to be with a man who had murdered her former partner."

With respect to the author's redrafting of 4.3 and the insertion of verses insisting that the narrator was blameless for the younger sister's death, there is no infallible explanation. Why, on the night of the murders, did the author try to make her demise look like an accident? Did it even have anything to do with events at Mills Apartments? Was it, as the author would be loathed to admit, mere coincidence? Did the author even know of the Bracewell deaths when he died? Did he feel that the novel's narrator was just not capable of murder? Did he determine that pushing the younger sister off the cliff top as a result of a heated argument was too extreme a course of action, and hence an unrealistic scenario? Had his resentment towards Rose faded and thus did he wish to depict her fictionalised self dying tragically but not being murdered? Did he ever have Bracewell in mind when he wrote the scene? These are just some of the many questions that have arisen in the light of the most recent revelations; disclosures that have led James Chilcott to dub *Broadlake*, "the book that became famous by mistake".

Mistake or not, the knock-on effect of recent events has been nothing less than extraordinary. On 19th December 2022, work began on reinstating the author's vandalised grave. Dubbed "The Tomb of the Unknown Author" by Arthur Hamlin, a new headstone was installed, paid for by public donations in the wake of Lucy Freeman's confession. As of 7th February 2023, it is estimated that over 8000 people have already visited the site, and the grave is soon to be listed in the latest *Top 20 Things to Do in Alice Springs*. Additionally, an evening vigil on 2nd February attracted approximately 400 enthusiasts and included several readings from the novel's most popular passages, as voted for on the recently created *Victory for Broadlake* Facebook page. Notably, during the recital of one such excerpt, *Jake, Klaus & Twain* (2.6), an effigy of the novel's greatest denigrator, Jacob Manson, was burnt at the graveside, sparking rapturous scenes amongst the crowd; footage of which has since gone viral on social media. It was also announced that David Balkan, the book's editor and champion, had been posthumously shortlisted for The Trident Medal, a national award for editorial excellence. This announcement inevitably delighted those gathered - self-proclaimed 'Broadlakers' - not least a group of four individuals dressed as the Falstaffian Blair, sporting the "vomit green shirt and rainbow shorts" detailed in 2.3, complete with the *Tug On My Fuel Pump* caption. Another Blair devotee braved the high temperatures in a Cheshire Cat onesie whilst carrying a set of Slazenger golf clubs; a red hunting hat replacing the driver head cover. Such celebratory scenes and clear affection for *Broadlake* are a far cry from the sinister legal battle that plagued the novel for so long. It again begs the question of how a text infused with such humour - amongst its starker plotlines - could ever have become implicated in the Bracewell murder case.

From a commercial perspective, sales of the book have risen by over 340% and poetry in general is seeing a renaissance due to what has been termed 'the *Broadlake* effect'; this despite the novel's roots in rhyming prose. Given the overdue success, for those who now wish to personally pay tribute to the late writer, the new gravestone's inscription simply reads:

Here lies the author of 'Broadlake'

Wordsmith and innovator

Justice at last

Jay Burgess, March 2023.

Bibliography

Allenby, Trudy: *A Brief History of The Anti-novel*, Sydney, Cloud Cover Press, 2004.

Bates, Catherine: *Post-Modernism at a Glance*, Sydney, Challenger Books, 2004.

Bates, Catherine: *Blood on the Pages*, Sydney, Challenger Books, 2005.

Balkan, David: *Otherworld - First Sight* (*Broadlake* extract preface), Sydney, Otherworld, 2003.

Balkan, David: *Broadlake* (1st edition preface), Sydney, Liger, 2004.

Brown, Toby: *Melbourne Times*, Melbourne, 24th April, 2004.

Brown, Toby: *Broadlake - A Confession and Suicide Note*, Melbourne, Crowley & Argyle, 2005.

Browning, Robert: *Selected Poems*, London, Faber & Faber, 1974.

Chilcott, James: *Writing for Freedom*, New York, Red Gloss, 2005.

Foster, Daniel: *Abandoned Logic*, Dublin, Watchtower, 1982.

Grey, Damien: *A Review Revised*, Sydney, Stormside Press, 2005.

Hamlin, Arthur: *The Kookaburra Killer*, Melbourne, Blindside Books, 2006.

Kipling, Geoff: *The Australian*, Sydney, 1st July 2005.

Manson, Jacob: *The Australian*, Sydney, 23rd April 2004.

Manson, Jacob: *Poetry? What Poetry?* Sydney, Darman & Chapman, 2004.

Manson, Jacob: *Damascus - Broadlake's Saviour*, Sydney, Darman & Chapman, 2005.

Melbourne Times, Melbourne, Stacey & Roundtree, 23rd June 2005, 1st July 2005.

Ratchet, Edith: *Changing of the Guard - The New Faces of Modern Fiction*, Melbourne, Hot Space, 2004.

Ratchet, Edith: *The Jury is Still Out*, Melbourne, Long Range, 2005.

Salinger, Jerome David: *The Catcher in the Rye*, USA, Penguin Books, 1951.

Shakespeare, William: *The Complete Works of William Shakespeare*, Glasgow, HarperCollins, 1994.

The Australian, Sydney, Steinhouse Publications, 16th June 2005, 19th June 2005, 11th October 2005.

The Northern Territory News, Darwin, Waterline, 19th June 2005, 21st June 2005, 1st July 2005.

The Sydney Morning Herald, Sydney, Red Rising, 21st June 2005, 27th June 2005, 28th June 2005.

Printed in Great Britain
by Amazon